Four-stroke Motocross and Off-road
Performance Handbook

By Eric Gorr with Kevin Cameron

First published in 2011 by Motorbooks, an imprint of Quarto Publishing Group USA Inc., 400 First Avenue North, Suite 400, Minneapolis, MN 55401 USA

Motorbooks titles are also available at discounts in bulk quantity for industrial or sales-promotional use. For details write to Special Sales Manager at Quarto Publishing Group USA Inc., 400 First Avenue North, Suite 400, Minneapolis, MN 55401 USA.

To find out more about our books, visit us online at www.motorbooks.com.

Library of Congress Cataloging-in-Publication Data

Gorr, Eric, 1957-
 Four-stroke motocross and off-road motorcycle performance handbook / Eric Gorr with Kevin Cameron.
   p. cm. -- (Motorbooks workshop)
 Summary: "This how-to manual tells the off-road motorcycle enthusiast how to get the most out of their motorcycle. The book covers everything from basic maintenance to performance modifications, including Engine rebuilding - Transmission rebuilding - Clutch repair and rebuilding - Big-bore kits - Cam kits and valve timing and tuning - Suspension revalving and kits - Tuning stock suspension - Jetting and tuning carburetors - Tuning electronic fuel injection - Wheels, tyres, and brakes - Chains and sprockets - Radiators and hoses - Electrical systems - Specific tuning tips for the most popular models of the past five years - Converting off-road bikes for dual-sport use"--
Provided by publisher.
 ISBN 978-0-7603-4000-4 (pbk.)
 1. Trail bikes--Maintenance and repair--Handbooks, manuals, etc. 2. Trail bikes--Performance--Handbooks, manuals, etc. I. Hamp, Ron. II. Cameron, Kevin, 1941- III. Title.
 TL441.G665 2011
 629.28'775--dc22
 2011000274

Editors: Kris Palmer and Charles Everitt
Layout by: Tom Heffron

Printed in China

On the cover: David Pingree on his Red Bull Honda. *Simon Cudby*

Inset: *Evans Brasfield*

On the title page: When your bike fits properly and is tuned perfectly, riding is more natural and speed comes more easily. *Yamaha Motor Corporation*

On the back cover: *Evans Brasfield*

About the authors

Eric Gorr is a motorcycle mechanic and performance machinist whom has worked in the motorcycle industry since 1971. Eric owns Forward Motion Engines, an international mail-order service business located in Madison, Wisconsin. Eric started freelancing for magazines in 1980 and has contributed hundreds of technical features in the past 30 years. He has also authored seven books, one SAE paper, and holds two U.S. patents. Eric's favorite motorcycle journalistic influences include the late Gordon Jennings and Gordon P. Blair, and iconic personalities Kevin Cameron, Rick "Super Hunky" Sieman, and Rich Rohrich. You can find out more about Eric's tech tips and forthcoming books at www.ericgorr.com

Kevin Cameron has been writing about motorcycles and racing since 1974, and is considered one of our times premier motorcycle journalists. The former tuner has provided insights into how technology works in *TDC*, his popular column at *Cycle World* magazine. He also has provided some of the most insightful profiles of racers and races ever written.

Contents

Introduction

Take a walk around your local motocross or hare scrambles track, and you are going to see a wide variety of people gathered to compete. Some will have achingly clean, wonderfully prepared motorcycles, brand-new gear, and brand new bikes in $25,000 enclosed trailers. Others will be riding ten-year-old bikes with beat-up plastic, throw-back gear, and a tool chest that is a living history museum.

The constant is that the bikes that are well-prepped will almost invariably finish better in the standings or, at the worst, are more likely to be standing at the end of the day. Are there a few riders out there so talented they can leap on a falling-apart wreck and win? Of course. Is it likely you are one of those one-in-a-million riding phenoms? If you have a factory contract and you have Stewart, Carmichael, or Villopoto monogrammed on your jersey, the answer is, "Yes." If not, well . . . you are going to get better results if you learn how to care for your bike.

Getting your hands on your motorcycle is part of the off-road riding hobby. This is true of all motorcycles, but it is particularly true with off-road bikes. The machines are sophisticated weapons, and the four-stroke engines are jewels of technology.

These high-performance baubles require maintenance in order to stay running in such a high state of tune.

The XR400s and DRZ400s of the world were built with fairly simple technology. Those machines were legendary for enduring even when riders did little more than filll them with gas and spray some chain lube in the bike's general direction once a season.

High-performance four-strokes are different. These machines are very fast, high-tech and somewhat fragile. If you neglect to change the oil and the air filter, you will soon find yourself with a very expensive engine rebuilding tag to pay.

Working on a motorcycle is also one of the joys. Every time you clean it, do a bolt check, and sniff around the bike a bit to see if all is right, you are spending quality time with your machine. That time gives you a familiarity with the bike that is key to staying on top of the maintenance regime.

Part of off-road riding and racing is bike preparation. Want to get faster, or simply have a better experience? Take care of your machine and set it up to match your riding style and needs. *American Honda*

Off-road riders need to take great care with their machines. If they break, they can be stranded miles away from the truck and trailer. *KTM-Sportmotorcycle AG*

Tuning is deeper level of commitment and relationship. Start making simple changes to the stock settings, and your bike's performance will improve. Properly set sag and perfect jetting mean your machine responds as it should, and you are free to progress and grow as a rider.

This book provides you with the tool you really need to keep your bike alive and well. That's knowledge. You'll find some theoretical information from the master of technology, Kevin Cameron, along with a lot of practical advice from two day-to-day tuners, Eric Gorr and Ron Hamp. Use the information wisely and you'll get the most of out of your machine. Whether that means better finishes or simply a more rewarding ride is up to you. The ardent student of the sport will be rewarded with improvements. Read on and let it rip.

Chapter 1
Basic Maintenance

How often have you seen a rider on the track who is sporting a brand-new exhaust pipe on a ratty bike? If you spend time at the track or on the trails, you've met this guy. Let's call our pal Rat Bike Johnson. The hundreds of dollars Rat Bike spent on his motorcycle could have gone to fixing, for example, worn swingarm bushings, adding fresh fork oil, or shimming the valves.

But it was spent on a shiny, new exhaust pipe in the hopes of improving performance on the racetrack. It made the bike louder, but Rat Bike didn't bother to re-jet so he actually has less horsepower. And the rest of the bike still works poorly.

Performance modifications are of little value when the machine is not performing up to stock capabilities. The best way to ensure your bike is performing its best is to maintain it rigorously. Don't be like Rat Bike.

Proper maintenance requires a little time, attention, and elbow grease. The time you spend out in the garage with your bike can be very rewarding, both in terms of performance on the track and for simple peace of mind (working on a bike can be a great form of relaxation).

In general, you need to go over the bike every time you ride it. You'll want to go over the list later in this chapter and keep an eye on each item.

You will also want to record how many hours you ride. You can do this with a log book in which you write down how many hours you rode each day.

A better method is to use an hourmeter. You can purchase them from Dubach Racing for less than $40. This little device records how many hours you have ridden your motorcycle, which is the guideline you will need to determine when to perform specific forms of maintenance.

Regular maintenance keeps your bike working its best. Four-stroke engines are particularly sensitive. If you neglect to clean the air filter or regularly change the oil, the engine will ingest dirt and require expensive service and rebuilding. *Beta*

MANUALS AND BOOKS

Let's go back to our friend Rat Bike Johnson with the ratty bike and the new pipe. The same stereotypical, mythical track creature probably has a few other interesting modifications on his bike.

Perhaps the chain is overly tight, steering head bearings overly loose, and the top end is about six seconds from hand grenading in the first turn—or on the face of that big double he's clearing through some unbelievable act of God.

The tight chain is robbing horsepower and screwing up his suspension, which is why he bought the pipe. The tight chain is also making his suspension stiffer, so he's loosened up the preload until the bike sags like a stink bug until he gasses it, and the chain stiffens the back end up so it's unrideable.

Due to the loose steering head bearings, the bike wobbles and shakes like a jello bar on a paint mixer.

And because he hasn't done any scheduled maintenance—to his knowledge, there is no schedule—the engine is about to blow sky-high.

What is Rat Bike missing? Many would say a few brain cells and probably they would be right. But the key component this rider is missing is information. He needs to know what needs to be done to the bike when. Without that, he's doomed to performing poorly on the track at best and needing a hospital ride at worst.

And, as an aside, if you happen to be a lot like Rat Bike, relax. You've come to the right place to change your course.

The information necessary to transform a rat bike into a mint moto monster can be found in two places. You are reading one of the best. Note that this book is intended to augment, not replace, an owner's manual. We're going to tip you off to the things you won't find in the manual, but you will still need an owner's manual for specifics. And, if you intend to do any service work yourself, you'll want to have the factory shop manual as well.

If the shop manual is not available, you can make do with a Haynes manual. They are decent books that give good information. They are famous for offering, at times, too broad of guidance. But they have more detail than the owner's manual and are much better than working with no information.

If you want to maintain the bike, you will need the proper literature. It's just that simple.

RECOMMENDED TOOLS

Once you have the literature you need, the next things you'll need are tools, decent ones, in order to maintain your machine. The list below will get you started.

You'll want a tool box to take with you to the track or the trailhead. Purchase a good tool box large enough to hold all the tools below, yet small enough to lift. Boxes with a top lid and several drawers in front are ideal.

Note that you can find good tools at Sears—Craftsman tools are sturdy and guaranteed for life. You can spend more

if you like—high-end brands such as Snap-on are wonderful to use, but Craftsman stuff will get the job done.

You will need specialty tools for working on your bike, and those can be found at your local shop or favorite online catalog. Some sources for them include Kiowa, Motion Pro, Race Tech, Race Tools, Scott's, White Brothers, and Moose Off-Road dealers.

Basic Tools

Start with these tools and you can perform most basic tasks:

- Combination wrenches in 8–19mm sizes
- T-handles in 8–17mm sizes
- Screwdrivers: one wide and one narrow flat-blade (10mm and 3mm wide) and No. 2 and No. 3 Phillips
- Allen wrench set (2.5, 4, 5, 6, 8, 10mm)
- 3/8-inch impact driver
- Specialty tools: spark plug socket, spoke wrench, rear-axle wrench, and carb main-jet wrenches
- Miscellaneous tools: feeler gauges, air-pressure gauge, measuring tape, cable-lubing tool, chain brush, pliers, and plastic mallet

To do more advanced maintenance, add the following to the list above:

- 3/8-inch-drive ratchet wrench and shallow, six-point sockets in 8, 10, 12, 14, 17, 19, 22, 24, 27, 30, and 32mm sizes; Allen bits in 2.5, 4, 5, 6, 8, and 10mm sizes
- Combination wrenches in 22, 24, 27, and 32mm sizes
- Needle-nose and channel-lock pliers, side cutters, chain clamp, and tweezers
- Hand-powered, electric, and/or pneumatic impact driver
- Two torque wrenches (inch-pounds and foot-pounds)

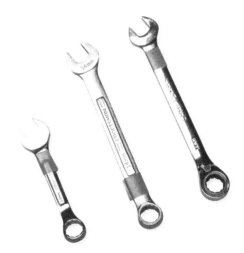

The right set of tools is key to performing maintenance. Combination wrenches are one of the most basic and essential tools. Here you see short, regular, and ratcheting socket wrenches, all color-coded by size (in this case, the 14mm are all blue). *Evans Brasfield*

A good set of socket wrenches is vital. These strips organize the sockets by type, and the color coding indicates size. *Evans Brasfield*

A socket wrench drives the sockets. From top to bottom, a ½-inch drive torque wrench, breaker bar, 3/8-inch drive torque wrench, flexible head ratchet, and simple ratchet. You are going to want all of these in your tool box.

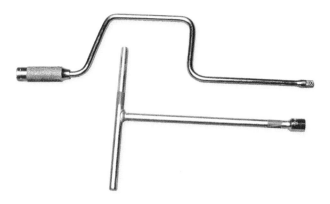

T-handles are the fastest, most convenient way to remove fasteners. The top tool works with sockets, while the bottom T-handle has the socket attached. A high-quality set can be purchased for about $50.

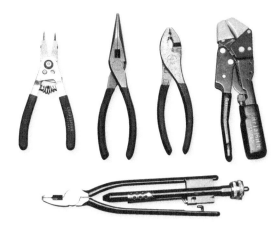

Pliers grip and grab. Here you see circlip, needle-nose, blunt-nose, locking, and safety-wire pliers. A good start. *Evans Brasfield*

- Ball-peen hammer
- Rat-tail, big flat fine and triangular files; set of needle files and a thread file
- Large- and small-diameter round punches and a 1/4-inch-wide flat chisel
- Parts washer
- Miscellaneous tools: flywheel puller, chain breaker, magnet, flashlight, and propane torch
- Air compressor

The tools below you will need to rebuild a four-stroke engine (plus all tools above). You might also need some brand- and model-specific tools, such as case splitters, flywheel pullers, or blind-side bearing removers.

- Bearing and seal driver set
- V-block and dial indicator
- Machinist's square
- Crankcase-splitting tool

- Stud remover
- Flywheel puller
- Dial caliper
- 20-ton press

These are the tools you will need to rebuild Showa and Kayaba forks and shocks:

- Scribe set
- Oil-level setting tool
- Nitrogen cylinder with regulator
- Bladder-cap remover
- 14mm Allen bit
- Vise
- Cartridge wrenches
- Seal drivers
- Bleeder rods
- Digital caliper

YOUR WORKBENCH

You are going to want a decent workbench or space. Maintenance can be done sitting on a bucket. But a bench will make you more efficient and productive—and a lot happier.

At the most basic level, you can draw up a simple plan, go down to your local home improvement store, and buy a pile of two by fours and nail a bench together. You can accomplish this with less than $20 (you can find plans for a $20 bench at http://www.hammerzone.com/archives/workshop/bench/below20.html).

If you do one of these quick-and-dirty home-builds, include a heavy-duty top in your design. Two-inch pine works well. If you can find arrow-straight two by twelves, two of them make a solid, level top. One-inch plywood is another good choice to provide a stout, sturdy work surface.

If you are made of money, kitchen countertops make great workbench tops. Better yet, go down to your local retailer and see if they have some scrap in the back. You just might find something long enough that the storekeeper is looking to unload for cheap.

The surface of your workbench should be from 24 to 36 inches deep. Any deeper and you won't be able to reach the back easily; go any narrower and you won't have enough space to work.

A good workbench should be 30 to 36 inches tall. Taller benches should be above elbow height, while benches designed for working on engines or other heavy equipment should be just below your elbows.

Length is a matter of taste and need. If you rarely use your bench and don't plan to install a vise or other bench-mounted equipment, an 8-foot bench is adequate.

But who wants adequate? If your space permits it, go for 12 feet or longer.

Purchasing Workbenches

If money is no object, you can find some incredible workbenches out there. Most come in packages that include matching cabinets, so you can outfit and color coordinate your garage.

You can find these packages made out of aluminum, stainless steel, and galvanized sheet metal. You can purchase a number of attractive benches that will help you pimp out your dream garage.

A well-outfitted, clean work area is key to good service. A corner of a garage could be transformed into a nice little work area with a few hundred dollars and some ingenuity. *KTM-Sportmotorcycle AG*

Rolling Workbenches

A portable workspace is a great addition to nearly any garage. When working on cars, motorcycles, tractors, or even bicycles, a portable place to rest tools, parts, and whatever else you need for the job is extremely useful.

You can build a portable wooden bench fairly simply. Find a plan for a small bench that includes casters or modify an existing plan to include casters.

You can also purchase metal and plastic rolling benches at your local home improvement store.

Whether you build or buy, look for a bench that is sturdy and includes a lip around the edge so that parts don't roll off and onto the floor.

A Better Homebuilt Bench

Cheap benches are fine for the practical-minded, but if you were that type, you probably wouldn't have bought a book about your garage. One of the great things about the increased interest in DIY these days is you can find some terrific plans for high-quality home-built furniture.

So here's a better option for the DIY types who want a bench that is both functional and attractive: http://www. plansnow.com/wkbmechanic.html.

Folding Workbenches

Another option for the portable workspace is a folding bench. These are pretty slick if you have a small garage or don't use your bench all that often. They don't tend to be as sturdy as the permanent variety, but they often are cheap.

Lighting Your Workbench

Once the bench is built, string up some good light. A nice mix is an overhead light above the space with a retractable light to provide extra illumination when you need it.

Putting the bench under a garage window will provide some natural light during the day and is particularly nice if you spend a lot of time working there.

Computerize Your Bench

Are you using your computer in the garage? More and more people are, whether to adjust tunable ignition systems or to do a Google search to find out how to adjust valve clearances. You can order racks with swinging arms to hang your laptop off the edge of the bench, or you can just build the bench a little wider.

NOW ADD THE TOOLS

Once you have your workbench sorted out, you'll want to have the tools you use regularly out in the open. Position the tool boxes where they fall readily at hand, and watch for opportunities to incorporate the tool boxes into the work bench.

Cover the wall behind the bench in pegboard, and you can have the tools you use most often here. You can also suspend tools from a two by four beam that runs over the

Work bench space on which to spread out tools and parts is important. Stainless steel countertops are lovely. A tightly built two by six pine top works nearly as well and is much more affordable. *Evans Brasfield*

A workstand for your motorcycle gets the bike off the ground and accessible. On a simple stand like this one, you can strip this motorcycle right down to the frame. *American Honda*

LIGHT AND POWER

You are going to want plenty of outlets on the workbench, of course. On the actual bench, consider adding switch boxes so you can turn on your lights, grinder, air compressor, or even the radio.

Drop-down lights are ideal for workbenches, as they put good light right on top of your project. If you mount shelves above the workbench, which is a good way to use that space effectively, you can mount the lights under the shelves as well.

WORK STAND

Go down to your local shop and buy a solid aluminum or steel motorcycle stand. This allows you to put the bike up with both wheels off the ground, and it's a must-have for working on your bike.

Some are simple hard stands that require you to lift the bike. Others will lift the bike with some kind of mechanism. The simple nonlifting types give you the most bang for your buck, and they can be had for less than $50. If you do get one that lifts the bike for you, pay a little more and purchase one of the higher-quality units. The bargain-priced lift stands tend to bend or fall apart.

GETTING TO KNOW YOUR BIKE

Whether you just brought that new bike home or are headed out for a ride on the same old machine, a great way to get started with your machine is to go over the basic checkpoints. You should go through this process every time you ride. Checking out all the basic functions of the bike is a great way to keep tabs on your machine and find things that are wearing out.

So here you go—get out your basic tool set, pull the bike up to the bench, and start to work.

BOLT CHECK

Check all the bolts on the bike to make sure they are tight. This is best done with your T-handle wrenches. Go methodically over the bike, front to back. Dirt bikes vibrate a lot—things come loose. If you don't check the bolts on occasion, parts might eventually fall off.

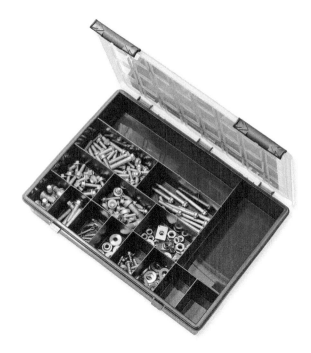

You will need a box of fasteners. A plastic box like this one can be found at an auto parts supply, and you can put spare fasteners in it. Motion Pro offers an off-road motorcycle-specific fastener kit. *Motion Pro*

ENGINE OIL

Check the oil. Make sure the bike is perfectly vertical when you do so. Your stand will come in handy for this.

Change your engine oil regularly—after every ride. The more often you change oil, the longer your engine will live. And if you don't change oil regularly in high-performance four-stroke dirt bikes, your engine will wear out quickly. Having a four-stroke engine rebuilt costs between $1,800 and $3,000. Oil is relatively cheap.

A four-stroke engine has two designs, one with a separate cavity for the tranny and one that shares the oil in the crankcase. For engines with separate tranny cavities, you can use three different types of oils. The different oils are used for specific reasons. The oils are crankcase (SAE 10W-40), ATF (auto trans fluid), and gear oil. Gear oil is available in hypoid and standard. The designation set by the SAE denotes the number of tons of pressure (psi) that it takes to make metal-to-metal contact with an oil film. SAE 80W gear oil is used in the gear cases on autos, and hypoid 80-gear oil is used in the tranny of a dirt bike because it pours thinner than standard gear oil. Standard gear oil available from auto parts stores is too thick to put in the tranny of a dirt bike. It gives good lubrication, but it causes too much drag on the tranny. SAE 10W-40 oil is inexpensive but requires more frequent service than gear oil. Pros use ATF because it gives good clutch action and poses minimal drag on the tranny, but it is one-ride oil.

Check your owner's manual to be sure you are using the proper oil for your bike, and change the oil after every ride.

CLEAN THE AIR FILTER

Oil is the blood of your machine, and air is the, er, air. If dirt and grit get into your bike's engine, it's going to wear out more quickly. The air filter is the gateway, and the filter the keeper. Keep it clean or pay the price.

Remove the filter, clean it in a half-and-half mixture of Simple Green and water, squeeze it dry, and coat it with air filter oil.

With the filter being exposed to dirt, it requires frequent service. Air filter oil must be resistant to breakdown from fuel and trapped dust particles. The best filter oils are those that pour thin and saturate the foam cells of the filter, then dry and become sticky.

No-Toil is a brand of biodegradable air filter oil. This type of oil can be cleaned with degreaser detergent and water. It's suitable for municipal sewer systems and it's easier on your skin and sinuses.

Buy a couple of filters and you can clean all of them at once, then put one back on the bike and a couple others can be oiled and sealed into ziplock bags so they are good to go.

Latex (or nitrile for those with an allergy to latex) gloves are great for both cleaning and installing air filters. Buy a box of 100 of the disposable gloves and keep them on your workbench. Toss a few in your race tool box for good measure.

Every time you clean the filter, inspect the seams for tears, and replace it every twenty washings. If time is of the essence, buy the cheap disposable air filters. They come pre-oiled and you toss them out when you are done.

AIRBOX AND BOOT

It's easy to overlook the air boot and box when you don't even want to clean the filter, but consider this: A small leak in the air boot or box flange can allow dirt to bypass the filter and go directly into the engine. Here are some tips to consider when servicing the filter:

- After you remove the filter, look into the air boot from the other side. Look for dirt that indicates a leak. The chain roller might wear through it, or sticks or rocks could puncture it.
- Never aim a power-washing wand directly at the boot-to-box flange. There is sealant at that junction, but the high-pressure detergent can easily penetrate the flange and blow out the sealant. Twin Air makes special air boot covers that block off the boot while you wash the box. This serves to flush the drain located on the bottom of the box.
- Seal the flange-to-box junction with weather-strip adhesive only. Never use silicone sealer because it is fuel-soluble.
- When washing the bike, remove the seat and air filter. Install a Twin Air filter cap to seal off the carburetor from water, wash the dirt out of the airbox, and flush out the drain.

CHAIN LUBRICATION

There are three different types of chain lubricants: petroleum lube, white lithium grease, and chain wax. Petroleum spray-lube products are the most popular and easy to use, but the oil tends to sling off and splatter other parts of the bike. Lithium grease can only be used after a chain is degreased and dried. Chain wax is gaining popularity because it stays right on the chain. Petroleum lubes can also be used for cables and chain guides. O-ring chains are sealed with grease so they don't require lubrication from spray lubes. After washing a bike, water-displacing sprays can be used on an O-ring chain, but take care not to soak the links. The water-displacing sprays will penetrate the links and dilute the grease.

CHAIN ADJUSTING

The two most important things to know about chain adjusting are to maintain alignment of the sprockets and to correctly set the chain free-play when the swingarm is parallel to the ground. There are a few ways to set the sprockets in alignment—by adjusting the axle to the stamped marks, using an alignment gauge, or visually sighting down the top chain line. All dirt bikes have marks stamped in the swingarm at the axle mounts. The chain adjusters have marks denoting the center of the rear axle. Normally, you would use the marks to keep the rear wheel centered in the swingarm while adjusting the chain's free-play. However, many production frames are robot-welded, and there can be slight tolerance differences that will put the stamped marks out of alignment. That's why race mechanics prefer to use an alignment gauge, which fits into the centers of the rear axle and swingarm pivot bolt. Race Tools in New York makes a simple alignment bar that fits all dirt bikes. You simply fit it in the center of the axle and pivot while you adjust the wheel position for the proper chain free-play. The easiest way, however, is to sight down the top chain run. If the rear wheel/sprocket is out of alignment with the countershaft sprocket, you'll be able to see a slight kink in the chain. Simply adjust the rear axle position so the chain run is straight.

No matter how much travel a dirt bike has, the ideal chain free-play is 0.5 inch or 13 millimeters measured when the swingarm is parallel to the ground. At that point, the rear axle is at the farthest point from the swingarm pivot and the chain free-play will be at its minimum. Just because the wheel is aligned when the bike is stationary doesn't mean it will stay in alignment when the bike accelerates up a bumpy hill. Whenever you set the chain free-play, try to wiggle the rear wheel and the swingarm. If any of the bearings are worn, the drivetrain can run out of alignment, causing a big power drain.

RADIATOR FLUID LEVEL

(CAUTION: Always let the engine cool down before releasing the radiator cap; otherwise, the hot coolant could rush out and burn you. Also, antifreeze is a dangerous fluid

Servicing your air filter is one of the basic must-dos of off-road performance. Most popular off-road bikes make the filters easy to remove. *KTM-Sportmotorcycle AG*

to leave in open containers, especially if you have a dog. Dogs are attracted to the smell of antifreeze and often drink it, causing a slow death from the poison.)

A dirt bike's cooling system should be flushed and changed once a year. Before you drain the cooling system, add four ounces of an aluminum radiator flushing fluid. Several companies make the product, and it is available from any auto parts store. Run the engine for about ten minutes and then drain the cooling system. Take care when disposing of the old coolant. Some states have strict EPA regulations regarding the disposal of used coolant. Call your local auto repair garage and ask if it has a recycling drum for used coolant. Now there are nontoxic, biodegradable coolants available.

Remove the water pump cover and check for corrosion and debris. Check the water pump's bearings by grasping the water impeller with your fingers and trying to move it up and down. If you feel any movement, the water pump bearings and seals need to be replaced. If you see oil leaking into the water pump housing, it is a sign the seals and bearings are worn too. Sometimes, the bearings will be so worn they cut a groove in the water pump shaft. In most cases, when the water pump seals and bearings are worn, so is the shaft. It's best to replace the parts as a set because they aren't that expensive. The water pump is gear-driven by the crankshaft. Some bikes use gears made of plastic; other bikes use metal gears. Metal gears are more durable but are very noisy. Plastic gears are vulnerable to melting, especially when the gearbox oil is low and at very high temperatures.

FILLING AND BLEEDING TIPS

Some bikes have bolts on top of the cylinder head or water spigot that are used to bleed trapped air in the coolant system.

If the air isn't bled from the system, the air pocket will prevent the coolant from circulating and the temperature will rise until the radiator cap releases. The proper way to bleed the trapped air is to fill the system to the top of the radiator, leave the cap off, and loosen the bolt until coolant streams out. Then tighten the bolt, top off the radiator, install the cap, and run the engine for ten minutes before checking the coolant level.

CABLE CHECK AND FREE-PLAY

Our good friend, and perennial whipping-boy, Rat Bike, can't figure it out: Why is his throttle control so haphazard mid-corner? And why does he hear crunching noises when shifting gears, even if he uses the clutch?

Throttle control first: Rat Bike's woes are almost certainly because he has—figuratively speaking—close to a yard of slack in his throttle cable(s), rendering precise throttle control impossible. Frayed cables can also lead to a sticking throttle, which will make Rat Bike utter words his mother never imagined. If your bike has kinked or frayed cables, throttle or clutch, replace them, period. As for free-play in the throttle, follow the instructions in your owner's or service manual to get it to the minimum. A good way to check if you've gone too far is to start the bike while it's on a work stand. While it's idling, rotate the handlebars through their full range of travel. If—usually at the lock stops—engine rpm increase, increase free-play until the condition no longer occurs.

The crunching noises our friend hears are most likely due to a similar condition with his clutch cable: excess free-play. Here again, the owner's or service manual is your best source for the specified amount of free-play at the lever, as well as the appropriate means for setting it and whether the adjustment should be made at the clutch itself or at the adjuster on the lever perch.

WHEELS AND TIRES

Check the tire pressure and make corrections based on track conditions. For, muddy conditions, use front 8 psi, rear 6 psi. For dry conditions, use front 14 psi, rear 12 psi. Always use heavy-duty inner tubes because they allow you to run lower tire pressure without the threat of a puncture. There are some good tools available for the purpose of restoring the edges on the knobs between motos.

The best way to tighten the spokes is to start at the valve stem and tighten every third spoke 1/8 turn. When you get to the stem again, start with the next spoke and repeat the procedure. Once you have tightened three spokes from the stem, you will have tightened every spoke equally. Check the spokes for loose ones and tighten them to the same tension as all the others. Don't use the "tap the spoke and listen to the pitch of the sound" method. It doesn't work. You have to develop a sense of feel for spoke tension. If the spoke is too tight, you'll hear stress relief sounds.

DIRT BIKE CLEANING

Pressure washers are either electric- or gas-powered. Degreasers can be used to break down dirt and oil, but don't use pressurized detergent because it can damage components, such as oil seals and brake pads.

Techniques

Rat Bike Johnson would probably think, "Why do I need to read this? Cleaning a bike just means using strong degreaser, such as Formula 409, or blasting the hell out of the oily areas of the bike with a power washer."

Actually, cleaning a dirt bike takes a lot of caution, and a pressure washer can do more harm than good. You will do less damage by cleaning the bike gently than by leaving it a muddy mess. Power washers can force dirt and water into areas where they can damage expensive engine components, as well as corroding electrical components and connectors. Strong detergents work similarly to acids in the way they tend to corrode certain materials. For example, alkaline can break down the bonding agent in the brake pads, causing them to disintegrate quicker.

Here is an easy guide to cleaning a dirt bike—easy enough even for Rat Bike Johnson to follow. Start by scraping off the big clods of mud under the fenders, on the tires, and around the engine. Next, remove the seat, air filter, and associated parts. Clean the outside of the seat with a brush because the foam can absorb water like a sponge. The water will cause the seat foam to break down and lose its cushion effect.

Stuff a rag in the intake air boot or buy a Twin Air filter cover and fasten it in place. Cap the end of the silencer with a rubber plug to prevent water from entering the pipe.

When washing a bike, a bucket of water and a wise selection of brushes are just as effective as a power washer. If you routinely use a power washer, remember to try to deflect the dirt away from the bike rather than chase it into crevices.

A power washer will make clean-up quick and easy. Just beware—the powerful spray can ruin bearings. Direct the nozzle with care.

After you clean the bike, spray certain parts with some chemicals. Remove the magneto cover and spray the flywheel and coils with nonchlorinated brake cleaner. Spray the disc brake rotors to remove the dirt and water. Next, spray the steel parts with WD40 or LPS to displace the water. Spray the tires and plastic parts with silicone to protect them from drying out and cracking. The silicone will cover the scratches in the plastic, renewing its look. The silicone also will reduce the chance of dirt sticking to the plastic, making it easier to clean the bike after your next ride.

The chain requires special maintenance similar to that of servicing air filters. First, place the chain in a container with a mild solvent. Then scrub it with a nylon brush to remove the dirt and debris. Next, let the chain drip dry and lubricate it once dry. The latest product in chain lubrication is chain wax. It doesn't attract dirt or make everything around it sticky and filthy.

FUELS, LUBRICANTS, AND FLUIDS

The harsh conditions in dirt biking require performance fuels, lubricants, and fluids to protect different components of the bike.

Fuel

There are several different forms of fuel available in the United States and some specific types for Europe. In the United States, the popular racing fuel brands are ELF, Klotz, Phillips, Powermist, Sunoco, and VP Racing. Racing fuel enables a dirt bike to rev higher before misfiring or popping. Some models of dirt bikes are designed with compression ratios and combustion chamber profiles that require racing fuels to run properly. Racers use racing fuel because it is consistent in quality and blended specifically for certain engine configurations.

It's possible to run super-unleaded pump fuel in a dirt bike if the ignition timing is retarded and the cylinder head modified. Oxygenates are added to pump fuel to reduce emissions. That type of fuel makes a dirt bike run leaner and hotter than normal. Pump fuel is graded seasonally. The boiling point is changed in order to make it easier for cars to start when the temperature changes. If you buy pump fuel for cold temperatures and run it in hotter weather, it will make the engine prone to bogging, pinging, and eventually piston failure. Octane booster additives can be mixed with pump fuel to help reduce pinging, detonation, pre-ignition, and flat spots in the powerband.

Lubricants make motorcycles go round. You'll need a pile of them. *Evans Brasfield*

HOW TO WASH YOUR BIKE

This seems like a very simple thing, but washing a bike incorrectly can cause more damage than racing. Start by scraping the majority of the mud from the bike to reduce the amount of water needed to wash the bike and keep your pit area clean. Remove the seat and air filter, and then cap the silencer end and the air boot. Seat foam manufacturers warn not to power-wash seats because the foam acts like a sponge to absorb water (added weight), and the water and detergent can break down the seat foam. Never point the power-washing wand directly at rubber seals (forks, shock, sprocket, wheel bearings). Never spray detergent on the brake pads or disc to clean them. The detergent bonds to the disc and glazes the first time you use the brakes, rendering the pads useless. The best way to wash the bike between races is with a stiff brush, sponge, and a bucket of water.

After you wash the bike, you need to do some things immediately. Drain the carb's float bowl (if your bike isn't fuel-injected, that is), just in case water seeped past the air filter cover. Dry the airbox and boot with a towel. Grease the air filter flange and install a clean filter to prevent anything from accidentally falling into the exposed air boot. Lastly, use a wire brush on the chain and spray it with chain lube to prevent it from corroding.

For race days when dust and water are minimal, you can use a thin disposable sock over the filter. Rather than changing your filter between motos, you can simply pull off the sock and have a clean filter. Some systems allow you to pull off the sock without even removing your seat. Several companies sell them in the United States and Europe.

Performance Tip: Use a steel container rather than a plastic one to hold your fuel. Plastic absorbs the additives that affect the octane rating of the fuel. The best fuel container is called a safety can and is marketed in automotive racing. These steel containers have mesh material inside them that collects vapor, the fuel component that is easiest to ignite.

Safety Tip: Never fill a fuel storage container when it is sitting on the plastic bed liner of a truck. The container will be insulated from ground and prone to static electricity sparks. Always place a fuel storage container on the ground when filling with fuel.

Suspension Oil

Modern suspension components require low-viscosity oils with additives that guard against fade, which is the oil's ability to transmit loads when the oil temperature rises. Use only oils designated for use in rear shocks and cartridge forks. Otherwise, the damping characteristics could be negatively affected.

Grease

Grease seals out water and dirt and provides lubrication to components. The most important areas of the bike that require grease are the air filter's sealing edge, swingarm and linkage pivot bolts and bearings, wheel bearings and seals, fork and

A quick-fill gas can helps speed pit stops. And keeps your petrol happily stored. *KTM-Sportmotorcycle AG*

PARTS CLEANING FLUIDS

Cleaning is a part of dirt biking. Having the right kit can make it easy to maintain your bike. Choosing the right chemicals and cleaning methods can be environmentally conscious and safer for your health. Much of the maintenance tasks that you'll need to perform on your bike revolve around a parts washer. You'll use it to do preliminary cleaning, such as degreasing. You can buy the components of the parts washer, the tank and the chemicals, but the disposal of the chemicals can be expensive. Companies such as Safety Kleen offer rental on parts washers, a variety of chemicals, and disposal service. Its services are fair, about $80 for solvent and the disposal. That's about the same amount that it would cost you to either buy the solvent or dispose of it legally.

The cleaning chemicals used in parts washers are either mineral spirits solvents or alkaline detergents. Some areas of the country prohibit mineral spirit solvents because of air pollution or flammable considerations. The alkaline detergents are advertised as biodegradable, but don't be fooled into thinking that you can just pour it down the drain when it's spent. As soon as you clean an oily part in it, it's contaminated and fits into a different waste category. The alkaline detergents tend to be harsher on unprotected skin than mineral spirit solvents. Some solvents have lanolin, a skin moisturizer, mixed in with them. Solvents are also graded in flash points. Generally speaking, the higher the flash point, the better the cleaning action. Most local fire departments have the right to inspect your parts washer and specify what type of chemicals you use, the flash point temperature, and the type of fusible link fitted to the tank's lid. Fusible links are used on all dedicated parts washers. They are built into the hinge of the lid and will melt if the solvent catches fire, closing the lid and smothering the fire.

Always use gloves when cleaning parts in solvents or detergents. You don't have to wear big clunky gloves anymore. The latest thing is a nitrile glove; it fits like a second skin. Over the years my skin has become hypersensitive to solvents and detergents, yet the tactile nitrile gloves keep my skin from breaking out in a rash. Kevlar-reinforced gloves from Ringer Racing provide additional hand protection for mechanical and machining tasks. These sturdy gloves are used by NASCAR teams for heat and abrasion protection.

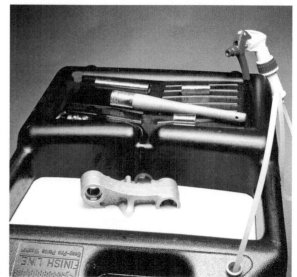

Washing dirty parts is done most easily with a parts washer. The fluid you choose stays in the holding tank, ready for that nasty brake caliper or axle bolt to be spiffed up nicely. *Evans Brasfield*

Part of keeping your bike looking fresh is crisp graphics. A new set of stickers won't make you go any faster, but they will keep the bike looking sharp. *KTM-Sportmotorcycle AG*

Save your forks with a brace like this, which is inserted just before you tie the motorcycle down in the back of your truck or trailer. *KTM-Sportmotorcycle AG*

shock seals, and the steering head bearings. There are three types of greases used for dirt bikes: petroleum, molybdenum, and PTFE-based (Teflon). Most manufacturers specify the use of moly grease for the swingarm, linkage, and steering head bearings. Such grease contains molybdenum disulfide, which offers a low coefficient of friction and holds its viscosity with temperature. Petroleum grease is good for all applications of a dirt bike, but it requires more frequent service. PTFE-based grease is ideal for suspension components.

Brake Fluid

There are two types of brake fluid: denatured alcohol and silicone-based. The designations DOT 3 and 4 are for denatured alcohol fluids; DOT 5 is for silicone fluid. These two types of fluid should never be mixed in the same brake system. DOT 3 and 4 fluids tend to absorb water, reducing the fluid's boiling point and subsequently require more frequent maintenance. Most motorcycle manufacturers recommend DOT 4 for use in dirt bikes.

Chapter 2
Fit the Bike to You

Rat Bike couldn't figure it out. No matter how hard he tried, his front end was pushing in the soft sand on the motocross track. He ran the bike in slow or fast, and the front end washed. In fact, he lost the front end entirely in the first moto and turned a better-than-average start into a long race spent chasing down the slowest guys in the pack—including his nemesis, Spit Polish Pete.

Spit Polish always had the cleanest bike on the grid. The thing gleamed like a Ferarri. But he always finished near dead last, because even though the machine was clean and bright, the setup was completely awful. Spit Polish couldn't ever leave well enough alone, and he was always turning suspension adjusters and jets. The result was his 450 bucked like bronco due to too-stiff settings in the rear and sunk like a stink bug in the front. And the engine often coughed and

hiccupped at low rpms. More times than not, Spit Polish finished the moto kicking his bike back to life, or upside down due to an endo in the whoops.

In moto one, Rat Bike's crash let Pete slip by. And damned if Pete didn't keep the bike upright long enough to stay in front of Rat Bike. Rat Bike would have passed him on the last lap to regain some pride, but the front end gave out again in the same sandy turn. Rat Bike limped across the line behind Pete. He would never hear the end of this from his buds.

So Rat Bike had to do something. He happened to be parked next to a veteran A rider who had seemed willing to help others in the pack. So he swallowed his pride, mustered some courage, and walked over to ask for some help.

The rider ambled over to check out Rat Bike's ride. He had Rat Bike put the bike up on the stand and climb aboard.

When your motorcycle fits you perfectly, riding is more natural. Note how this rider is in perfect position, with controls falling readily at hand. *Suzuki*

"Look at where you are sitting," the A rider said. "You're way back on the seat, with no weight on the front wheel! We can fix this."

What the rider knew that Rat Bike didn't is that how you and your motorcycle interact is key to being effective on the track. One of the keys to making you and your motorcycle work together well is the fit. If all of the controls fall naturally to hand, you will find that you are more relaxed and typically faster on the machine.

Follow the steps below to set up your bike right for you. Then keep refining—small adjustments over the course of a season can make you and the bike one. All that is required is time, a little thought, and possibly a new set of bars.

The reward is speed. Performance doesn't get any cheaper than setup.

BIKE SETUP 101

The starting point for Rat Bike (and you, for that matter) is to get the handlebars in the right position. Rat Bike's were leaned way back, as he liked to rest on the rear of the seat. It felt comfortable to him, just like his days riding a Triumph chopper around the hood.

Those days are gone for Rat Bike, and anyone who rides dirt bikes. Where you want to be is right on top of the front wheel. Modern four-strokes are built to center you in that position. Being in the right place is called body position, and it's the single most important factor in becoming a better rider.

Watch the pros. They are in the right spot, all the time. You don't see them coming off jumps hanging awkwardly off the back of the bike. They are centered and positioned perfectly, getting the most out of their motorcycle.

Set up your bike right, and you will more naturally be in the right spot. Set it wrong and, like Rat Bike, guys like Spit Polish will beat you to the checkers.

The starting point comes in your garage. Put your bike on the stand so it's nice and solid. Put on your riding gear, or at least your boots, and swing a leg over your motorcycle.

Fitting the bike starts with the handlebar position. You can rotate the bar forward or back in the mounts. Some motorcycles also come from the factory with adjustable bar mounting positions. *Yamaha Motor Corporation*

Position yourself on the seat so you are scooted forward, right up to the close to the bars. Now close your eyes and reach out to the handlebars. With your elbows bent just a bit and extending out, the grips should fall naturally in front of you. If you feel like you are reaching too far, loosen the bar clamps and move the handlebars back a bit so they are closer.

Rat Bike had his bars rotated way back, which was pushing him back on the seat. You want the bars positioned so they encourage you to be in the right spot.

Fine-tune the bar adjustment until they fall naturally to your hands when sitting forward on the bike.

Next check the bar height with the same method. If you need to lower or raise the height of the bars, you will have to buy a higher handlebar or add a handlebar riser (see below). Some bikes have adjustable top clamps (the clamp that holds the handlebar to the triple clamp) that allow you to move the bar forward and back. You can also purchase aftermarket top clamps that are adjustable forward and back, and have different heights.

For most of us, you can make do with adjusting the stock bars or changing to a bar that you like. Note that dirt bike magazine tests often have suggestions on how the riders in the test fitted the bike. Find a rider who is about the same size as you are, and the magazine test may give you some clues to help you get the bike set up perfectly.

Once you have the seated position of the bars feeling about right, stand up and do the same exercise. The bars should fall naturally at hand when you stand. Fine-tune, adjust, and keep tuning until you are comfortable either sitting or standing on your bike.

And note that if you can't get this adjustment right, particularly if you find that the standing position is fine but the bars feel wrong when you are seated, you might need to adjust the seat foam.

HANDLEBARS

Handlebars are available in all sorts of configurations. Handlebars are rated for rise, height and sweep-back distance. Handlebars are made of steel or aluminum. Thick-walled aluminum bars without crossbars are designed to flex a bit and absorb vibration.

Fitting Aluminum Handlebars

There is nothing worse than the sinking feeling you get when you land from a big downhill jump and the bars fall to the tank, preventing you from steering. This section provides tips on how to custom fit aluminum handlebars and keep them tight in the clamps. First, determine the optimum width of the handlebars, based on your body positioning and riding needs. For example, if you are tall with wide shoulders, leave your bars at the maximum width. If you ride enduros through tight woods sections, cut the bars down so the bike fits between trees.

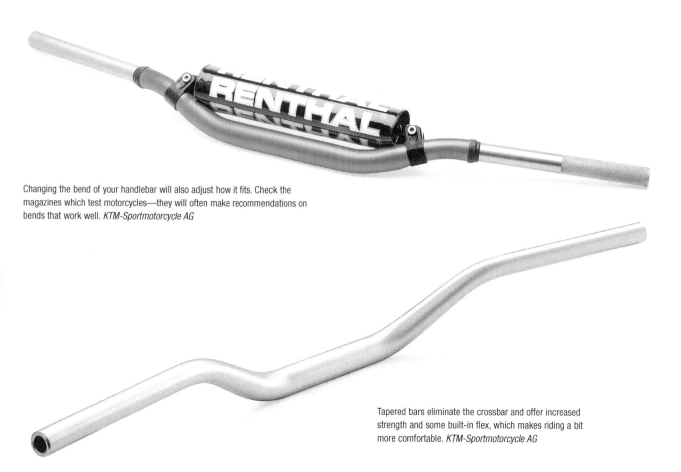

Changing the bend of your handlebar will also adjust how it fits. Check the magazines which test motorcycles—they will often make recommendations on bends that work well. *KTM-Sportmotorcycle AG*

Tapered bars eliminate the crossbar and offer increased strength and some built-in flex, which makes riding a bit more comfortable. *KTM-Sportmotorcycle AG*

Cutting and Polishing

In general, cut the bars to a width that matches the width of your shoulders. You may want the bar a bit wider or narrower than this to suit your personal taste and riding conditions. Motocross riders tend to use wider bars for a bit more leverage, and enduro riders tend to cut them narrower (down to about 28 inches) for maneuvering through tight trees.

Measure and mark the area of the bar that you need to cut and wrap a piece of black tape around the bar. This will help guide your hack saw and enable a smooth, straight cut. After cutting the bar with a hack saw, wrap a piece of medium-grit emery cloth around the rough edge and polish it smooth. The rough edge of the saw cut could gouge the inside of the rubber grip or plastic throttle grip and cause the throttle to stick wide open! Remember to install the end plug in the bar after you have finished sawing and polishing. Some aluminum handlebars do not have diamond-shaped knurling for the handlebar clamps. It may be difficult to keep these bars tight, especially if the clamp and bar surfaces have deformities. It may be necessary to lap these surfaces together to increase the clamping surface area.

Lapping and Fitting the Bars and Clamps

Factory mechanics in Europe recommend using medium-grit valve lapping compound ($3 at auto parts stores) to lap the surfaces of the bars and clamps so the clamps can get a tighter grip on the bars. To begin the process, apply the compound between the handlebar and clamps. Then snug the clamps down and rotate the handlebars back and forth. This procedure polishes the high spots off the surfaces of the bar and clamp and effectively increases the clamping surface area. After lapping, the handlebars will stay tight in the clamps, eliminating any chance of slipping. This method of clamp-to-bar lapping is also recommended for the crossbar clamps. Normally, they have a locking agent applied to the clamp from the manufacturer, but a couple of hard landings cause the locking agent to break bond with the bar. The lapping method is a reliable way to keep the crossbar tight.

Handlebar Tightening Warnings

Pay attention to the manufacturer's recommendation on how to tighten your handlebar clamps and to what torque specification. Some handlebar clamps are designed to have equal-distance gaps on each side of the bar and some are designed for zero gaps on one side. For example, Honda stamps one side of the clamp with a dot mark. That indicates the dot should face the front of the bike and that clamp bolt should be tightened until the clamp has zero gap. This is a common clamping system used on late-model Japanese motorcycles. Honda uses this system on all the front-end clamps from the handlebars to the controls and the front-axle clamp. Some other manufacturers use arrows to denote directions of forward or up. If you are ever unsure which direction a clamp should face, refer to your factory service manual or call your local dealer.

Vibration in Handlebars

If vibration in the handlebars is making your hands go numb, then you might want to consider some options. You can fill the inside of the bars with liquid foam to isolate vibration. This foam is sold at home improvement stores under the category of spray-on insulation. Also there is a product specifically designed for handlebars called the Bar Snake. It is a solid piece of rubber that can be threaded through the bars.

When you can't get the bar position correct by changing bars or settings, you can change the mounts. *KTM-Sportmotorcycle AG*

These mounts are adjustable, and bar height can be changed with spacers. *KTM-Sportmotorcycle AG*

Another option is to use a tapered-wall-tubing bar without a crossbar. On some models you can adapt top triple clamps that use rubber-mounted bar clamps. Rubber-mounted bar clamps tend to get damaged easily in a crash but offer a lot of insulation from vibration.

Notes on Tapered-Wall-Tubing Bars

Aftermarket handlebars, such as the Answer Pro-Taper and the Magura Bulge Bar, are tapered-wall-tubing bars designed to incorporate a bit of flex. These handlebars do not use crossbars. The extra flex is intended to absorb some of the vibration and shock of impacts transferred up the forks. These types of handlebars might require different top clamps and handlebar clamps. Check with the manufacturer as to the availability of clamping kits for your model of bike before purchasing these products.

CONTROLS

Once you have your bars set, the next step is to properly position the controls. The clutch and brake levers need to fall easily to hand, and their position will help keep your elbows up nice and high.

Another way to adjust handlebar placement is replacing the entire triple clamp. This can also adjust the way your bike handles. Note that this clamp offers three different bar positions. *KTM-Sportmotorcycle AG*

The right set of grips makes riding a motorcycle a pleasure. Choose grips that suit your taste in feedback and tackiness. *KTM-Sportmotorcycle AG*

When your elbows are up, you are in the attack position and can better manage the bike. You can apply pressure to the handlebars, and keep the wheel straight when it deflects—or control the bike in a turn or in the air.

A key to keeping your elbows up is positioning your control levers down a bit. You don't want them positioned parallel to the ground. This encourages you to get lazy, drop your elbows, at which point the bike will ride you rather than vice versa. Take charge.

So let's do our fitment drill again. Sit on the bike and reach out to those bars. Fits perfect, right? Now extend two fingers to the clutch and brake lever. With your elbows high, straighten your fingers and reach out for the levers. They should fall readily to your fingers.

If you have to bend your fingers down or up, loosen the bar clamp for the lever and turn them until your fingers hit them with an easy reach.

Note that if you are reaching too far, you can sometimes slide the lever clamp on the bar and change the distance between the grip and the lever. Move the clamp left and right until the lever nestles neatly under your fingers.

Tighten up the bar clamp again, and you are ready to go. Note that if you want to save a few bucks, tighten up the clamp just enough so that it stays in place but can be moved

Levers are another item that can be changed to suit your riding style. *Motion Pro*

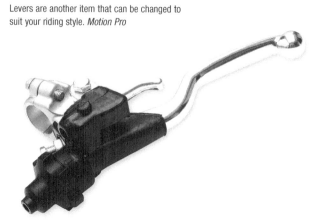

When mounting levers, place a sheet of this material on the handlebar under the lever clamp. This will allow your clamp to rotate rather than break in a fall. *Motion Pro*

by hand if you really lean on it. This way, when you crash, the clamp will spin on the bar before the lever breaks off. This not only saves you money, but it might mean you can get back on the bike and finish the race (or the day) with an operating clutch or front brake.

SEAT

A step back here. If you find that you just can't get your seated position right on your motorcycle, changing seat foam can make it work.

Let's say that you sink down into the bike too much when seated, leaving your hands too high on the handlebars and your legs folded too tightly up on the pegs. This is typical for taller riders, or even for riders who like to stand a lot of the time. Taller seat foam will raise you up, and your legs will get a little more breathing room. This also typically makes the transition from sitting to standing quicker and more natural.

For shorter riders, thinner seat foam can be a big help. Shaving the foam, or using a thinner aftermarket foam, lowers the seat height, making touching the ground a little easier. This will also help shorter legs reach the pegs. You can either shave the stock seat foam with a utility knife or purchase new foam. You can reuse the stock seat cover, or buy a new one.

Fitting Seat Covers and Foam

Have you ever spent fifty dollars on a seat cover and botched the installation, leaving it looking like the ruffled trousers of a wobbly old man?

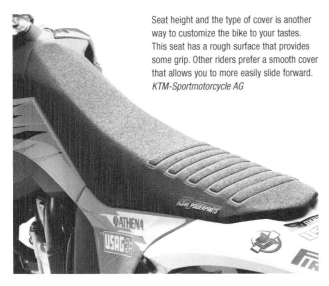

Seat height and the type of cover is another way to customize the bike to your tastes. This seat has a rough surface that provides some grip. Other riders prefer a smooth cover that allows you to more easily slide forward. *KTM-Sportmotorcycle AG*

While you can install a new cover on top of your old one, that is not likely to lead to good results. Strip off the old one first, and then put a new one on top of the foam. Quality seat covers are designed to fit tightly, and they can only do so if you remove the old cover.

One important thing to consider when installing a new cover is the foam. Seat foam deteriorates when you power wash the seat with detergent. When you strip off the old cover, you may find that pieces of the foam underneath have crumbled off. This is an indication the foam has gone bad and must be replaced as well.

Aftermarket Seat Foam

Aftermarket companies offer many different types of seat foam. You have the option of stiffer foam in two degrees or foam both shorter and taller than stock. Before you buy a new seat cover and foam, consider your height, weight, and riding style. A very tall, heavy rider needs the tallest, stiffest foam possible. Stiffer foam makes the seat seem taller.

Gutz Racing specializes in making tall, stiff foam for riders over seventy-four inches in height. The foam is stiffer than stock and more resilient over time and is available in two heights. If you are not a tall rider and want to lower the stock seat foam, you might want to trim the foam. This enables you to rest your foot flat on the ground when coming to a stop or waiting at the starting line. Trimming the foam lower is accomplished with a "hot wire." Most upholstery shops can handle this task. Afterward, you will need to stretch the seat cover tighter and reposition it on the seat base.

Use a pneumatic staple gun to secure the seat cover.

Fitting the Seat Cover

You will need a staple remover, utility knife, and staple gun to fit the seat cover correctly. A pneumatic staple gun is best because it uses significant force to inject the staple into the plastic seat base. If you try to do it with a hand-squeeze stapler,

it will be difficult to get the staple to bite into the base while keeping the cover taut. If the staple doesn't connect the seat into the base, the cover will just tear apart and the staples will fall out. If you doubt your abilities, take the seat and cover to an upholstery shop and make a copy of this section on seat cover installation tips to guide the person doing the work.

Here are the steps to doing it yourself:

1. Remove the old seat cover by extracting the old staples with a hooked staple remover. You can also use a flat-blade screwdriver and sidecutter pliers.
2. Hook the seat cover to the front of the seat and pull it tight at the back. Remove all the wrinkles along the length of the seat before you staple it. Install the staples at least a half inch from the edge so they don't protrude out the sides.
3. Start stapling the seat at the back. Just put four staples in to begin.
4. Staple the seat at the front corners. Pull the cover tight and put two staples on each side.
5. Now take a utility knife and cut the cover to accommodate the seat-mounting tabs. Cut two vertical lines on each side of the tabs. Pull the cover tight on each side equally and put a staple on each side of the tabs. Take care in aligning the seat equally on each side. Now that the cover is set into position, you can staple it every one and a half inches around the perimeter.

FOOT CONTROL ADJUSTMENT

Another way to make your motorcycle fit you is to adjust the rear brake properly. You want the lever high enough so you can depress it easily, but not so high that it interferes with your boot when it is on the peg.

The same is true of the shift lever height. Adjust it so you can easily shift the motorcycle, but don't make it so high that you have to bend unnaturally to change gears. The shift

Wide footpegs make standing up a bit more comfortable. *KTM-Sportmotorcycle AG*

Setting your sag is the most important performance setting for your bike's handling. Set it up properly, and you will be amazed at how much better your machine will work. *Evans Brasfield*

lever is splined and has a lock bolt. Loosen the bolt, and you should be able to pull the lever off the spline, rotate it a bit to adjust it, and slide it back on. Note that some shift levers require you to remove the bolt before pulling the lever off the shaft.

Also, take care to keep the pinch bolt tight. If it loosens up, the shift lever can fall off.

SETTING THE SAG

Another key adjustment is setting the suspension sag. This is the single-most important setup item on a dirt bike. It controls how the bike sits and rides, and it ensures the bike is properly balanced. How to do this is covered in the suspension chapter. Flip to that, and be sure to do it. Setting your sag is the best way to improve your motorcycle's performance. The cost? Zero. Nada. Zip.

CHAIN TENSION

Another oft-overlooked setup item is proper chain tension. Sit on the bike in all your gear, and the chain should have about one to two inches of free play. Don't make the mistake of checking chain free play when you are not on the bike. Overtightening the chain will affect the rear suspension and totally upset how your motorcycle performs.

WHEELS AND TIRES

Tire pressure is another key facet of setting up your motorcycle properly. Setting the correct pressure is a balancing act between enough pressure so that you don't flat and low enough pressure to give good traction. In general, you want your tires inflated with between 8 and 15 psi. See chapter one for information on setting up your motorcycle with the correct tire pressure. Also refer to the chart on page 73, which gives recommendations for tire pressures for different conditions. Rat Bike took in all the information above from the old vet. He adjusted his handlebars so that he sat forward on the seat and also moved his levers to put his elbows in the attack position. He found that his front spokes were so loose the wheel could bend a bit, and the vet helped him tighten those so the wheel was true and tight.

These covers protect your brake rotor and rear sprocket during storage and tire removal. *KTM-Sportmotorcycle AG*

While you can get by with one set of general-purpose off-road tires, the ideal situation is to have several compounds and tread patterns available.
KTM-Sportmotorcycle AG

Tire pressure has a significant effect on performance. Check your tire pressure before every ride, and adjust for conditions. Even one to two pounds of pressure can change how the bike handles. *Mark Frederick*

In the second moto, he got a solid midpack start, and he was able to slice through the sandy corner without his front end washing a bit. He ran hard, didn't crash, and worked his way up to a top 10 finish—his best of the season.

Spit Polish Pete, in the meantime, hadn't tightened a bolt on his shiny machine in three weeks. The shift lever fell off, and he trolled around the track stuck in second gear. He finished last.

PROJECT 1
Adjusting Your Bike to Fit You

Time: Less than 30 minutes

Cost: 0-$

Tools: Basic mechanics tools and stand

Parts: Possibly aftermarket replacements for controls

Experience: 1

Every manufactured product is built to some standard. In the case of dirt bikes, they are sized to fit the vast majority of riders, making them more attractive for purchase. Once you've taken your shiny new ride home, there's only one person the bike needs to fit: you. You may be taller or shorter than the manufacturer's average. Your riding position may be aggressive or laid back. All of these things affect how you interact with the bike's controls. Simply adjusting the controls to fit the way you're built and the way you ride will make you more comfortable and give you more control of your bike. So, why bother with average settings when you can make your own?

When the motorcycle fits your body, you will be faster and more relaxed on the track. Controls that fall naturally to hand allow you to more easily fan the clutch for a little extra juice out of a corner or on the face of a jump. The handlebar position is also key. The most common mistake made when riding is improper body position. When you are in the right spot on the bike--scooted up tight to the tank with your elbows out and parallel with the bars--you are superman. You can do almost anything because you are balanced and in control of your motorcycle. The minute you get out of position, you are unable to make inputs quickly because it can cause you to lose control of the machine.

Positioning your bars so that they are not just comfortable and natural, but also put you in the proper position, can and will make you a faster rider. The starting point for you is to fit the motorcycle that you bought to your body. These simple steps are the most important performance upgrade you can do. Better yet, this upgrade is free!

Once you get used to making the bike fit you, instead of the other way around, you may find yourself looking to the aftermarket to provide you with even more flexibility. Adjustable levers are one popular way to get the fine-tunability you desire. A nice side benefit is that some of these levers also provide a means to prevent them from breaking in a tipover.

You can also change the bars to a different bend that suits you. You can also move the bars forward and back with aftermarket triple clamps and mounts. Some of these mounts and triple clamps are adjustable, which gives you more options.

While we don't all have a shop as flashy as the one provided by the Motorsports Aftermarket Group (www. maggroup.com) for photographing these projects, you can do this all alone in your garage or in your driveway with a stand for your bike.

1

Begin by sitting on the bike in your riding position and consider how comfortable you are operating the controls. Wearing your gear helps the riding simulation.
Evans Brasfield

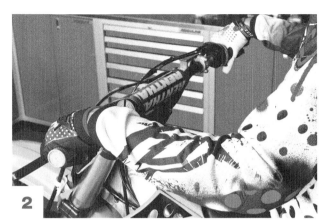

2 Handlebar position is the best place to start. Wrap your fingers around the grips and look at your wrist position when your arms are comfortable. Note how bent down the wrists are in this photo. The bar is too high. *Evans Brasfield*

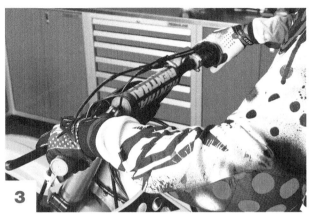

3 With the bar in the sweet spot for your height and arm length, you'll find that your wrists have a slight bend in them. *Evans Brasfield*

4 Once the bar is locked into position, lay your fingers across the levers from your position on the grips. If a lever is too low, you'll be forced to bend your wrist down at an awkward angle. *Evans Brasfield*

5 When the lever is set at the right height, the best compromise for riding both in and out of the saddle is achieved. You may notice that you like your brake and clutch levers in slightly different positions. Also, your preferred lever position may change over time as your ability and riding style develops. This is not unusual. *Evans Brasfield*

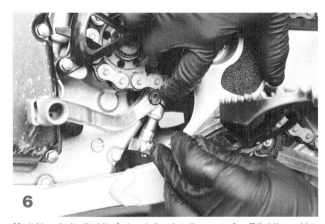

6 Most riders don't adjust the foot controls unless they are so far off that they get in the way. To adjust the shifter, remove the pinch bolt and slide the lever off the shift shaft. Rotate the lever one or two splines on the shaft and bolt it back in place. *Evans Brasfield*

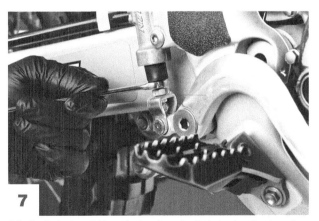

7 Adjusting the brake pedal is as simple as loosening the lock nut on the plunger's shaft and then rotating the adjustment nut to move the pedal up or down, as needed. *Evans Brasfield*

Chapter 3
The Intake System

Ol' Rat Bike Johnson has a size-large problem: His latest, greatest piece of racing hardware, barely two weeks old, has seized tighter than a banker's grip on money. And money—lots of it—is precisely what it will take to make things right. Johnson is by equal turns outraged and dismayed. His cars and trucks have traveled 30,000-plus miles before needing new air filters. What happened?

Simply put, by neglecting his bike's intake system he allowed the engine to ingest dirt, either by not cleaning the air filter, by pressure-washing junctions in the intake system, or other crucial acts of omission or commission. According to oil and filter retailer Amsoil, there are more than 400 tons of suspended dirt and other contaminants in a cubic mile of air over a typical city; things do not improve on a motocross

track or out on a trail. What's more, it's widely accepted that dirt and grit approximately 20 to 25 microns wide (1 micron = 0.001mm, or 0.000039 inch) can cause severe engine wear if they get past the air filter. For comparison, a human hair is approximately 50 to 100 microns wide.

AIR INTAKE SYSTEM

The air intake system comprises the airbox, boot, air filter, and box drain. A cheap piece of foam and a thin barrier of oil—the filter, essentially—is all that protects expensive engine parts from becoming a pile of melted metal. Consequently, if you don't learn the basics of air filter maintenance, you won't be riding for long, just like Johnson.

Dusty conditions quickly dirty air filters. When riding in heavy dust, be sure to change your air filter. *Yamaha Motor Corporation*

CLEAN AND INSPECT

Every time you clean the air filter, check the seams for tears. Some filters are sewn together, while others are bonded with adhesives; over time the seams will split. Professional racing teams only use a filter for one moto. That might seem extreme, but the point is to replace the filter often, preferably after about 20 cleanings.

The best way to clean a filter is with two stages of a petroleum degreaser. Gasoline is a bad choice for two reasons: one, it can ignite, causing burns, and two, it disintegrates the filter's seam glue. Filter oil manufacturers make specific filter cleaner products. The second stage of filter cleaning is with detergent and water. I recommend mixing equal parts of water and Simple Green, a biodegradable detergent made by Gunk sold at most hardware and auto parts stores. Let the filter soak for five minutes and then work it with your hands. Squeeze the filter to remove water; do not wring it out, which could damage it; plus, wringing pushes dirt particles deeper into the foam.

OIL AND GREASE

The filter needs special oil for the foam, and grease for the mounting surface. Filter oil is blended with chemicals that keep the oil diluted so it pours and spreads throughout the filter. These chemicals evaporate quickly in the open air, allowing the filter oil to become very tacky. Don't be tempted to use substitutes for filter oil. Filter oil is available from most motorcycle shops. Apply oil evenly and sparingly across both the inner and outer surfaces of the filter, and squeeze the filter several times, adding oil periodically until the foam is lightly saturated with oil.

Apply a thin layer of grease to the flange-mounting surface to help prevent leakage at the mounting surface. I recommend Bel-Ray waterproof grease.

MAKING IT EASY

Nobody likes to clean and oil air filters, but there are a couple of things you can do to make air filter maintenance easier. I recommend buying two additional filters; if you can clean and oil three filters at once, you'll save yourself time. Store the clean, oiled filters in clear plastic bags. Then, if you have to service the filter at the racetrack or riding area, you don't have to clean it—just replace it with one of the pre-oiled spares. Disposable nitrile gloves are great for keeping the goop off your hands when changing filters between motos. The gloves come in boxes, typically of 100 for about $15. You can find nitrile gloves at cleaning supply, industrial, and hardware stores.

Filter covers can extend the service interval of air filters. There are two types of filter covers: a cloth sock for the filter and a plastic lid for the top of the airbox. These things shield the filter from dust and mud. Some people think airbox covers choke off airflow to the airbox, hindering performance, but that's not true. The covers are designed

to reduce intake noise; when you remove it, the bike makes more noise, and you're liable to be fooled into thinking it has more power. Leave the plastic cover on. It will save you from cleaning the filter as often.

The latest trend in air filter maintenance is convenient, pre-oiled disposable air filters sold in packs of ten. This is a great idea, but you still have to take care to distribute the oil evenly before installation.

AIRBOX AND BOOT

It's easy to overlook the air boot and box when you don't even want to clean the filter, but consider this: a small leak at the air boot or box flange can allow dirt to bypass the filter and go directly into the engine. Here are some tips to consider when servicing the filter:

- After you remove the filter, look into the air boot from the filter side. Look for dirt that indicates a leak. The chain roller might wear through the boot, or sticks and rocks could puncture it.
- Never aim a power-washing wand directly at the boot-box flange. The high-pressure detergent can easily penetrate the flange and blow out the sealant located there. It is advisable to wash the airbox from the top. Twin Air makes special air boot covers so you can block off the boot when washing the airbox. This serves to flush the drain located at the bottom.
- Seal the flange-box junction with weather-strip adhesive only. Never use silicone seal because it is fuel soluble.
- When washing the bike, remove the seat and air filter. Install a Twin Air filter cap to seal off the carburetor from water, wash dirt out of the airbox, and flush out the drain.

Servicing air filters varies from manufacturer to manufacturer. Most have made accessing the filter a fairly simple process. *KTM-Sportmotorcycle AG*

FUEL DELIVERY SYSTEM TUNING

One of the most important changes you can make to your bike's engine management system is to modify the fuel delivery. Whether your bike uses a carburetor or an electronic fuel injection (EFI) system, the delivery settings from the factory typically need some help to work perfectly for you.

This section will give you insight into the fuel delivery system tuning process, from diagnosing mechanical problems that mimic poor jetting, to tuning tools. It will also provide tips on a jetting method I've developed called the ride and feel method, which I consider to be the best. You don't need any fancy tools, just the ability to make observations while you ride.

FUEL DELIVERY SYSTEM PARTS AND FUNCTION

A carburetor or fuel injector is a device that enables fuel to mix with air in a precise ratio while being controlled over a wide range. Carburetors use jets, which are calibrated orifices, such as pilot/slow jets, pilot air screw, throttle valve/slide, jet

A quick-disconnect fuel coupling makes tank removal a snap. Consider installing one if you frequently remove the fuel tank. *Motion Pro*

needle, needle jet/spray bar, air jet, and main jet. Fuel jets have matching air jets, and these jets are available in many sizes to fine-tune the air-fuel mixture to the optimum ratio.

HOW FUEL INJECTION WORKS

By Kevin Cameron

Electronic fuel injection is now the definitive fuel system for high-performance off-road motorcycles. Its accuracy facilitates meeting emissions regulations, and its ability to compensate for a changing atmosphere keeps mixture—and therefore power—much closer to optimum. As always, "The first instance of superior principle is invariably defeated by the developed example of established practice." Some early EFI systems washed the oil off cylinder walls, or produced throttle hiccups, but these troubles were solved.

In a typical system there is an electric fuel pump inside the fuel tank, supplying a constant fuel pressure (such as four to five atmospheres) to the injectors. In place of a carburetor on each intake tract there is a throttle body, typically containing a butterfly valve on a rotating shaft. When automotive-inspired slide throttles were tried in MotoGP, their extra friction proved troublesome—just as it had years before in slide-throttle carburetors.

Most often there is one injector just below the butterfly to cover the range from idle through, say, sixty percent of peak rpm. As the engine revs up, injection may switch to a second, or showerhead, injector located to spray straight into the bell mouth of the intake pipe. This is a system adopted from earlier development for Formula One and is typical on Japanese sportbikes. Ducati, after 1999, developed its solutions around a single showerhead injector.

Each injector is actually an electromagnetic valve. Early types sprayed through a single hole, but in the interest of more thorough fuel evaporation, multi-hole injectors with up to twelve tiny holes are now used. When fuel is to be delivered to the cylinder, the computer determines when injection is to begin, and then opens the electromagnetic valve. Fuel quantity is determined by how long the injector is turned on.

Fueling information is stored in a three-dimensional map in electronic form, relating injector on-time to engine rpm and throttle angle. When a given system is described as an n-alpha system, n is rpm and alpha is throttle angle. The computer modifies the data it takes from the map as necessary, according to both atmospheric and engine variables. Air pressure and temperature are measured by sensors, and various means are used to compensate for the reduced fuel evaporation that results from reduced engine temperature. Some earlier fuel injection systems required use of a manual cold-start enrichment system, but newer systems perform this automatically. After years of struggling with motorcycle and car carburetors, I must confess that I love electronic fuel injection. Engines start, run, and respond regardless of temperature, cold or warmed-up. Wonderful.

Map data are originally obtained by running an example engine at many operating points on a dynamometer. This process assumes that all production engines, whether brand-new or well-worn, will be alike enough to operate well from the resulting map.

Owing to ever-tightening exhaust emissions regulations, motorcycles increasingly monitor actual fuel mixture with exhaust oxygen sensors. This permits the engine computer to hold mixture in the zone that allows the best operation of exhaust catalysts.

An early complaint against mapped fuel injection was that it had to be re-mapped each time the machine's owner made a modification, such as substituting an aftermarket exhaust system. One way around this has been the use of external electronics which fool the engine computer into supplying the desired changes. Dynojet's Power Commander III has become the tool of choice here. The modified machine, with the device plugged into its electronics, is run on a dyno while its exhaust oxygen is monitored by a sensor. Several pulls are made on the dyno, and the feedback from the oxygen sensor allows the system to learn to modify the fueling to obtain best power from the modified engine.

It is possible to effectively build this capability into the engine control, as S&S has done on its X-Wedge large V-twin. Bolt on the chosen modifications, then ride the bike around your favorite road loop a few times, and the system learns what it must do to fuel the engine correctly.

Racing engine controls are computer-addressable, so that the current fuel map may be altered in detail as desired.

It may be that in future, engine controls will become completely self-optimizing, using cylinder pressure sensors to constantly measure where, in crank degrees, peak combustion pressure is reached. Such a system would do away with the ignition map by finding optimum timing continuously, and would do away with a fixed fuel map through use of oxygen sensors.

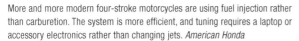

More and more modern four-stroke motorcycles are using fuel injection rather than carburetion. The system is more efficient, and tuning requires a laptop or accessory electronics rather than changing jets. *American Honda*

Engine tuning on fuel-injected motorcycles is done with components rather than jets. The injection system can be tuned with aftermarket components such as the Power Commander, which typically can be adjusted with a laptop computer. *American Honda*

Extracting maximum performance from the intake tract requires that the channel is smooth and direct. Experienced tuners can adjust ports by grinding and polishing the tract. Don't try this at home, and only use a well-known tuner to perform this work on your bike. *American Honda*

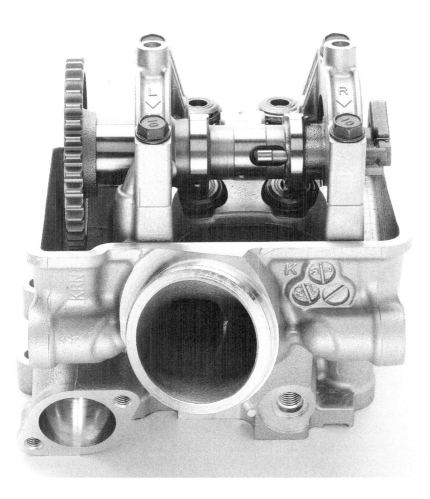

EFI units inject the fuel into the intake with precisely metered electronically controlled sprays. Tuning of an EFI unit is done with a computer.

For four-strokes something closer to the stoichiometric (ideal) ratio of 14:1 works best; 13:1 is usually the default, especially for EFI systems.

For carbs, when you raise the clip, the jetting from one-third to full throttle becomes leaner because the needle lowers into the needle jet, thereby decreasing the area of the needle jet. When you lower the clip, it makes jetting richer.

FUEL JETS, AIR JETS, AND THROTTLE POSITIONS

Three circuits control the air: the air screw, the throttle slide, and the air jet. Four circuits control the fuel: the pilot/slow jet, the spray bar/needle jet, the jet needle, and the main jet. The different air and fuel circuits affect the carb jetting for the different throttle-opening positions as follows:

- Closed to 1/8 throttle—air screw and pilot/slow jet
- 1/8 to 1/4 throttle—air screw, pilot/slow jet, and throttle slide cutaway
- 1/4 to 1/2 throttle—throttle slide cutaway and jet needle
- 1/2 to full-open—jet needle, spray bar/needle jet, main jet, and air jet

(**Note:** On many modern carburetors, the spray bar/needle jet and air jets are fixed-diameter passages in the carburetor body and cannot be altered.)

BASIC CARB SERVICE

Nobody likes to fiddle with a carb if they don't have to. Wedged between the engine and frame with tubes, cables, and wires sprouting out like spaghetti, carburetors are a pain to work on. But they require cleaning just like anything else, and some careful observations can save you big money in the long run. Start by carefully washing the bike, especially around the bottom of the carburetor where roost from the tires and oil from the chain tend to accumulate. Take care when removing the carb—it's easy to damage the cable. It's better to remove the subframe so as to enable unrestricted access to the carb. This will also make it easier to route the vent hoses in their proper positions.

When you remove the carburetor, look at the vent hoses. Are they melted from heat or clogged with mud? If so, that can cause vapor-locking in the float bowl and make the engine bog. Remove the top of the carb and disconnect the cable from the slide. Is the cable frayed or kinked? Is the rubber dust cover missing? If so, replace the cable and dust cover. Now remove the float bowl, jet baffle (white plastic shroud around main jet), float and fuel inlet needle, and the air screw.

To adjust the float level of Mikuni VM, PM, TM, and Keihin PJ and PWK carburetors, set the carb upside-down on a flat surface. Pivot the float lever up, and slowly set it down to the plunger tip of the inlet needle. Observe the

Jet wrenches make removing and adjusting carburetor parts a bit easier. *Motion Pro*

seam line or float lever in relation to the float bowl gasket surface—they should be parallel.

Shake the floats and listen for fluid that might have seeped inside. Replace the floats if there is fluid present or the engine might suffer from constant fuel flooding. Check the fuel inlet needle. It has a Viton rubber tip and occasionally fuel additives and dirt can damage it. Also check the spring-loaded plunger on the opposite end of the tip. Replace the spring if it doesn't push the plunger all the way out. Check the air screw; there should be a spring and O-ring on the end of the needle. The spring provides tension to keep the air screw from vibrating outward, and the O-ring seals out dirt and water from entering the pilot circuit. Next, check the mouth of the carburetor. Look for the two holes at the bottom of the mouth. The one in the center is the air passage for the needle jet and the other hole offset from center is the air passage for the pilot circuit. It's typical for those passages to get clogged with dirt and air filter oil. That would cause the engine to run rough, because without a steady stream of air to mix with and atomize the fuel, raw fuel droplets make jetting seem rich.

Once the carb is stripped down (pilot/slow and main jet still in place), you can flush the passages. Get an aerosol can of brake or carb cleaner from an auto parts store. Make sure you get the type with the small-diameter plastic tube that attaches to the spray tip. Direct the tip into the air-screw passage. When you spray the cleaner, you should see it flow out the pilot/slow jet and the air passage in the carb mouth. Next, spray through the pilot/slow jet, and look for flow through a tiny passage located between the venturi and the intake spigot. Spraying cleaner through these passages ensures the low-speed air and fuel circuits are open and free-flowing.

The last areas to flush with cleaner are the slide bore and slide. Dirt tends to get trapped there, causing the mating surfaces to develop scratches that could cause the throttle to stick. Just a small amount of water and dirt trapped in the tiny passages of the carb can cause havoc with jetting or even engine damage. How often should you service the carb? Whenever it gets dirty. For example, if you ride in muddy, wet conditions, you should check the vent hoses after each ride. If the riding conditions are dusty and your air filter is covered with dirt, then it's a good idea to do a basic carb servicing.

BASIC CARB TROUBLESHOOTING
Weak Spark
When an ignition coil deteriorates, engine performance becomes erratic, developing a miss at high rpm. Check the coil's condition with a multimeter.

Clogged Carburetor Vent Hoses
When carburetor vent hoses get clogged with dirt or pinched closed, jetting will seem lean and the engine will be sluggish. Always check the condition of your carburetor vent hoses. Make sure there is no mud in them and they're not pinched between the suspension linkage.

Carburetor Float Level
When the float level is too low, jetting will appear lean and engine performance will be sluggish. When the float level is too high, jetting will appear rich.

Worn Carburetor Fuel-inlet Needle
When the fuel-inlet needle wears out, excess fuel enters the float bowl and travels up the slow jet and into the engine. This makes carb jetting seem too rich. Replace the fuel-inlet needle and seat every two years.

JETTING SHOULDN'T BE SCARY
Jetting is the process of making adjustments to the air- and fuel-jet sizes in order to fine-tune carburetion to suit the load demands on the engine and make power delivery consistent and optimal. Too much anxiety is spent on jetting. Most people just want to call me on the phone and ask what jets they should put in their carb. That's an impossible question the big dirt-bike magazines attempt to answer just to increase readership. People get confused because they read jetting specs in a magazine, put those jets in their bike, and seize the engine. Any quoted jetting in this book is just a baseline. Most magazines don't list parameters for jetting specs such as: brand-new bike running with VP fuel and an NGK 8 spark plug, ridden by a really slow, lard-ass editor twisting the throttle on a hard-packed track—often someone such as our Rat Bike Johnson.

Some part numbers and jet sizes are given in this book for models that definitely need certain jets in order to get the bike near a baseline. There is an old saying that you can fish for a man and feed him for a day or teach him to fish and enable him to feed himself for life. Here is a quick lesson on how to jet your dirt bike.

THE RIDE AND FEEL METHOD
The most basic method of determining correct carburetor jetting is something I call the ride and feel method.

This method requires you to determine if carburetor tuning is too rich or too lean by the engine's sound and feel. The first step is to mark the throttle on the right side of the handlebars in one-quarter increments, from closed to wide-open, with tape or a Sharpie felt-tip pen. Then ride the motorcycle on a flat, open course. To check jetting for up to one-half throttle, ride in second or third gear. Roll on the throttle slowly from one-quarter to one-half open. If the engine is slow to respond and bogs, then the jetting is too lean. You can verify lean jetting by engaging the choke or enriching lever to the halfway position. This will make the air-fuel mixture richer and the engine should respond better. If the carb jetting is too rich, the engine will feel unresponsive and sluggish. Careful engagement of the choke can help you determine if the jetting is rich or lean. Change the jets one increment at a time, either richer or leaner, until the engine runs better. Most people are afraid to change a jet because they think the engine will be in danger of seizing. Believe me, one jet size won't make the engine seize, but it could be the difference between running poorly and running exceptionally.

To check the jetting for throttle positions from one-half to wide-open, ride in third and fourth gear. Check the jetting in the same manner as listed above. The jets that affect the fuel metering from half to full-throttle are the jet needle, main jet, power jet (electronic carbs), and the air jet.

If you want to take this technique out to the racetrack, you can test the pilot/slow jet when accelerating out of tight hairpin turns, the needle clip position on sweeper turns and short straights, and the main jet on the big uphill or long straights. Of course, be careful if you try to use the choke technique because you could lose control when riding one-handed.

JETTING FOR RIDING TECHNIQUES
Certain types of riders require jetting to complement their technique. For example, beginner mini-bike riders might need slightly richer jetting on the pilot/slow jet and the needle clip position to mellow the powerband and make it easier to ride. Conversely, desert racers who hold the throttle wide-open for long periods of time need rich main jets to compensate for the high load.

WEATHER MAKES THE BIGGEST DIFFERENCE
The weather can have a profound effect on carb jetting because of changes in air density. When the air density increases, you will need to richen the air-fuel mixture to compensate. When the air density decreases, you will need to make the air-fuel mixture leaner to compensate. Use the following as a guide to correcting your jetting when the weather changes.

Air temperature—When the air temperature increases, the air density becomes lower. This will make the air-fuel

The key to tuning your motorcycle is to make careful, subtle adjustments and then ride and pay attention to the results. *KTM-Sportmotorcycle AG*

mixture richer. You must select jet sizes with a lower number to compensate for the lower air density. When the barometric pressure decreases, the opposite effect occurs.

Humidity—When the percentage of humidity in the air increases, the engine draws in a lower percentage of oxygen during each revolution because the water molecules (humidity) take the place of oxygen molecules in a given volume of air. High humidity will make the air-fuel mixture richer, so you should change to smaller jets.

Altitude—In general, the higher the altitude, the lower the air density. When riding at racetracks that are at high altitude, you should change to smaller jets and increase the engine's compression ratio to compensate for the lower air-density.

TRACK CONDITIONS AND LOAD

The conditions of the terrain and the soil have a great effect on jetting because of the load on the engine. Obstacles, such as big hills, sand, and mud, place a greater load on the engine, which then requires more fuel and typically richer jetting. In motocross, track conditions tend to change over the course of the day. Typically, in the morning the air temperature is cooler and the soil wetter, requiring richer jetting. In the afternoon, when the temperature rises and the track dries out, leaner jetting is needed in order to keep the engine running at peak performance.

Other changes for mud and sand riding might include changing to a lower final-drive ratio (rear sprocket with more teeth) to reduce the load on the engine and help prevent overheating. Advancing ignition timing will make the engine more responsive at low-to-middle rpm.

TUNING GAUGES

There are three types of gauges that professional tuners use to aid carb jetting:

1. Relative-air-density (RAD) gauge
2. Air-fuel (AF) ratio meter
3. Exhaust-gas-temperature (EGT) gauge

The following is a description of how each gauge functions and its advantages.

RAD Gauge

A RAD gauge is the best choice for dirt bikes because of the convenience, but it's no good unless you get the jetting perfect. The RAD gauge provides you with an indication of how much the air density changes, helping you compensate for the effects of changes in the air temperature, altitude, and barometric pressure.

The gauge is calibrated in percentage points. Once you set the jetting with the ride and feel method, you can set the calibration screw on the gauge so the needle is pointing to 100 percent. When the air density changes, the RAD gauge will show the relative percentage of change. Using a calculator, you can multiply the percentage change shown on the RAD gauge by the jet size and determine the corrected jet size for the air density. The pilot/slow and main jet have number sizes that correlate with the RAD gauge, but the needle-clip position can only be estimated. Normally for every two main jet increments, the needle clip must be adjusted one notch.

AF Ratio Meter

The AF meter measures the percentage of oxygen in the exhaust gases and displays the approximate air-fuel ratio of the carburetor. The gauge displays AF ratios from 10:1 to 16:l. The AF gauge utilizes a lambda sensor that is inserted into the center of the exhaust stream, approximately six inches from the piston in the header pipe of a four-stroke.

A permanent female pipe fitting (one-quarter inch) must be welded to the side of the exhaust pipe in order to fasten the sensor. The weld-on fitting is also used on the temperature gauges, and the fitting can be plugged with a quarter-inch male pipe fitting when the gauge is not in use. This gauge is ideal for four-stroke engines.

EGT Gauge

An EGT gauge measures the temperature of the gases in the exhaust pipe by means of a temperature probe fastened into the exhaust pipe, six inches from the piston. This type of gauge enables you to tune the carb jetting and the pipe together, taking advantage of the fact that exhaust pipes are designed with a precise temperature in mind.

An exhaust pipe is designed to return a positive-pressure wave to the combustion chamber just before the exhaust port closes. Most pipes are designed for a peak temperature of 1,200 degrees Fahrenheit. Most dirt bikes are jetted too rich, which prevents exhaust gases from reaching their design temperature, so power output suffers.

Sometimes just leaning the main jet and the needle-clip position makes a dramatic difference.

Digitron is the most popular brand of EGT gauge. It measures both EGT and rpm. The gauge is designed for kart racing and is not suited for wet weather conditions. It is designed to mount on the handlebars so the rider can see it clearly. Once you perform baseline jetting, send the rider out on the bike with the EGT. The rider observes the EGT to give you feedback on the necessary jetting changes. Once jetting is dialed, use the tachometer to check the peak rpm of the engine on the longest straight of the racetrack. For example, if the peak rpm exceeds the point of the engine's power-peak rpm, change the rear sprocket to a higher final-drive ratio (rear sprocket with fewer teeth) until the rpm drops into the target range. An EGT gauge is ideal for when peak rpm temperature is crucial.

EFI TUNING

Just as with cars and street bikes, electronic fuel injection (EFI) systems have become the order of the day for most competitive dirt bikes. They provide more accurate fuel metering for best power and fuel consumption, but they have another benefit as well: greater ability to tune than even the hardest-core carburetor fanatic could ever imagine.

EFI tuners allow you to tailor your engine's powerband to specific track conditions, as well as tune the EFI system to certain modifications, such as aftermarket exhaust pipes. They're available from Honda, Husaburg, Kawasaki, KTM, Suzuki (Yoshimura), and Yamaha, as well as other manufacturers, and Bazzaz, FMF, and Power Commander to name but a few aftermarket sources.

After purchasing an EFI tuner, just follow the device's enclosed instructions, as well as consulting your service manual for any information there. Then, with your computer, use the tuner or available software maps to get the throttle response you're seeking. It's really that simple, although some systems allow you far more complex tuning options, such as resetting ignition maps as well. If you don't understand some of the complexities, it's best to stick with the supplied or downloadable maps for the time being. Lastly, one of the greatest advantages of such devices (especially for maladroits such as Rat Bike Johnson; not you, the reader, of course) is that, should you get lost in the forest of possibilities, you can always return the EFI system to stock parameters.

PROJECT 2
How to Clean Your Air Filter

 Time: 30 minutes or a couple of hours if air-drying a filter

 Cost: $

 Tools: Sockets, ratchet, stand, clean rags, compressed air

Parts: Air filter cleaner, air filter oil

 Experience: 1

Dirt and sand are major killers when it comes to dirt bike engines. That's why we put those great, big foam filters inside the airbox. However, there's another thing that dirt and sand kill over time: performance. Keeping your filter clean will help your engine produce maximum power with the smoothest delivery. Trying to suck air through a clogged filter will reduce your gas mileage, drop your horsepower significantly, and make your engine feel soggy. Why skimp on an easy chore, one that takes only a half hour—mostly waiting for the filter to dry—when the benefits are so great?

When it comes to cleaning filters, there are two schools of thought. One uses a solvent that you dip the filter in to cut the filter oil and float out the crud. The other (shown here) uses spray-on solvent. Although each method has its supporters, each method is equally valid. The same goes for spraying on or pouring on new filter oil. Most importantly,

do not use gasoline or other solvents that are not specifically designed to clean air filters or you risk damaging the filter by degrading the glue used to hold multipart filters together. Similarly, you can actually swell the filter material, making the filter holes larger and less effective at stopping dirt. Simply put, use the right products for the job.

Purchasing one or two extra filters allows you to clean and prep 2-3 filters at one time. Oil the extra filters, and then store them in ziplock bags with all the air squeezed out of the bag. This way, you have a clean filter ready to go. This is ideal when you are on a several-day trail ride or racing motocross in extremely dusty conditions, as you can change filters between rides.

If you want to avoid this process entirely, you can purchase disposable pre-oiled air filters. These add cost to your ride, but make life a little simpler.

1 Since dirt bikes are so elemental, getting to the air filter couldn't be easier. Usually you just unbolt the seat. *Evans Brasfield*

2 Lift the seat free of the frame and you'll see the soiled filter in all its glory. *Evans Brasfield*

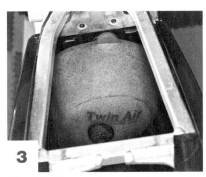

3

Although air filters come in a variety of shapes and sizes, the vast majority of dirt-oriented filters will be foam, like this one. Before you jump right in and pull the sucker out, make sure that no rocks or sand are loose on top of the filter. You don't want to accidentally drop abrasives into the intake while you're removing the filter, and sand is remarkably good at weaseling its way past the wire mesh blocking the intake. *Evans Brasfield*

4

Brush off the exterior of the filter to get rid of any loose grunge. Remove the filter from the cage, and inspect both the cage and the filter for any breaks or tears. Since filter cleaners tend to be smelly, noxious stuff, go outside before spraying down your filter. Wearing gloves is also a nice idea. Completely saturate the filter, making sure that all the dirtiest parts get a liberal coating. Let it soak in for a few minutes before rinsing. *Evans Brasfield*

5

Use warm water to rinse the cleaner and dirt out of the filter. Although you want a good flow of water, don't use such a strong stream that you risk damaging the filter. If you're using one of those fancy cotton filters, this is even more important—along with using cold water and only rinsing from the inside of the filter out. Foam filters aren't as finicky. Take your time and get the filter as clean as possible. *Evans Brasfield*

6

Shake and squeeze the excess water from your filter and set it aside to dry. The sun on a nice, hot driveway will speed the process a little. The filter needs to be completely dry prior to oiling. Again, cotton filters are a bit more sensitive than foam. Resist the urge to use a hair dryer to speed things up. *Evans Brasfield*

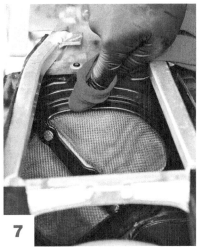

7

While the filter is drying, use the time to clean out the airbox. Wipe any excess grease from the filter's mounting surfaces. Remove the sand and dried mud from the bottom of the airbox. *Evans Brasfield*

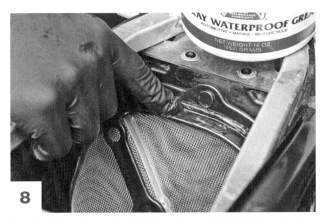

8

Once the airbox is clean, apply a liberal layer of grease to the filter flange. Sand and dirt want to work their way into any intake orifice, like cockroaches into kitchen cracks. This grease will thwart their nefarious goals. *Evans Brasfield*

9

When applying the filter oil, you'll want to be outside. It's stinky and will get all over the place, if you're not careful. Using a pattern to spray the oil will help if you miss any spots. After the oil has soaked in for a couple minutes, check the filter over to make sure you didn't miss any places. Reinstall the filter and button up your bike, and you're good to go. *Evans Brasfield*

Chapter 4
The Exhaust System

BY KEVIN CAMERON

Aftermarket pipes are a popular addition with off-road motorcycles. They reduce weight and typically make the bike louder. Unfortunately, bikes with aftermarket pipes too often have powerbands less smooth than with the original equipment manufacturer (OEM) pipe. Aftermarket pipes may affect carburetion for the worse and usually need additional tuning work to give their best.

What can you expect from a pipe, as compared with your stock system? A lot less, unfortunately, than you could 10 years ago. Older four-stroke bikes, XR400s and such, had less sophisticated exhaust systems, so a modern pipe was a significant performance upgrade. But recent high-performance off-road bikes have highly engineered pipes.

What aftermarket pipes can do is relocate and concentrate your engine's torque for some special purpose.

A complete exhaust system with a less restrictive muffler, for example, will boost roughly the top 3,000 rpm of your engine's performance—but don't be surprised to find a good-sized flat spot just below that. Other pipe designs and features can alter this basic tendency, but none can completely avoid it, as we shall see.

With off-road motorcycles, you also have to be concerned about passing sound tests. Many competitive events, group rides, and off-road riding parks have noise level restrictions. These vary by state and riding organization. Note that many race events have a decibel meter present at the tech inspection, and you will not be able to ride if your motorcycle is too loud.

An exhaust system is more than just tubing to carry away your engine's smoke. It is also a pump, using the energy in exhaust pressure pulses (as much as 100 psi) to help empty

Carbon fiber mufflers reduce weight and add some flash to your bike. Carbon fiber is easier to clean than titanium, and remains cooler than metal mufflers. *American Honda*

and refill your engine's cylinders. This pumping action has negative as well as positive effects, however. While it can create peaks on your torque curve—rpm regions in which the engine pulls more strongly because exhaust waves are pumping more mixture into the cylinders—it also generates other rpm zones, so-called flat spots, in which your engine's pull is weakened.

All production pipes have to meet sound standards, and there is only one way to do that—with plenty of silencer volume. This is why a few stock systems have two silencers, one on each side.

The general rule is, therefore, that a quiet system is a big system, while a small, racy-looking system will tend to be loud.

HOW PIPES WORK

As an exhaust valve opens, a pulse of high-pressure exhaust gas is released into the pipe. It travels down the header tube at high speed until it reaches the junction with the collector pipe. Here, pipe area suddenly expands, so the pulse expands, too. It expands in all directions, including back up the pipe from whence it came. This means that an expansion wave (suction) travels back up the header.

If the pipe is correctly dimensioned, and the engine is operating in the rpm band for which the pipe is designed, this negative wave arrives back at the exhaust valve during valve overlap. Overlap is the period near TDC (top dead center) at the end of the exhaust stroke, when the exhaust valve is just closing and the intake valve just opening. During overlap, both valves are slightly open for some time period—with street cams, overlap may last less than 30 crank degrees, but with race cams, it may be 60 degrees or more.

The expansion, or negative pipe wave, travels in through the open exhaust valve, and its low pressure helps to pull residual exhaust out of the small space above the piston.

Remember, this occurs near TDC, so the piston is essentially stopped for about 30 degrees at the top of its stroke.

As the suction wave pulls cylinder pressure down, it also travels out of the intake valves into the intake tract. This causes immediate flow of fresh charge from the intake system toward the cylinder—even before the piston has begun its suction stroke. This early acceleration of the intake flow gives the intake process a valuable head start, causing the cylinder to fill more completely than it would if there was no exhaust pipe negative wave. This boosts torque, making a positive area, or bump, on the torque curve.

This tuning effect works over a range of rpm a few hundred revs wide because: 1) the valve overlap period has some duration, allowing the effect to work even if the suction wave is a little early or a little late, and 2) the exhaust pipe's suction pulse itself has some duration; if its leading edge arrives before overlap begins, its trailing edge can still do some good work.

Now for the bad news. At lower rpm, each revolution of the crank takes longer, but exhaust waves travel at the same speed as before. The result is that the "good" negative pipe wave now reaches the cylinder *before* the overlap period, *before* the intake valves have begun to open, thus it can't reach the intake system. Moments later, when overlap does begin, it is a positive wave that arrives, not a negative one. This is because negative and positive waves alternate in the pipe in an unending series, bouncing from end to end, just as they do in an organ pipe.

This unwanted positive wave pushes hot exhaust gas back into the cylinder, maybe all the way back through the carburetor and clear into the air box. The result delays the intake process and dilutes it with exhaust gas. It also makes the engine run very rich (unless it has fuel injection, more about that later) in a process called multiple carburetion.

Stock head pipes work well with a stock engine or intake system. The factory designers put a lot of time into the flow, so don't automatically replace it unless you understand the performance gains you desire. This is the exhaust on the Beta 520RR. *Beta*

Multiple carburetion works this way. Carburetors are devices for adding fuel to moving air by use of Bernoulli's principle: Moving air has less pressure than still air. But carburetors are dull-witted and don't care which way the air is moving through them, or even whether what's moving is air or not.

So when a positive exhaust pulse blows back through the carburetor, it picks up fuel on its way into the airbox. Remember, this is exhaust gas, with all the oxygen already burned out of it. It can't support combustion a second time. Once the piston gathers speed on its downward suction stroke, carburetor flow reverses and the fuel-rich exhaust gas swirling in the airbox is drawn through the carb a second time, picking up even more fuel. Pure air follows it later, but the damage is already done.

This episode of reverse flow has diluted this cylinder's charge with exhaust. It has also made it very rich—maybe even too rich to burn, in which case the engine misfires, or at least stumbles. You, riding the bike, feel this as weak acceleration or a hesitation. Even if it doesn't misfire, the rich mixture burns poorly and with reduced effect, and cylinder filling is poor because of the delayed intake process. Torque

is weak. You feel the dreaded flat spot, an rpm zone of poor acceleration. This mechanism causing momentary richness is called multiple carburetion because the charge passes through the carb more than once.

Countless riders, discovering this flat spot after fitting a new pipe, have devoted themselves tirelessly to trying to tune their way out of the hole they've made. Soon discovering that their engines are rich in the flat spot, they jet down. Power in the flat spot improves, so they jet down again. But when they check overall performance, they find that their engines are almost too weak (lean) to run everywhere else across the band.

Sadder but wiser now, they have to accept the flat spot and just ride around it—or try another pipe.

Only one thing is guaranteed when you buy an aftermarket pipe: It will be a bunch lighter than your stock system, which is built with heavy materials. This may be the ultimate bottom line in the pipe world; a lighter bike is a better bike, every time.

Stock pipes are heavy because they're designed to last. Heavy-gauge metal, large mufflers with complex internal

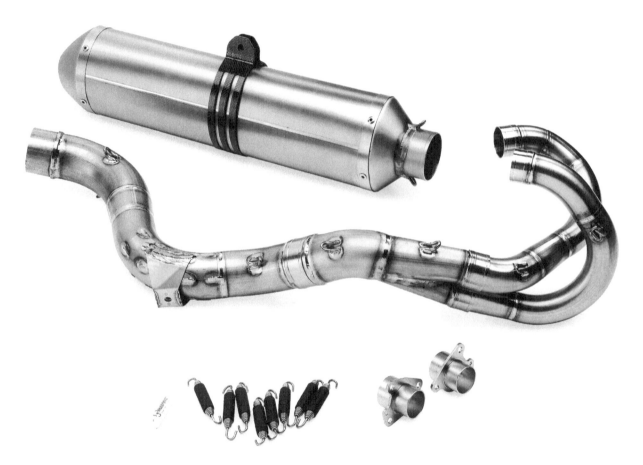

A complete exhaust system often gives you a more significant performance upgrade, as the header pipe and the muffler have been designed to work in concert. They are typically lighter than stock units. Provided you choose a quality exhaust system that is well-designed, the only disadvantage of a full system is the cost.
KTM-Sportmotorcycle AG

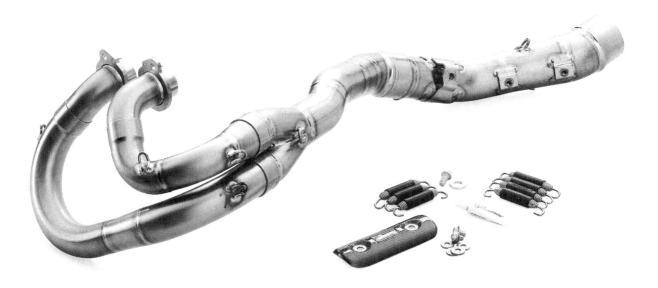

An upgraded exhaust is best used in concert with a variety of other upgrades. Consult a tuning shop on package upgrades—a good combination of upgrades may include an exhaust pipe, EFI tune, and a change in cam. *KTM-Sportmotorcycle AG*

flow paths, and the need for compliance with noise standards make them that way. With an aftermarket pipe, you will have to consider its little sacrifices. To be made thinner and lighter, aftermarket pipes are often made of corrosion-resistant stainless steel or titanium. Lacking a production pipe's internal tubes and baffles, your aftermarket muffler canister is going to be louder than stock—maybe too loud for even your own taste. More reasons to inspect before you buy.

HEADER TUBE SIZE

Some pipes have bigger header tubes, some have smaller. Why? The answer is that header-tube size is related to exhaust valve-open area—valve circumference multiplied by max lift, times the number of exhaust valves per cylinder. Play-

A slip-on exhaust is an easy way to reduce weight and add modest performance gains, depending on the motorcycle. This works well with off-road motorcycles when you want to make them breathe better, or motocross bikes on which you are adding a spark arrestor. *KTM-Sportmotorcycle AG*

bike engines have moderate lift because they are supposed to last at least as long as the payments. Therefore, they have small header tubes. In high-performance off-road motorcycle engines with more exhaust-valve lift, bigger tube pipes can be considered.

The rule of thumb is that header-pipe inside area should be 1.16 times exhaust-valve open area.

What happens if you put on the big tubes and don't have exhaust area to match? It's just like oversized carbs; slowing down the gas speed tends to hurt bottom-end performance and may not help the top-end either. Exhaust gas must accelerate to high velocity to duck under the exhaust valve and get through the port throat. If the header tube size is too big, the gas then has to slow down again.

If the pipe is too small for the valve area, the pipe will be the restriction. Too high a pipe velocity creates friction loss. Too low a velocity makes it too easy for pipe waves to reverse flow when it shouldn't happen.

SLIP-ONS

For the rider who wants a different look but doesn't care to wrestle with all those bolts and nuts, there is the slip-on—a replacement muffler that takes the place of the stock part. There is likely a weight saving and there may be a drop in back pressure, but the bottom line, I fear, is no pain, no gain. But, again, if you are just starting out with modifying, it's an easy place to start, with reversible consequences.

Slip-ons are also a good option for riders who want to add a spark arrestor, which is needed to ride in many trail systems and in hare scrambles and enduro competition. Several aftermarket companies offer slip-on mufflers that incorporate a spark arrestor.

IS PERMANENT BEAUTY POSSIBLE?

My metallurgist friend likes to say, "Metals can hardly wait to get back to their natural state," which means they oxidize—rust—and return to mineral form. It is, therefore, pleasing that today's stainless-steel and titanium pipes resist such decay, and make unnecessary the primitive practices of painting and plating. Paint burns off, rubs off, and weathers off. Plating peels, chips, and discolors.

The fact is off-road motorcycles look good only if their owners take the time to make them look good. Race bikes look good because they are frequently maintained and always indoors in comfortable shops or transporters, perhaps paid for by deep-pocket sponsors to whom appearance is important. For myself, I find beauty in a strong dyno printout. I appreciate the look of a bike that is actually ridden, with some wear and tear visible. I happily leave the cosmetics to others.

INSTALLATION

It would be nice to have a set of metric combination wrenches—box and open-end—and even some sockets for tackling this job. Often, getting at the attachment of the pipes to the cylinder head requires removing the radiator or hinging it forward. Each header pipe is held in place against its exhaust port by a collar, which in turn is held in place on a pair of studs by nuts. The muffler itself is supported on brackets and detaches from the pipe system by means of a large clamp.

Find all the fasteners, and then remove the muffler first. After unfastening the headers from the cylinder head, the rest of the pipe can be removed as well. Expect to hurt your knuckles—it comes with the territory. As with anything that has been together for a while, some wiggling may be necessary to free the parts. Note whether sealing washers are used between the pipes and head. If new ones are not included with your pipe kit, get them from your dealer or via mail order.

Race pipes are flexibly mounted to save them from vibration-induced cracking. Instead of being held into the head by bolts, the header pipes slip into couplers that bolt to the head. The pipe ends are held into these couplers by springs. While this is racy, it also will leak slightly, giving your engine a bad case of the brown dribbles, or embarrassing backfires on deceleration. If your pipe kit is spring-mounted this way, invest in a spring hook or make one out of a screwdriver. Many a mechanic's knuckle carries scars inflicted when trying to hook up pipe springs using only a pair of pliers.

Once you have the stock pipe removed, inspect the exhaust ports with a strong light and remove any crud that would be trapped by the new pipe and its fittings. If your pipe is spring-mounted, you can bolt on the couplers now, using whatever seal or washer is required. It's a good idea to be sure the hole in the washer is at least as big as the hole in the coupler, so there is no partial masking of the port by the washer.

On some engines, the pipe or coupler actually fits deeply into the head. This is done to make the port in the head shorter. A lot of the heat that the engine's cooling system must get rid of is picked up right here, around the exhaust port, because velocity, and therefore heat transfer, is large here. In this case, the pipe is held in place by a piece of tubing split down the middle to make a pair of collets.

To install, put in the seal washer, slip the pipe or coupler in on top of it, and then slide the pair of collets in against the back of the flange on the pipe's end. Next, slide the collar up the pipe to bear on the outer ends of the collets and over the pair of studs projecting from the cylinder head. Put the nuts loosely on the studs to hold everything together, but don't tighten yet—everything must be lined up first.

Some pipes are welded in one piece, while others may have slip joints to allow for some adjustment during installation. If your kit uses couplers, present your pipe to the couplers now for a trial fit. On some engines, all ports face the same direction, but on others this is not so, requiring some jiggery-pokery to get everything in place. With the header pipes inserted into the couplers now, snug up the mounting nuts.

Bear in mind that 6mm studs should be tightened to no more than about 50 in-lb, or 8mm studs to 150 in-lb. It's very unpleasant to pull or break a stud on a cylinder head because getting a broken stud out or a thread repair into a stripped hole is tricky and may require removing the head. You want this to be an easy job, so be careful when tightening!

On a spring-retained pipe, bring the pipe to its final position, and you'll be able to see if the rest of the kit—the canister and its associated brackets—is going to fit nicely in place.

If your pipe is rigid-mounted, with the pipe and flanges in place, snug up the mounting nuts to bring the pipe firmly against the head, thereby positioning the rear part of the pipe. Jiggling the pipe slightly as you tighten the nuts can help align things and prevent binding. You can now see if everything else is going to fit nicely.

A word of caution about mounting brackets: It's common for there to be small misalignments, and the temptation is to force everything into alignment and slap the bolts through, tighten them up, and forget it. But that will build tension into your installation, and the vibration of operation will add to that tension, making cracking and breaking more likely. Better to take some time making things line up, using a round file or whatever is needed to create stress-free alignment. Then you can put the mounting bolts in without having to be Tarzan. Also be sure any fasteners tighten against flat surfaces, not irregular blobs of weld.

Whatever man can put together, vibration can take apart, so at this point, you may want to consider what to do about it. Your kit may come with self-locking fasteners of some kind, which you should use. Plastic-inserted self-locking nuts may not, however, be much use on the hot exhaust flanges, so consider using nuts drilled for safety wire, and then wiring

Spark arrestors are necessary for riding on most public land and competing in some enduro and hare scramble races. They prevent sparks from escaping the exhaust. *American Honda*

the nuts in place. You may also be able to find deformed thread nuts that work in hot applications.

If you have drained and removed your radiator for this job, refer to your service manual for the proper procedure for refilling and bleeding your cooling system. Start up the engine. Enjoy the rich, mellow sound. Investigate the possible other benefits.

But wait! You're not through yet because most pipes require changes to what I will loosely call "carburetion." If your bike is equipped with fuel injection, you will need a means of altering the fuel mixture to suit the new conditions. The usual way of doing this is to buy a Dynojet Power Commander III (referred to as a PCIII in ads and available for select off-road motorcycles) and either obtain the mapping for your particular pipe from Dynojet or book in at a dyno facility that can map your system.

In former times, carburetor jet kits were the tool for this, with settings for widely sold pipes often available. There are three ways to go here. One is a full kit, including new needles, needle-height adjusting washers, and possibly instructions on how to modify the rate at which the CV throttle pistons open during acceleration. Another is just

needles and washers. A third possibility is to adjust the position of the stock needles by thin shim washers.

In any carburetor work, prepare to display all the patience of which you are capable. Getting at the carburetors on a dirt bike isn't always easy. There are going to be regiments of resisting fasteners, knuckle-barking opportunities, and occasion to doubt the sanity of those bright young engineers who designed your bike.

All this, let me assure you, is normal, and you'll overcome it. Just keep thinking about the outcome: You want your bike to run right, and you want to learn something about carburetion in the process. These goals make the nonsense worthwhile. Soon you'll be an ace at whipping all those parts on and off.

All the foregoing is made obsolete by electronic fuel injection. Whether you use a PCIII or a laptop, your only connection with hardware is via electrical signals. Tools, jets, needles, and throttle slides are eligible for the museum now. Even our current era of ignition timing and fuel injection mapping stands ready to be swept away in its turn by the next flood of self-optimizing electronic controls.

Why, the only skill left for us to learn will be riding itself.

PROJECT 3
How to Repack Your Muffler

 Time: 1 hour

Tools: Sockets, ratchet, Allen keys, flat head screw driver (or putty knife), dead blow hammer

Experience: 1

Cost: $

 Parts: Muffler packing material

One maintenance item that has become much more common with the move from two-stroke to four-stroke engines in dirt bikes is the need to repack the muffler. Those big power pulses beat down and actually break the packing material in the muffler. Gradually, cavities open up in the packing, and as they get larger, their power-robbing appetite grows. If you let this process go too long, the packing's insulating properties can't fight back the heat, leading to a scorched appearance to the outside of the muffler. Some lighter-weight alloys can actually burn through from extended neglect. All of this is long after the engine's performance has taken a major hit, though.

In order to make sure that you keep your muffler performing at its peak, you doubtless want to know when you should repack it. The answer to that is: "That depends." Your bike's factory service manual probably says something like every 15 hours of operation. However, you may need to do it sooner if you've been running through the wilderness with the throttle wide open for extended periods of time. In case you're wondering, the pros have their mufflers repacked after every race weekend. That's how important it is to top performance.

1 The folks at FMF who repack all the mufflers for their sponsored riders took the time to demonstrate how to do it the right way. The technician on the left is packing a new muffler, and the one on the right is starting out on a well used one. *Evans Brasfield*

2 Begin by removing the bolts that hold the canister together. The instructions that came with your repacking kit will tell you which end to open. *Evans Brasfield*

3

Hold the muffler off the work bench by the endcap that you've unbolted and rap on the mounting bracket with a dead blow hammer. *Evans Brasfield*

4

With a twisting motion, remove the endcap and the baffle assembly. The packing will usually come out with the baffle. *Evans Brasfield*

5

The technician is pointing to one of the cavities that has developed inside the packing. While this one isn't big enough to rob the engine of power, it will grow quickly once it has formed. *Evans Brasfield*

6

Inspect the baffle for any holes in the mesh. If you find any, you will need to replace the mesh before you repack the muffler. *Evans Brasfield*

7

Roll the packing tightly around the baffle. If you don't do this as tight as possible, you'll have a hard time squeezing it into the canister. Note how some of the material has extended over the end. It will slide back over the baffle as you insert it in the canister. *Evans Brasfield*

8

Twist the baffle in the same direction that you wrapped the packing material as you insert it into the canister. This will help to keep the wrap tight. *Evans Brasfield*

9

Check to see if any of the packing is preventing the baffle from being slipped into the other endcap. If so, use a putty knife or screwdriver to slide it back over the baffle. *Evans Brasfield*

10

Using a dead blow hammer, carefully tap the endcap until it is about a quarter inch from being fully seated. *Evans Brasfield*

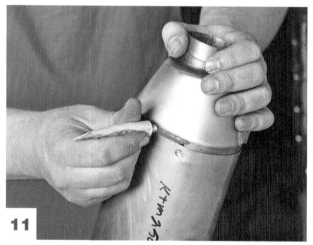

11

Apply a bead of heat tolerant sealant before pressing the endcap into its final position. *Evans Brasfield*

12

After the endcap is in position, wipe away any excess sealant before it has a chance to set. *Evans Brasfield*

13

Bolt the endcap and canister back together but don't over tighten the bolt. They can strip easily. *Evans Brasfield*

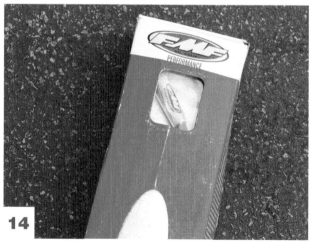

14

Most exhaust system manufacturers sell repacking kits for their mufflers. They should have everything you need to perform the task. *Evans Brasfield*

PROJECT 4
How to Install a Spark Arrestor

Time: Less than 30 minutes

Tools: Basic mechanics tools and stand

Experience: 1

Cost: $$

Parts: Aftermarket spark arrestor

Spark arrestors and reasonable sound output are increasingly important for anyone who wants to ride the trails. More areas are being regulated, and those regulations almost invariably include lowering the sound output of your bike and adding a spark arrestor.

The guys at Pro Moto Billet have come out with an endcap that is fitted to your stock exhaust, providing a cleanable spark arrestor and an insert that reduces sound output. The cap is CNC machined from 6061 billet aluminum and is a handsome, nicely finished part.

The unit sounds very close to stock with the spark arrestor in, and we found no noticeable power change. With the optional noise-reducing insert installed, we found the output dropped to about 96 decibels.

About the only drawback with the unit is the installation, which takes a bit of time and effort. It's nothing extraordinary and well within the means of the average garage wrencher. The unit looks great and is nicely finished, and it is reasonably priced at $134.95.

Pro Moto Billet offers the units for most high-performance four-strokes, including Yamaha YZFs, Honda CRFs, Kawasaki KX-Fs, KTMs, and Suzuki RM-Zs.

1 In order to mount the unit, the stock endcap needs to be removed. On our CRF, this proved to be the most difficult part of the installation. The stock rivets need to be drilled, and then the endcap has to be pulled out. Use a rubber mallet and a blunt-ended chisel to hammer the stock piece out. *Mark Frederick*

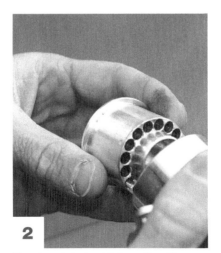

2 The noise-reducing insert fastens with an Allen screw. With the insert installed, the sound level of the CRF450R dropped to 96 decibels. *Mark Frederick*

3 The entire body of the unit then can be slid into the muffler and screwed tight. This means you can easily pull it off and remove the spark arrestor for a weekend motocross ride. *Mark Frederick*

Chapter 5
The Electrical System

Dirt riding is not touring and a rutted forest trail or motocross course is not bound by the rules of the road. The range of demands on the electrical system is therefore narrower on a dirt bike than a road bike—no radio, turn signals, heated grips, GPS, fancy gauges. Many off-road bikes don't even run lights. Yet electricity is still essential to an internal combustion engine. No electricity means no spark, means no ignition, means no BROOOM-BROOOM!

Electrical troubles can stop the show altogether or make for poor performance, such as when timing is off or ignition components are worn or out of adjustment. The band of assailants—moisture, heat, vibration—can wear down or take out electrical parts with their ceaseless onslaught. You can imagine Rat Bike's steed, hard-ridden, seldom maintained, jolted by jumps, pelted with mud, sloshed through creeks and rainstorms and put away wet, has lost the kick it had when new.

Fortunately, modern electrical and ignition systems are typically well engineered and robust. What's out of tune can be brought back to spec, flagging parts can be swapped out with new, and preventive maintenance can keep Rat Bike's refreshed bike riding stronger, longer.

The electrical system on a dirt bike is simpler than that of a street bike, but no less crucial. Lights and accessories need to be powered on off-road motorcycles, and motocross bikes require plenty of juice for spark as well as EFI and engine management operation. *Yamaha Motor Corporation*

BASIC IGNITION SYSTEM MAINTENANCE

The most cost-effective way to keep your bike running well is to maintain it. Your owner's manual will provide the bike manufacturer's recommendations in this regard. There are some other time-proven tricks that can also promote and prolong good performance.

Apply Dielectric Grease to Connectors

Auto parts stores sell dielectric grease. If you apply it to the wire connectors, they will never corrode. Clean the connectors with brake or contact cleaner, let the connectors dry, and then apply a light coating of the grease. Wipe the connectors' plastic covers with the grease to seal out water. Take care to route wires and connectors clear of the exhaust system and away from the rider's boots. Use electrical tape to route the wires, not zip ties, which can pinch or sever the wires, and then ground them to the frame.

Clean and Check the Magneto

A dirt bike magneto consists of a stator plate for mounting the generator and signal coils, and a flywheel rotor that houses the magnets. Special precautions must be taken when attempting to remove the flywheels from four-stroke dirt bikes. The end of the crankshaft might be part of the lubrication system, as it is on Honda's CRF450. Trying to use the wrong puller could mushroom the end of the crank, possibly leading to loss of oil pressure. The factory Honda flywheel puller features a protective end cap to use with a traditional bolt-type puller.

With the stator plate removed from the engine, you can use extremely fine-grit sandpaper to remove the corrosion from the coil pickups. Clean the stator plate coils with brake cleaner. Check the coils for dark spots that would indicate a shorted wire and a heat buildup. In previous years, when the stator plate coils shorted out, you had to replace the whole generator assembly. But now, Electrex makes primary and lighting coils for most late-model dirt bikes. These kits require you to solder the wire connections with a simple soldering iron and rosin-core silver solder.

Adjust Ignition Timing

Ignition systems are designed with specific timing curves. The typical Japanese ignition system fires at about 6 degrees before top dead center (BTDC) at idle, and then advances to 20 degrees BTDC at the rpm of peak torque. At high rpm, the timing changes back to the retarded position of 6 BTDC. This serves to reduce the heat in the cylinder and shift it into the pipe to prevent the engine from overheating and seizing. The black box, or igniter, controls the timing curve. That is the small plastic box located under the fuel tank on most dirt bikes.

The black box has either analog or digital circuitry. Analog circuitry uses a series of Zener diodes to trigger the spark based on the amount of voltage generated by the rotor magnets and stator coils. Analog black boxes produce and are vulnerable to heat. Digital ignition systems use chips that sense rpm and adjust the ignition timing to suit.

It isn't possible to change the timing curves of OEM black boxes but companies like Vortex offer aftermarket black boxes with several ignition maps that can be accessed by changing the position of a series of dipswitches. Vortex ignitions are made in Australia and distributed by MT Racing in California (www.mtracing.com). Vortex offers some interesting accessories like a programming kit that works with a PC and enables tuners to custom program an ignition map in conjunction with a chassis dynamometer. They also sell a handlebar switch that enables the rider to

The heart of the electrical system is the magneto. Off-road bikes use larger magnetos that provide more amperage. The additional flywheel weight is often welcome to make throttle response more controllable. *Yamaha Motor Corporation*

Performance upgrades for your ignition system can consist of a higher-amperage magneto and/or an improved ignition controller.

Trickle chargers are great if your motorcycle uses a battery and sits for extended periods of time. They provide the battery with a light level of current, keeping it fresh and ready to go. *Husaberg*

change to map to one which helps gain traction on starts and on slippery mud tracks..

Aftermarket Ignition Systems

The Vortex ignition system is designed for motocross racing but many off-road riders are looking for generating capacity. Electrex is a company that makes aftermarket replacement parts including stator plates that include generating coils with up to 130 watts of output. That's enough to run a lighting system and heated grips. You can find them at www. electrexworld.co.uk.

DIAGNOSING ELECTRICAL PROBLEMS

Even good maintenance won't sustain a bike forever. Thrown and jumped and crashed in the dirt, a bike is subject to many forces that can cause electrical problems. Approached logically and with the right tools, most of these can be solved at home.

Kill Switch

A faulty kill switch is the most common electrical problem. The kill button can easily be checked with either a continuity light or a multimeter. Link the two test leads between the two wires from the kill switch. When the switch is depressed, the circuit will be continuous. Neither wire should ever be grounded to the handlebar.

Spark Plug Caps

Spark plug caps can break loose from the coil wire after repeated removal of the cap. Most caps thread in to the wire. Whenever you reinstall a cap, cut 1/4 inch from the end of the wire to ensure the cap threads bite into fresh wire. Nology sells an aftermarket wire and cap. It's a high-quality item that

requires you to thread on and glue the wire into the coil. Spark plugs can also be faulty. Refer to the section on spark plugs for more information.

Igniter Box

The igniter box, or black box, contains sensitive electronic circuitry that controls ignition timing in accordance with changes in engine rpm. All sorts of things can cause a black box to fail, and it is difficult to test for anything but complete failure. Heat and vibration are the main causes of black box failure. The electronic circuitry is encased in an epoxy material.

Black boxes are usually mounted in areas of free airflow, such as the frame neck, under the tank, or under the seat. Sometimes water gets into the black box, or the epoxy encompassing the electrics inside the box cracks and causes damage to the circuitry.

There are some simple ways to test a black box for complete failure using a multimeter. Manufacturers generally publish wire connection and ohms specs for their black boxes.

The black box can also be tested dynamically with an inductive pickup timing light (plastic body). Remove the magneto cover, start the engine, and point the timing light at the flywheel. Look for timing marks to appear at one side of the flywheel and focus the strobe light there. You should see T, F and I marks. The T means TDC (top dead center), the F means fire at low and high rpm, and the I means full advance. The F mark should line up with a fixed point on the crankcase at idle. When the engine is revved to mid-throttle, the timing mark will advance to the I. When the engine is revved higher, the timing mark will jump back to the F mark. If ignition timing doesn't go to the F mark at high rpm, the piston might seize from too much cylinder pressure and heat.

Magneto

The magneto consists of a flywheel with magnets (rotor) and a stator plate with a few types of coils mounted to it. The two basic coils are the generating coil and the signal coil. The generating coil is also known as a primary coil, and the signal coil is also known as a pickup coil. The generating coil produces the primary AC voltage, and the signal coil is the trigger that releases the voltage to the igniter. Any additional coils mounted to the stator plate are charging coils for a lighting system. Some manufacturers put all the coils under the flywheel rotor, and some mount the signal coil outside of the flywheel.

Individual coils can be tested for resistance and AC voltage output. Manufacturers publish resistance testing specs in their factory service manuals. They specify which two wires to connect to the multimeter and the correct ohm value. The output of the generating coil also can be tested with a multimeter.

TROUBLESHOOTING GUIDE

PROBLEM: The engine is hard to start and dies periodically.

SOLUTION: Unplug the kill switch. If it cures the problem, replace the switch with an OEM part.

PROBLEM: The engine coughs under hard midrange acceleration and misfires at high rpm.

SOLUTION: The generating coils on the stator plate may be breaking down or metal debris in the oil could be shorting the connections. Remove the generator cover and inspect the coils for damage from metal debris and wipe clean the flywheel's magnets and look for deep scratches. Check the wire connections for frays that can cause shorts. Check the generating coils for ohms resistance with a multi-meter.

PROBLEM: The engine runs fine on flat ground but misfires when riding over a series of whoops or braking bumps.

SOLUTION: Check the top coil mounted under the fuel tank. Make sure the ground wire, coil mounts, and spark plug cap are tight and clean. There is also a slim possibility that the black box is faulty. These units are potted with epoxy to hold the fragile circuits from breaking apart. Sometimes the epoxy material breaks down, allowing the circuits to vibrate and short out when you ride over rough terrain. Unfortunately, there is no reliable way to test an intermittently faulty black box, but an ohm test can determine if the unit has completely failed. See your factory service manual for testing procedures.

PROBLEM: A Japanese 250F has progressively poor performance and is hard to start and pops on top end.

SOLUTION: Most 250Fs have secondary ignition coils built into the spark plug cap like an automobile. Unfortunately coil/caps such as these are vulnerable to moisture. Although the caps have rubber seals from the topside of the spark plug hole, there is a drain hole built into the cylinder head. Before you attempt to power-wash a bike, insert a golf tee inside the drain hole just like you plug the end of the tail pipe to protect it from water damage.

OTHER COMMON PROBLEMS

Dirt bikes may experience other common problems that are easy to identify once you know the basics.

Cold Fouling

This occurs when the bike and engine are still cool. On the extreme, cold fouling occurs when the plug's electrode temperature falls below 800 degrees Fahrenheit. At this point, carbon deposits accumulate on the insulator (the ceramic part

Dual-sport and off-road racing motorcycles often have computers designed to record mileage, riding time, and other figures useful for enduro racing and street riding. *Beta*

of the spark plug that holds the center wire). The voltage will travel the path of least resistance. Deposits such as these are a path for the voltage to follow to ground rather than arcing across to the plug's electrode. Keep in mind that it is more difficult to fire a spark plug under compression pressure than at atmospheric pressure. Just because a plug fires in the open air doesn't mean it will work inside the engine.

Melted Plug

When you find a plug that has melted or is coated with globules of melted metal, something is seriously wrong. Combustion pre-ignition occurs when the spark plug or anything in the combustion chamber reaches a temperature over 1,800 degrees Fahrenheit. At this point, a hot spot could ignite unburned mixture gases before the spark occurs. Hot spots can be caused by everything from too-lean jetting, air leaks, lack of cooling, lack of lubrication, or a sharp burr in the head.

Heat Ranges

The length of the insulator nose largely determines a plug's heat range of operating temperatures. Colder range plugs have a short heat-flow path, which results in a rapid rate of heat transfer. The shorter insulator has a smaller surface area for absorbing combustion heat. Conversely, hotter range plug designs have a longer insulator nose and greater surface area to absorb the heat from combustion. It is most important to install a spark plug of the heat range specified by the manufacturer as a starting point. When tuning racing engines, it is not uncommon to go up or down three heat

ranges of plugs to optimize performance. For example, when your jetting is slightly rich but not enough to require a jet change, you could select a plug one range hotter to achieve the target exhaust-gas temperature. Each step in heat range will effect a 50-degree Fahrenheit change in the exhaust-gas temperature.

TYPES OF SPARK PLUGS
Fine-wire Plugs

Fine-wire electrodes provide easier starts and reduced cold fouling, partly because they require slightly less voltage to fire the plug compared to standard-size electrode center wire. The fine wires are made of precious-metal alloy and are excellent conductors of voltage. Fine-wire spark plugs produce a more direct and confined spark that is better for igniting the air-fuel mixture.

Resistor Plugs

Nonresistor spark plugs give off excessive electromagnetic interference (EMI), which can interfere with radio communications. That is the primary reason why manufacturers recommend resistor spark plugs. In North America, engine manufacturers must install resistor plugs in new engines because many people in rural areas depend on CB radios for their communication needs. In Canada, it's actually a law that you must use resistor plugs in your off-road vehicle. Dirt bikes manufactured after 1996 may have some type of sensitive electronic engine management controls that require the use of resistor plugs.

Spark plugs can tell you how your engine is performing. Read them carefully. *NGK*

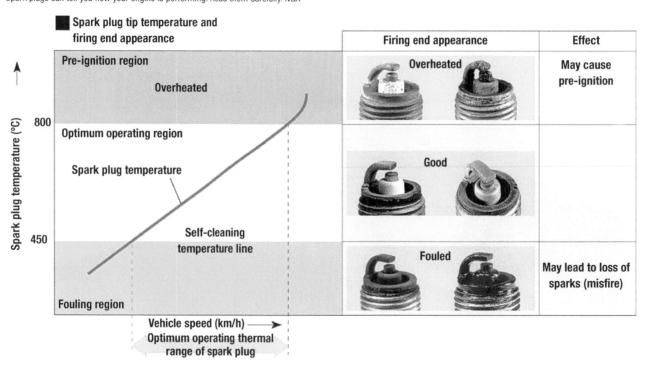

The right plug is key to your engine's performance. Check your manual carefully—many modern four-stroke engines use unique spark plugs. *Bosch*

Heat rating and heat flow path of spark plugs

Hot type		Cold type
BKR5E-11	BKR6E-11	BKR7E-11

Longer insulator nose · Shorter insulator nose

Spark plugs ignite the air-fuel mixture, and they also dissipate heat. *NGK*

THE THROTTLE

Obviously the best ignition system for your bike can't perform well when paired with a dodgy throttle. Factory mechanics routinely disassemble and clean throttles between races, and sometimes between motos if the conditions are muddy. Use the following tips to clean a throttle and identify trouble signs.

Basic Cleaning and Inspection

After removing the throttle's rubber dust cover and plastic housing, examine the throttle pulley for dirt and the cable for frays. Examine the plastic guide for cracks, which can cause the cable to fray or catch on a tree branch, pulling the throttle wide open. If this happens to your cable, don't try to fix it with tape, just replace it with an OEM part.

The throttle pulley generally is made of nylon and doesn't require more than perhaps a touch of lubricant, but

One of the key parts of an electrical system on a modern four-stroke dirt bikes is the fuel pump, which is typically located inside the gas tank. *Yamaha Motor Corporation*

the cable does. Use a cable lubing tool to force lube into the cable housing.

Remove the carburetor slide and stuff a clean rag into the top of the carb to prevent any dirt from entering. Make sure you disconnect the cable from the slide first; otherwise, dirt and lube from the cable will flow down into the slide, which can cause the throttle to stick open.

Clean the throttle tube and pulley with brake cleaner. Lube the throttle tube and handlebar with penetrating oil.

Replacing the Throttle Tube and Grip

Most stock throttle grips on modern off-road bikes are molded to the throttle tube. If you damage the grip and need to replace it, it's a tedious job to remove the old grip. Plastic throttle tubes are susceptible to crash damage and sticky operation. The best setup is to install an aftermarket aluminum throttle tube. There are two types: closed- and open-end. Closed-end tubes are the best for MX applications; open-end tubes are needed for off-road because of the mounting fixtures used in handguards. Throttle tubes' exteriors often are knurled to improve the bond to the grip. Grip glue is an easy way to bond the rubber grip to the throttle tube; some brands of grips are designed with small grooves to accommodate safety wire.

PROJECT 5
How to Install Heated Hand Grips

Time: One hour

Tools: Basic mechanics tools and stand

Experience: 1

Cost: $$

Parts: Heated hand grip kit, grip glue

Heated hand grips help your hands stay warm during long, cold rides. They also help you warm up more quickly, which means you will be riding more efficiently.

Heated grips are available in many types. The most common type is the membrane type. This consists of two heated membranes with adhesive that wrap around your grips. This allows you to use any grip you like. Each membrane has wires that are routed to a central high/off/low switch. The 12-volt power needed to run these is tapped off a power source on the motorcycle. This can be the headlight, or battery, or an ignition-switched power source. These types of grip heaters are branded and sold through many outlets, but for the most part they are all the same. If care is taken when routing the wires from the grips, and the connections are good, you should expect a long service life out of them.

Heated hand grips work on bikes with and without a battery.

The grips will keep your hands warm on cool days, and are perfect for riding when it is wet and 40 degrees or so. They are wonderful for riders who race on ice and snow, but bear in mind they don't provide as much heat as do the hardwarmers on touring motorcycles or snowmobiles. This is mainly because dirt bike's electrical systems don't generate as much power as touring motorcycles or even snowmobiles.

The grips are also useful to help you get warm a little more quickly on a cool day. Staying warm will mean your body is more relaxed, and your riding will improve and odds of getting hurt will decrease.

Note that you can purchase electrically heated grips with the heating coil embedded in the grip itself. These tend to provide a bit more heat on your hands, but they also tend to be grip patterns that aren't as desirable. If you are riding in sub-zero temperatures, the embedded-membrane heated grips may be the best choice.

1 Remove both grips and clean surface of all glues and grip debris. *Jeff Sangeorge*

2 Remove the backing paper from the switch and apply to the cleaned bar as shown, making sure the end of the membrane is inside the end of the bar. Once attached, gently roll the membrane around the bar to adhere it. *Jeff Sangeorge*

3 Repeat this on the throttle side. This is fully wrapped throttle body. Notice the membrane hangs over slightly. Trim the end of the heater before installing the grip. Take care not to cut the circuit path. *Jeff Sangeorge*

4 Install your grips as normal and begin wiring. Run the wires to the front side of the bars. Pay close attention to the throttle as it has to move freely to work properly. Loosely attach the wires to the bars between the throttle body and the front brake master cylinder. Zip tie them in place. *Jeff Sangeorge*

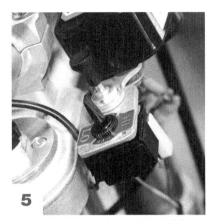

5 A small steel bracket was fabricated to attach the heater switch to the bike. Your bike may require other mounting. Keep in mind you need a place that you can reach and that will not interfere with the movement of the handlebars left or right. *Jeff Sangeorge*

6 Select one wire from each heater and crimp them together in this eyelet. This will be the ground. Attach this to a metal screw on the bike. *Jeff Sangeorge*

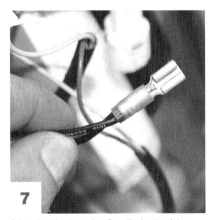

7 Crimp the other two wires from the heaters into a spade fitting. *Jeff Sangeorge*

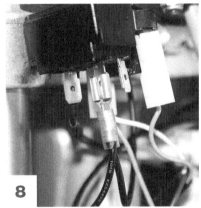

8 Attach the spade to the center post of the switch. *Jeff Sangeorge*

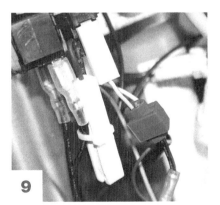

9 The grips need a 12-volt power source. If your bike has a battery, disconnect it at this point. Splice the single end into the power source. Attach the wire with the resistor to the Low plug and the remaining wire to the High plug. Check connections carefully. *Jeff Sangeorge*

10 Now that the wiring is all done, secure any loose wires with zip ties. Notice in this install the switch is in an easy to reach location just next to the light switch. Please note that if your bike does not have a battery and you run the light and grip heaters at the same time, your grip heat will be lower. *Jeff Sangeorge*

Chapter 6
The Drivetrain

Return with us now, not to those thrilling days of yesteryear, but to the present and the continuing travails of our good friend—and anti-role-model—Rat Bike Johnson. Once again RB is circulating at his local track, and things aren't going so well. Oh, he's on the gas, but he's not making a lot of forward motion. His knackered chain is slipping over the teeth of the bike's sprockets, which are hooked like a kestrel's talons; that is, when his clutch isn't slipping. Read on for another series of gripping tales on how not to be like RB.

CHAIN AND SPROCKET BASICS

The condition of the drivetrain has a significant effect on both the handling and engine performance of a dirt bike. The simple chain-and-sprocket drivetrain is still the most efficient way to transfer power from the engine to the rear wheel, especially on a motor vehicle with 12 inches of travel. The forces transferred through the chain and into the suspension can have a positive effect on handling. During acceleration, the chain forces push the rear wheel into the ground. That's

Sandy conditions are hard on the drivetrain, particularly the chain and sprockets. When riding in sand, keep a close eye on both. *KTM-Sportmotorcycle AG*

why when you land from a jump with the throttle on, the rear suspension has more resistance to bottoming. Pro racers depend on chain forces when pre-jumping and landing. If the chain is too tight, too loose, or the rear wheel is not aligned, you'll have problems, just like Johnson. When the chain and sprockets get packed with mud or corroded from lack of lubrication, they can generate a significant amount of friction, absorbing as much as 5 horsepower from the average 250cc dirt bike. Learning the basics of drivetrain maintenance can improve your riding because you'll be able to use the chain forces to your advantage.

CLEAN AND LUBE

After each ride, spray the chain and sprockets with degreaser, rinse the chain with water while scrubbing it with a wire brush, then spray the chain with a moisture-displacing chemical, such as LPS 1, Boeshield T-9, Motorex Joker 440 Synthetic, or similar—just not WD-40 or a powerful penetrating lubricant. WD-40 is composed largely of Stoddard solvent (similar to kerosene) and light mineral oils, and it has a bad habit of sneaking past a chain's O-rings and displacing the lubricant therein. Another hot tip: When spraying the moisture-displacing lube on O-ring chains, simply spray it at the chain. Don't spray it as you would a chain lube—that is, between the links. You do not want to force the spray past the O rings.

When you scrub the chain and sprockets, make sure to remove the dirt and oil deposits embedded near the sprocket's teeth. If you don't clean off the debris, the sprockets will wear faster.

There are many different types of chain lube—petroleum-based, lithium grease, and even wax. Each is designed for a specific use. Petroleum chain lube is good for street bikes because it doesn't make a huge mess, but it offers little resistance to water. Lithium grease lasts a long time and offers protection against water damage, so it is good for enduro and trail riding. Wax-base chain lubes were designed for motocross bikes that get serviced every moto or practice session. Chain wax is a light coating that seals the link and doesn't fly off or significantly attract dirt. This type of lube is easily stripped off when the bike is washed.

TIPS ON CHAIN ADJUSTING

The two most important things to know about chain adjustment are to maintain alignment of the sprockets and to correctly set free-play when the swingarm is parallel to the ground.

There are a few ways to set the sprockets in alignment: by adjusting the axle to the stamped marks, visually or with an alignment gauge. All dirt bikes have marks stamped in the swingarm at the axle mounts. Normally, you would use the marks to keep the rear wheel centered in the swingarm while adjusting the chain's free-play. However, most production frames are robot-welded, and slight tolerance differences can put the marks out of alignment. The simplest way to ensure alignment is to visually ensure the top of the chain runs

Adjust your chain slack when you are sitting on the bike, ideally with your gear on. The chain will be quite slack when the bike is on the stand. *Beta*

Don't skimp when the time come to replace your chain. Off-road motorcycle chains are exposed to horrid conditions. A high-quality O-ring chain that is well-maintained can last a full season under normal riding conditions. *KTM-Sportmotorcycle AG*

A chain breaker presses the pins out of the chain and allows you to remove it. You will eventually need this tool. *Motion Pro*

straight from the rear sprocket to the countershaft sprocket. Race mechanics prefer to use an alignment gauge, which fits into the centers of the rear axle and swingarm pivot bolt. Race Tools, Motion Pro, KTM, and others offer a simple alignment bar that fits virtually all dirt bikes. You simply fit one end in the center of the axle and the other in the swingarm pivot while you adjust the wheel position for the proper chain free-play. Then place in the same position on the other side of the bike to ensure the distances are the same. If not, you need to adjust the wheel position to make it so. There are also laser chain-alignment tools, if you're feeling flush. But visual inspection is the easiest and cheapest method.

No matter how much travel a dirt bike has, the ideal chain free-play is 0.5 inch or 13 millimeters measured when the swingarm is parallel to the ground. At that point, the rear axle is at the farthest point from the swingarm pivot and the chain free-play will be at its minimum.

Just because the wheel is aligned when the bike is stationary doesn't mean it will stay in alignment when the bike accelerates up a bumpy hill. Whenever you set the chain free-play, try to wiggle the rear wheel and the swingarm. If any of the bearings are worn, the drivetrain can run out of alignment, causing a big power drain.

TYPES OF CHAINS

There are two types of chain: conventional and O-ring. Conventional chains use steel pins with a press-fit metal bushing to form each link. These chains use a mechanical seal to protect the link, meaning there is minimal clearance between the rollers and links. O-ring chains (for practical purposes, we refer to O-ring chains to include all the various cross-sections of such seals) use an O-ring to seal lubrication in the link and keep out dirt and water. O-ring chains are more durable, more expensive, and slightly heavier. Such chains are great for long-distance off-road riding because they doesn't require quite as much maintenance as a conventional chain.

Some chains are advertised as having the ability to resist stretching, but this claim is misleading. No chain really stretches; it's most correct to say the chain elongates because of loss of lubrication (O-ring chains) or wear between the pins and rollers (all chains).

It's normal for a chain to wear at different rates at different points.

CHECKING A CHAIN FOR WEAR

There are a few different ways to determine if a chain needs to be replaced. Examine the chain for kinks—points where the link and roller have seized, preventing them from freely rotating—and replace the chain if kinks exist. Also, if the chain needs to be adjusted frequently and has many points where the free-play varies, then the chain needs to be replaced. Sprockets tend to wear twice as fast as the chain, so replace the chain when the sprockets are worn enough to need replacement and vice versa. If you install a new chain on worn sprockets, the chain will wear prematurely; likewise a worn chain will wear out new sprockets quickly.

MASTER LINKS

There are two types of master links: slip-fit and press-fit. Conventional chains use slip-fit links, and O-ring chains use press-fit links.

Press-fit links can be installed by using the appropriate chain-riveting tool. To install slip-fit links, simply push the link together with your fingers and install the locking clip with the closed end facing the direction of rotation.

SPROCKETS

Sprockets or chain rings come in many different colors, patterns, tooth designs, materials and sizes, and they are made of steel, aluminum, or titanium. Steel is a better material for longevity and cost; aluminum is lighter. More expensive alloys, such as stainless steel and titanium, offer advantages in wear and performance. Individual sprocket teeth tend to wear in a wave pattern.

When the profiles of the front and rear sides of the teeth look different, the sprocket is worn out. Once the teeth wear far enough, they'll allow the chain to skip over their tops. If the chain derails while you're riding it, the bike will stop abruptly and you could be injured. If the chain derails forward and gets jammed between the sprocket and crankcases, it can break the cases or shift shaft. It's best to retain the original front chain guard or buy a suitable aftermarket product. The chain guard prevents the chain from derailing forward and directs it downward.

TIPS FOR CHANGING THE SPROCKETS
Countershaft Sprocket

There are three different methods of retaining/securing the front-sprocket: bolts, nuts, and circlip. Circlip retainers can be removed with circlip pliers, available at any hardware store. However, the circlips can only be removed a few times before their shape is distorted. Factory mechanics use a coating of Yamabond 4 or ThreeBond 1104 to prevent the circlips from vibrating off or getting hooked by small rocks.

The bolt or nut retainers use either a cupped spring washer for bolts or a bendable retaining clip for a nut to prevent them from loosening. The average torque setting for a large-diameter nut is 24 ft-lb but only 15 ft-lb for a small-diameter bolt. Most cupped washers are marked OUT for the exterior face. If that wears off, install the washer with the highest part of the cup under the bolt head to provide spring

Gearing is a key performance tool. Changing the rear sprocket by one to four teeth will let you fine-tune final gearing.
KTM-Sportmotorcycle AG

tension for the locking effect. If you don't have an electric or pneumatic impact wrench to remove the sprocket's retaining bolt/nut, you'll need to prevent the sprocket from turning while you loosen the retainer with a hand wrench.

Applying the rear brake will prevent the sprocket from turning—assuming, of course, you did not remove the chain first. Never wedge anything between the chain and sprocket while removing or tightening the front sprocket bolt/nut because the wedge can come out and injure you or damage the chain and sprocket.

Once you remove the sprocket, clean the inside and outside of the countershaft bushing, which is the spacer that fits between the bearing and the sprocket on the countershaft. The bushing is sealed on the outer edge by the countershaft seal that fits into the crankcase and by an O-ring on the inside. If the seal and O-ring wear out, water and dirt can enter the countershaft bearing, and that is expensive to fix. You'd be surprised how much tranny oil can seep past the seal and O-ring while you're riding. After cleaning, apply a dab of waterproof grease to the inner and outer faces of the bushing to help keep out water and dirt.

Rear Sprocket

Rear sprockets are bolted to the wheel hub. Normally, a tapered-head bolt with a flanged nut fastens the sprocket to the hub. Sprocket bolts tend to loosen up. That makes mechanics over-tighten them, stripping the bolt head or nut. Avoid these problems by using a torque wrench to tighten the fasteners to spec and applying blue Loctite on the threads. Always use a six-point box wrench on the sprocket nuts, and tighten the bolts in an alternating diagonal pattern.

GEARING TIPS

You'll have to change gearing to suit different tracks. A simple rule of thumb: For more top speed, switch to a countershaft sprocket with one more tooth than stock; for quicker acceleration, switch to a rear sprocket with two more teeth than stock.

CLUTCH

A motorcycle's clutch has a significant effect on power delivery and handling. If the clutch doesn't operate smoothly, the bike's rear wheel could break loose and compromise traction or, worse, cause the rider to crash.

Does your bike lurch when you fan the clutch? Do the clutch plates break or burn out fast? Does the clutch make a grinding noise when the engine is idling in neutral? This section provides insight into the problems that affect clutches, and some tips on how to permanently fix clutch problems.

Common Clutch Problems

Too many riders replace clutch plates before the plates are worn out. They don't measure the plate thickness, plate warpage, or spring free length. One guy called me complaining he had

Clutches require regular service and rebuilding. A clutch kit consisting of fiber and steel replacement discs is fairly inexpensive, and installing the kit is something most home mechanics can do. *KTM-Sportmotorcycle AG*

spent over $600 on clutch plates in one riding season. He said his bike burned up clutch plates on every ride. I asked him to send me the entire clutch and all the old plates and springs. The problem was the springs were sacked out and didn't exert adequate tension on the plates, thus allowing them to slip and burn. All his clutch plates were standard thickness and none were warped. The average cost of replacing a set of clutch plates is about $100, which brings up the moral of this story: Spend some time looking for the cause of a clutch problem rather than just throwing money at it.

Measuring Tools

There are three inexpensive tools you need to perform basic measuring of clutch parts. A flat surface, such as a piece of glass or preferably a thick piece of steel, will give you a surface to check plate warping and deglaze the plates. A feeler gauge will enable you to measure plate warping. A dial caliper will allow you to measure the springs' free length and plates' thickness.

Before you attempt to measure the clutch parts, you will need the manufacturer's recommended dimensions, which you can find in the service manual. Dimensions such as clutch-plate thickness or spring free-length will be listed as standard and minimum.

Measuring the Plates

Clutch plates wear and become thinner with use. They also can warp if they become overheated. Use the caliper to measure each plate's thickness. If within spec, place each plate on a flat surface, such as glass or steel. Press the plate down evenly and try to insert a 0.020-inch feeler gauge between the plate and the flat surface. If the feeler gauge can be inserted under the plate, it's warped and cannot be repaired.

Measuring the Springs

Clutch springs sack out with use, so they become shorter in length. Measuring each spring's free length is the best way

to determine if they should be replaced. Use the caliper to measure the free length, and compare that dimension to the minimum-length spec listed by the manufacturer. Sacked-out springs will cause the plates to become glazed and the clutch to slip.

TROUBLESHOOTING CLUTCH PROBLEMS

What happens when you have a serious clutch problem, such as a grinding noise or a combination of dragging and slipping? This section provides some insight into troubleshooting common and serious clutch problems.

Grinding Noises

Warm up your engine, put the transmission in neutral, and turn the throttle so the engine runs steadily, just over idle. Slightly pull in the clutch lever. Check for a significant reduction in vibration and the grinding noise. If the noise is reduced, then the needle bearing and bushing that fit between the clutch basket and main transmission shaft are slightly worn. There is no way to measure the needle bearing, but the service manual will list a dimension for the bushing diameter. Always replace the needle bearing and bushing as a set.

If the grinding noise isn't affected by engaging the clutch, then the problem might be more serious. Check the bolt that retains the primary gear to the crankshaft and the nut that retains the clutch hub. If the nut and bolt are tight, then the crankshaft main bearings could be worn out.

Dragging or Lurching Problems

Dragging and lurching problems are primarily caused by deep notch marks that form in the clutch basket and inner hub. The notch marks are the result of wear caused by the clutch plates' tangs. Eventually, the notches become so deep that the plates just stick in one place and resist engaging or

Keep a close eye on your clutch basket. Once it becomes notched or grooved on the inside, where the plates move up and down, you will need to replace it. *KTM-Sportmotorcycle AG*

Automatic clutches are terrific for off-road use. They automatically engage, which means you don't have to grab the clutch in nasty terrain—you just stay on the gas. This is tremendously helpful on technical ascents or negotiating obstacles at low speed. This is the Rekluse Z-Start, which replaces the stock pressure plate. *Jeff Sangeorge*

disengaging. If the notches are less than 0.02 inch deep, it's possible to draw-file down the high spots of the notches. Be careful—filing too much aluminum from the clutch basket or inner hub will make the clutch prone to dragging. A common symptom of dragging is the bike creeping forward when you put it in gear.

Draw-filing refers to a method whereby you stroke the file in one direction, evenly along the length of a surface. This enables you to file down only the high spots of the notches equally. You will need two types of files: a flat file for the clutch basket and a triangulated file for the inner hub. You'll also need a file card to clean the aluminum debris from the file.

Before you attempt to draw-file the notches from your clutch basket, you must check the basket for hairline fractures at the base of each of the fingers. If you find any cracks, replace the basket. If the fingers break off, the debris will cause catastrophic engine damage. If you draw-file a basket with fracture cracks, it will fail much faster.

Aftermarket Clutch Baskets

Several aftermarket manufacturers, such as Hinson Racing, Wiseco, Vortex, and Moose Racing, offer replacement clutch baskets. Most of these products are machined from billet aluminum and hard-anodized for wear resistance. Hinson products are hard-anodized and coated with Teflon to reduce friction. Wiseco clutch baskets are forged from billet slugs. Installing aftermarket clutch baskets requires you to remove the original primary gear, kick-start gear, and rubber bushings from the clutch basket. That sounds difficult but it isn't. Here is an overview of installing any aftermarket clutch basket. You will need access to a drill press and a hydraulic press.

1. Start by cleaning the oil residue from the old clutch basket.
2. Use a drill press and a 0.25-inch drill bit to bore out the stock mild-steel rivets that retain the primary gear. Drill off the rivet heads deep enough to remove the thin sheet metal retaining plate.
3. Strip off the retaining plate, rubber bushings, and primary gear. Take care to remove the parts in order because it's possible to install the gear upside-down.
4. Use a hydraulic press and a bushing driver or large-diameter socket to press out the kick-start gear. Don't try to hammer it out because you'll fracture the hardened gear and you can't buy a replacement, only a complete new clutch basket.
5. Aftermarket clutch baskets use tapered panhead Allen screws to retain the primary gear. Always use red Loctite on those threads of the bolts and tighten them with a hand-impact driver. Wiseco clutch baskets use Plasti-Lok screws so you don't need a thread-locking agent, such as Loctite.
6. Wipe a dab of anti-seize compound on the kick-start gear before you press it into the new clutch basket. Take care to press it all the way on, but don't bottom it too hard or the basket might crack.

AUTOMATIC CLUTCHES GROW UP

The biggest innovation in dirt bike clutches is the automatic clutch. For decades, such clutches were used on smaller motorcycles, but they've now grown up and are becoming popular on much larger motorcycles in enduro, DTX, and supermoto settings. The automatic clutch is essentially a pressure plate with a set of centrifugal weights (steel balls), a wave washer spring, and a channeled ramp. Put the bike in gear and rev the engine until the centrifugal force of the spinning balls causes them to roll up the channel ramp far enough to overcome the spring force of the wave washer. I first rode a CRF450 with a Rekluse auto clutch. I found I could start in fifth gear from a dead stop and the clutch would engage smoothly. The other advantage to an auto clutch is it's nearly impossible to stall the bike. However, the downside is the fiber plates wear faster.

PROJECT 6
How to Replace Your Chain and Sprockets

 Time: 2 hours

 Cost: $$

 Tools: Sockets, ratchet, breaker bar, torque wrench (foot-pounds), wrenches, locking pliers, flathead screwdrivers, chain cleaner or WD-40, rags, chain breaker, rotary tool, tape measure

 Parts: Countershaft and rear sprockets, chain

 Experience: 1

If you ride dirt bikes, sooner or later you'll have to replace your chain and sprockets. Dirt and sand combined with friction can wear down even the toughest metal. Wear and tear isn't the only reason to swap chains and sprockets. As the terrain you're riding in changes, you may want to change the gearing of your bike to optimize its performance. Your power delivery needs can change pretty dramatically when switching from a tight and bumpy track to wide-open desert riding.

You won't need to swap out sprockets every time you need a new chain. So, learning to read your sprockets is the place to start. Look closely at the sprockets. Are the sides of the teeth worn? If so, expect to find a matching wear pattern on the inside of the chain. Do the teeth of the sprockets look like cresting waves? Are teeth missing? If you answered yes to any of these questions, you need new sprockets.

1

Begin with your bike on a stand. Once you've found the master link, you can put the transmission in gear to keep the chain from moving while you're working on it. *Evans Brasfield*

2

Circlip pliers can ease the removal of the clip. A flathead screwdriver will do in a pinch. Although you shouldn't reuse a master link's clip, saving an old clip as a spare in your tool box (or tool pouch out in the wild) can come in handy if your bike tosses a clip. *Evans Brasfield*

3 If you don't have a chain tool, you can use a screwdriver to pry the plate off of the master link, but the right tool makes the job quicker and easier. *Evans Brasfield*

4 Remove the rear wheel. With the chain already removed, you shouldn't have to move the chain adjusters on the swingarm, giving you a reasonably close starting point when the time comes to adjust the slack after the new chain and sprockets are installed. When reinstalling the rear wheel, be sure to put a good coating of grease on the axle. *Evans Brasfield*

5 With the wheel resting on a flat surface, remove the sprocket with a combination wrench and a ratchet. When you tighten the new sprocket, do it in a criss-cross pattern. Snug all the bolts down and then torque them in a two-step process, setting all at 50 percent torque before the final tightening. *Evans Brasfield*

6 Remove the circlip or bolts securing the countershaft sprocket to the countershaft. Take note of the sprocket's orientation since it may have a spacer. *Evans Brasfield*

7 Feed the chain over the countershaft sprocket from the top and then through the roller on the bottom of the swingarm. *Evans Brasfield*

8 If you're keeping the same size sprockets, you can lay the old chain out on a clean workbench and measure the new chain side by side. Mark the link you need to remove with a Sharpie. *Evans Brasfield*

9 If you're changing your gearing, measure the chain length by mounting it on the bike and marking where it overlaps with the end. You will need a rotary tool to grind off the top of the rivet and a chain tool to press out the pin. *Evans Brasfield*

10 Don't listen to your friends about chain slack. Consult your owner's manual or factory service manual to find out what proper chain slack is for your model bike. *Evans Brasfield*

11 Once you know the proper amount of slack, measure it with a metal tape measure. *Evans Brasfield*

12 If your chain is too tight, back the adjusters off two full turns and bang the wheel forward until the axle mates with the adjusters, then remeasure. When tightening the chain, work the adjusters in small increments and remeasure. *Evans Brasfield*

13 Torque the axle to factory specifications. Snug the chain adjusters an additional 1/8 turn before tightening the lock nuts. *Evans Brasfield*

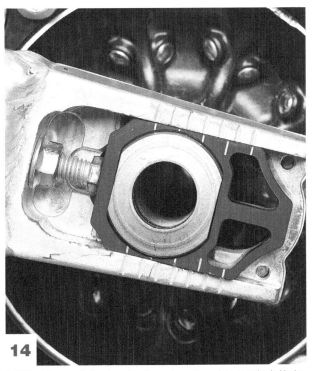

14 Don't trust the manufacturer's registration marks on the swingarm and axle blocks. Put the bike in gear, rotate the wheel until the chain is taut, and sight down the top. If the axle is straight, you will be able to see as the chain runs from the rear to the countershaft sprocket. *Evans Brasfield*

Chapter 7
The Wheels and Tires

As the parts that connect the motorcycle to the dirt, wheels and tires play a role in bike performance. You want a tire and tread design suited to your riding and wheels that are strong enough to do the job, but light enough that the suspension can push them back down as quickly as possible after a bump for maximum bike traction and responsiveness. Wheels and tires are below the suspension and therefore unsprung weight. Low unsprung weight provides better performance, as long as the strength is there for the wheels to hold up and not bend or break.

A guy like Rat Bike Johnson doesn't much care about his wheels as long as they rotate, nor his tires if there's air in them. But ignoring the dirt bike parts that actually pound and grip and navigate the dirt costs him time and comfort. Let's look at some wheel, tire, and maintenance tips that can provide a competitive edge and a better ride.

TIRES

Your tires are important because, even with the most expensive suspension revalving and a powerful engine, you'll still end up on your butt if your tires' knobs are all rounded or torn off, or the tread pattern and tire design is wrong for the terrain. In GPs, riders and mechanics regard tires as a suspension component. They are constantly fiddling with different tire patterns, compounds, and hybrid mousse inserts just to get a slight competitive edge.

TREAD PATTERNS, COMPOUNDS, AND PRESSURES

There are many different tread patterns and compounds for off-road tires. In general, hard compounds are better for soft terrain, such as mud and sand, while soft compounds are better for hard terrain, such as clay. The best patterns for

Fresh tires are a great performance upgrade that improves handling. The right tire for the conditions is key. *American Honda*

Compound	Hard	Intermediate	Soft	All-Purpose	Desert
Terrain	Clay, Churt, Dry Dirt	Loamy Soil	Sand, Mud	Most conditions	Rocks, sand and clay
Dunlop	MX71 or D745/D739	MX51 or D756	MX31, MX11 (sand) or D756	D952	MX71
Bridgestone Front/Rear	M603/604 (mx) or ED77/78 (off-road)	M403/404 (mx) or ED11/12 (off-road)	M203/204 or M101/102 (mud)		ED77/78
Pirelli Front/Rear	Scorpion 486 or 454	Scorpion 454 or 32	Scorpion 410	Scorpion Extra	
Maxxis	Dual SX	Radial SI	Radial SI or M7311/7312 SI	M7313/7314 or M6001	Desert IT
Recommended Pressure	12-14 psi	10-13 psi	9-12 psi	10-14 psi	12-18 psi

Chart 7-1 Tire Compound Chart

Dunlop MX71 front. *Dunlop*

Dunlop MX71 rear. *Dunlop*

Dunlop MX51 front. *Dunlop*

Dunlop MX51 rear. *Dunlop*

Dunlop MX31 front. *Dunlop*

Dunlop MX31 rear. *Dunlop*

Dunlop MX11 rear. *Dunlop*

Maxxis Maxxcross Dual SX front. *Maxxis*

hard-packed surfaces have tightly spaced, low-profile knobs. Soft-compound, short knobs can conform to the terrain without breaking loose. The best patterns for soft terrain feature widely spaced, tall knobs. Hard-compound knobs can penetrate the terrain and resist clogging, thanks to the open area between the knobs.

A tire's air pressure can be adjusted to take advantage of the tread pattern and compound. In general, lower pressure is used for soft terrain because it allows the tire to conform to the ground for maximum traction. On a muddy surface, there aren't as many sharp-edged bumps and it's difficult to get big air over jumps, so it isn't necessary to use high air-pressure to prevent the tube from being pinched or punctured. However, on hard-pack or rocky surfaces, it's necessary to run higher pressures for three reasons: to resist punctures from hard landings, to keep the tire from spinning on the rim, and to make the soft-compound tire conform to its proper profile.

PUNCTURE PROTECTION

There are some precautions that you can take to ensure against punctures. Heavy-duty inner tubes should be used on every bike except minis that are raced competitively in motocross. The reason is that the tubes are heavy and pose a bit of drag on small engines.

In some forms of racing, such as desert events held in rocky terrain, the risk of puncture is great, even with heavy-duty tubes. For this situation, you may want to use either a mousse tube or a combination mousse and inflatable tube, like the Dunlop Crescent mousse. Mousse is a dense, closed-cell foam tube-shape ring that cannot deflate. Many off-road racers riding large-displacement bikes choose to install mousse in the tires. The mousse enables the tire to absorb the impacts of rocks instead of bottoming and deflecting in a random manner. Mousse tubes do have some disadvantages, however. They are prone to shrinkage, and they have a high cost per usage.

Maxxis Maxxcross Dual SX rear. *Maxxis*

Maxxis Maxxcross Radial SI front. *Maxxis*

Maxxis Maxxcross Radial SI rear. *Maxxis*

Maxxis IT Desert rear. *Maxxis*

SNOW AND ICE TIRES

Riding in snow and ice can be as much fun as riding typical terrain. It also can be a way for riders in northern climates to stay sane during the winter. With good tires, the effect is not all that different from riding on loose sand. Off-road bikes can't handle deep snow, but studded tires allow the bike to navigate 12 inches or less with ease (not to mention throwing huge roosts). Ice riding and racing require a thick and basically flat ice surface.

There are several ways to get good traction in frozen conditions. The most common is to screw ice studs into your tires. Aftermarket studs are better than regular sheet-metal screws for several reasons. For one, they are actually unfinished sheet-metal screws. The finishing process smoothes the surface of the screws, which reduces their ability to get traction. Second, ice studs are coated, making them more durable than conventional sheet-metal screws. Put one or two screws in per knob. Keep in mind the studs

eventually will round off and might pull out of the tire. Replace the studs regularly.

Custom-Made Ice Tires

Several manufacturers offer an alternative to making your own ice tire. These hand-built custom tires are perfect for winter trail riding. You can find them at Moto Race (www. motorace.com). The rubber compound is designed for the cold and the studs are carbide-tipped points molded into the knobs. These tires are very durable and cost about the same as a tire and liner with 800 studs.

TOOLS FOR HOME AND TRAIL

You will need the following tools to change a tire: a 12-mm wrench for the rim lock and the Schrader valve, a valve-stem tool, an air pressure gauge, a set of short and long tire irons, a compressed air source, and a bottle of spray detergent. If

69

Dunlop D952 rear. *Dunlop*

Maxxis Desert IT. *Maxxis*

Custom-made studded ice tires provide solid traction on snow and ice. The studs are formed into the tire, and stay embedded much better than ice screws. The tires are not cheap, at more than $300 per tire. *Mark Frederick*

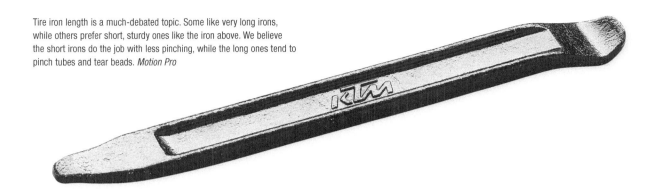

Tire iron length is a much-debated topic. Some like very long irons, while others prefer short, sturdy ones like the iron above. We believe the short irons do the job with less pinching, while the long ones tend to pinch tubes and tear beads. *Motion Pro*

you want to put together a collection of tools that fit into your trail-riding tool kit, get two short tire irons, a valve-stem tool, a pressure gauge, a bar of soap, and some compressed-air (CO2) cartridges.

WHEEL BEARING REPAIR

Top Grand Prix mechanics replace the wheel bearings after every race. In racing, you need every small advantage. Less demanding riders might only need to replace their bikes' wheel bearings once each race season. This section's tips show you how to check and change your wheel bearings the easy way.

Cleaning and Inspection

1. The seals in the hubs can be removed, cleaned, and greased many times before replacement is needed. You should also clean out the area between the seal and the

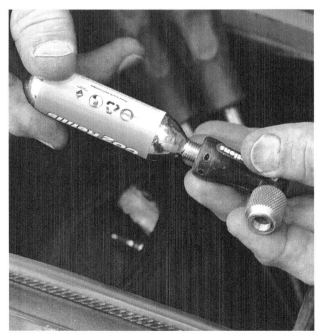

Quick-fill CO2 cartridges are great for airing up tires on the trail. *Mark Frederick*

sealed bearing. Now you can check the condition of the bearing.

2. Place your finger on the inside race and try to spin it. If the bearing is worn out, it will feel gritty and be difficult to turn. Check for excessive movement in the race. A wheel bearing should never have any movement.

3. Wheel bearings fit into the hubs with an interference fit. That means that the bearing is larger than the hole it fits into in the hub. The hub must be heated with a propane torch in the area around the bearing so that the hub expands enough to allow the race to be removed.

4. After the hub has been heated with a propane torch for about three minutes, use the following procedure to remove the bearings. From the back side, position a long drift rod on the inner bearing race and strike it with a hammer; rotate the position of the drift rod around the circumference of the race to push the bearing out of the hub evenly.

5. The wheel bearing assembly consists of two seals on each end, two wheel bearings, and one axle spacer. After removing one bearing, pull out the axle spacer. Then remove the second bearing. Notice how dirty and corroded the bearings and spacer become when the seals fail.

6. Clean the inside of the hub, and then heat it with a propane torch for about three minutes just prior to installing the bearing.

7. One side of each bearing is sealed (the side that faces out). Before installing the bearings, pack the open side with white-lithium or moly grease.

8. Use a hammer and a bearing driver to install one bearing. Universal bearing/seal driver kits are available from auto parts or industrial supply stores. Drive the bearing until it's completely bottomed into the hub. Now install the seal with a dab of grease to prevent water from penetrating the bearing. Install the axle spacer, and then install the second bearing until it is fully seated. Install the second bearing's seal with a dab of grease and you're done.

A good spoke wrench is your friend. Make a habit of checking spoke tension every second or third ride. *Motion Pro*

Spoke Check

Spokes in a spoked wheel hold the rim in the proper position, keeping it true by exerting equal forces from either side, and keeping it round by holding it equidistant from the hub all around the circumference. Over time and use, the heads of the spokes in the hub and the spoke nipples in the rim will begin to seat, pulling into each of these surfaces. As a result, the spokes grow looser and the wheel tends to go out of true.

Hard knocks will also distort a rim, creating either side-to-side motion, or a lumpy ride if a portion of rim is pushed closer to the hub than the rest. Side-to-side motion, if modest, can be corrected by truing the rim, adjusting spoke tension at the nipple to move the tweaked section back into place. Be careful not to make spokes too tight, as that can crack the rim.

Lighter rims and hubs improve performance. At the least, maintain your stockers well. And if you are made of money, invest in aftermarket hubs and rims that are lighter than stock. *KTM-Sportmotorcycle AG*

PROJECT 7
How to Change a Tire

 Time: Less than 30 minutes

 Tools: Basic mechanics tools and stand, tire irons, tire pressure gauge, air compressor

 Experience: 1

 Cost: $$

 Parts: New tube and tire

Mounting a crisp, fresh set of tires is one of the best performance-enhancing changes you can make to your bike. Doing so at home not only saves you a few dollars, but it also will come in handy as you will eventually need to change a tire while at the track or out on a ride. And if you think you can't do this, bear in mind that legend has it that pro rider Scott Summers can change a tire with his bare hands. Pro legend Dick Burleson demonstrates how he changes tires trailside.

Changing tires without tearing the bead or pinching the inner tube is just a matter of technique. You can struggle with the task, or you can stay patient and use your head.

1 When you change a tire at the trail, your bike is likely to be dirty. Wipe the rim clean before pulling it off. Loosen the axle nut.

2 Roll the chain off the sprocket, and remove the wheel. When the wheel is off, remove the valve stem and the bead lock nut.

3

Stand on the tire to break the bead. Remember to protect the disc rotor with a piece of cardboard so the ground doesn't scratch it.

4

Once you break the bead away from the rim, insert one tire iron at a time, folding the tire over the rim, alternating every few inches until the tire is two-thirds off. Use two to three tire irons to remove the tire from the rim. Two short levers and one long one often is a good mix. Once the tire is free, extract the tube and the rim lock.

5

Use the large tire iron and a hammer to remove the tire from the rim.

6

Before installing the tube in your new tire, line the inside of the tire with baby powder. This will prevent pinch flats. Be sure to wipe the bead clean before mounting the tire.

7

Place the rim inside the tire.

8 Put the brake disc side up and spoon the tire carefully on the rim. Take small bites with the levers so you gradually lift the bead on to the rim.

9 You can use your hands at times to work the bead over the rim.

10 As you get close to having the tire completely mounted, take smaller and smaller bites with your levers.

11 Air the tire up to set the bead. Make sure the bead is flush to the rim all the way around the tire and air isn't leaking before you mount the wheel. Remount the rear wheel, and tighten down the axle nut. Adjust the chain properly beforehand.

12 Air the tire up according to your riding conditions.

Chapter 8
The Brakes

Modern bikes have become so dependable that it's easy to take them—and their components' capabilities—for granted. We whittle our concerns down to the most basic question: Will it start? If it starts, it will go, and if it goes, it will stop . . . or so we might believe. But that's only true for a while.

Brake parts are consumables, components that get used up from riding. Though he hasn't given it much thought, Rat Bike Johnson's brake pads, discs, and fluid have limited life. The pads wear, the discs can distort, and the brake fluid absorbs moisture that will reduce braking efficiency and cause corrosion. The longer he ignores it, the more the system will decline and the harder it will be to hang with the pack.

In this chapter, we'll make sure shedding speed is as dependable and predictable as piling it on.

BRAKE SYSTEMS

The elements and the laws of physics punish a dirt bike's brakes. Water, mud, and sand attack your brake pads, wearing them down faster and raising maintenance requirements compared to car or street-bike brake systems. Because weight transfers to the front of the bike when you apply the brakes, it's the front brake that does the yeoman's work in slowing you down. The rear brake can help an advanced rider change a bike's attitude in the air by transferring the force of the spinning rear wheel to the bike frame, torquing the front of the bike downward to lower the front wheel. The rear grabber can also be applied lightly to keep the back of the bike tracking straight through whoops.

Dragging the brake accelerates pad wear, so check them often. The resultant friction also creates a lot of heat, which carries through the caliper piston to the brake fluid. Hot

Off-road motorcycle brakes are treated to horrendous conditions. Dirt, mud, sand, and water washes right over the rotors. Care of them is essential to top performance.
Maragni M/KTM-Sportmotorcycle AG

Motorcycle braking power is mostly generated from the front brake system. *KTM-Sportmotorcycle AG*

brake fluid breaks down more quickly, so it, too, must be checked often.

In addition to performing normal maintenance, you can tune your brakes in a number of ways. Manufacturers make different pad materials to improve longevity in various riding conditions. Metallic pads work best in sandy conditions, while composite pads offer superior braking power. Brake discs likewise vary in design and purpose. Following are the basics of brake system repair, maintenance, and tuning, along with some tips on troubleshooting braking problems.

COMMON BRAKE PROBLEMS Q & A

QUESTION: The front brake on my bike is weak. I change the fluid often and have tried different types of pads. Nothing helps much. I power-wash the brakes after I ride to keep out the dirt. What do I need to do to fix this bike's brakes?

ANSWER: Power-washing the brakes with soap is a bad thing. The soap film attacks the adhesive in the pad and bonds to the ridges in the disc. Soap can also glaze the disc. You can deglaze the disc with medium-grit sandpaper or have it resurfaced. The best cure is to install a stainless-steel disc and a set of composite or metallic pads.

QUESTION: The disc brakes on my bike start to get hot and lock up. The pads get wedged against the disc and I can't even turn the wheel until the brakes cool down. I have to bleed out some brake fluid when it gets really bad. What do you think is wrong?

ANSWER: This is a common problem. The two pins the pads slide on can become grooved and prevent the pads from moving away from the disc when the brake lever is released. Try replacing the pads and pins and changing the brake fluid to DOT 4. The best fix for preventing the problem of grooved brake pins is to use stainless-steel pins.

QUESTION: I put a set of expensive Kevlar brake pads on my bike and they are shot after only a few rides. The material is still on the pad, but I have to pull in the lever really hard just to get them to lock. What gives?

ANSWER: I'm guessing that you are a power-washing freak. That is a sure way to damage Kevlar pads. The strong detergents that commercial power-washing systems use can damage the Kevlar material used on the pads. The detergent bonds to the pads and causes them to form a low-friction glaze. That is why the pad material has not worn down, but the pad won't grip the disc. Don't try to file or sand the pad; just get a new set, and wash your bike with water only.

QUESTION: Why do my brakes drag when they get hot?

ANSWER: The brake fluid could be saturated with water. It's best to change the brake fluid twice a year, or more often if you're racing.

QUESTION: After only 15 minutes of riding, the rear brake pedal has no free movement and the brakes are very sensitive. What would cause this problem?

ANSWER: The brake pins could be bent or have divots that cause the pads to drag against the disc. The heat is transferred through the caliper piston and into the brake fluid. The water in the fluid boils and expands, and that causes a lack of free movement at the brake pedal. Check the brake pins and change the fluid.

QUESTION: Why would my brake lever or pedal pulse when the brakes are applied?

ANSWER: The disc is bent and is pushing the piston back into the caliper whenever the distortion is to that side. This force is transferred into the pedal/lever, making a pulse for every revolution of the wheel. Replace the disc because it cannot be repaired.

QUESTION: Why do my front brake pads wear on an angle?

ANSWER: The front caliper carrier bracket is bent; replace it.

QUESTION: The brakes make a squealing noise. Can this be eliminated?

ANSWER: The squeal is caused by glazing on the discs and pads. The glazing could have occurred from leaking fork seals, power-wash detergent, or chain lube accidentally sprayed on the disc. Medium-grit sandpaper can remove the glazing from the surface of the discs and pads. Afterward, clean the discs with brake cleaner—never with a detergent.

BASIC CLEANING AND PAD REPLACEMENT

Following are some basic tips on checking and changing brake pads. If you are having a specific problem with your brakes, see the troubleshooting guide at the end of this chapter. Always review the factory service manual for your bike before attempting any service procedures.

1. Before you attempt to change the brake pads, first power-wash the brakes clean with water only—no soap! The high-strength detergents used in power washers can damage the caliper seals, disc surface, and even attack the bond used on the pad, so avoid spraying the brakes when you wash your bike. Next, clean the dirt from the inside of the Allen-head caliper screws with a pick or brake cleaner so you can remove the screws without stripping the ends.

The rear brakes are used as much for control as they are stopping power. Wave rotors clean off more efficiently in heavy mud. They also wear pads more quickly. *KTM-Sportmotorcycle AG*

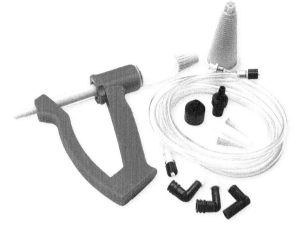

Change your brake pads regularly. Metallic pads offer superior stopping power, but more quickly wear down rotors. Semi-metallic, Kevlar, and ceramic pads are less abrasive choices.

Bleeding your brakes can be done without a brake fluid pump like this one. The process is much easier to do alone with the pump. *Motion Pro*

2. Remove the brake pins and check the pins' surfaces for divots, dents, and corrosion. These surface blemishes can cause the pads to drag when the brakes get hot. Replace the pins at least once a year, and never apply grease to them.

3. After you have removed the brake pins, you can pull out the pads. Check the pads for glazing or wear. If the pads are worn out, replace them.

4. Reinstall the pads, caliper, and pins, and tighten all fasteners properly. Always depress the brake lever several times after you have installed the wheel to enable the brake pistons to pump up to the pads.

FLUID REPLACEMENT

The brake fluid should be changed at least two times a year. Race mechanics change the fluid on their bikes every two races. There are two methods for replacing the brake fluid and bleeding the brakes: pump-and-purge or hand-operated vacuum pump.

The Pump-and-Purge Method

If you don't have a brake bleeder tool, this is the best method to change brake fluid:

1. Remove the master cylinder cap and top off the cylinder with brake fluid.

2. Put a six-point box-end wrench on the bleeder valve located on the caliper. Slip a 10-inch-long piece of clear plastic tubing over the end of the bleeder valve.

3. Slowly pump the brake lever two or three times, then hold it fully engaged. Loosen the bleeder valve a quarter of a turn for one second before retightening.

4. While frequently checking fluid level in the master cylinder and topping it off as necessary, repeat Step 3 until the fluid coming out of the tube is clean, clear, and without bubbles.

5. Remove the hose, tighten the bleeder valve, top off the master cylinder, and replace the master cylinder cap.

The Hand-Pump Method

A brake bleeder tool will speed up your brake fluid change. Use the following method to change your oil with the tool:

1. Connect a collection tank between the pump and a hose attached to the bleeder valve.

2. Remove the master cylinder cap. Be prepared to constantly replenish the master cylinder with brake fluid during the bleeding process.

3. Loosen the bleeder valve a half turn and use the vacuum pump to slowly pump the fluid through the brake system. Don't forget to replenish the master cylinder.

4. When the fluid coming out of the bleeder valve looks clean, clear, and free of bubbles, stop pumping and snug down the bleeder valve.

5. Detach the pump from the bleed valve, top off the master cylinder, and replace the master cylinder cap.

PROJECT 8
How to Change Front Brake Pads

 Time: 30 minutes

 Cost: $$

 Tools: Basic mechanics tools and stand, bleeder wrench, clear plastic hose, brake bleeding tool is a nice extra

 Parts: New brake pads, brake fluid

 Experience: 2

Modern disc brakes on a motorcycle are nothing short of amazing. They are lightweight, effective, and very reliable. They are technological and manufacturing marvels. One of the keys to maintaining this effectiveness is to have brake pads that are in top shape.

Brakes convert forward moving energy to thermal energy when the brake lever is pulled. The friction between the pads and the rotor generates heat and that heat is where the energy is dissipated.

Brake pads come in many types. Some come with metal; others have ceramic in them, and some are just simple old school organic compounds. The goal of each of these is heat dissipation, and some materials do it better than others. But like all things in life each has its costs. Better heat dissipation created by a more abrasive material shortens rotor life. Softer pads with less heat dissipation offer reduced stopping power, but longer-lived rotors. OEM equivalent pads offer a good balance of rotor life and braking performance, and they are also the most economical choice.

The front pads are the most crucial portion of your braking system. Most of your stopping power is up front.

1 Before you remove the brakes, make sure this area is free of excess dirt, mud, and muck. If they are full of dirt, spray them off with a hose. Changing the brakes can be done when they are wet so this will not slow your progress. This model of bike uses two clips to hold the brake pin. Other models use a screw-type brake pin. Either way they are usually located at the base of the caliper. *Jeff Sangeorge*

2 Before you remove the clips, you must push the caliper pistons back to allow for the thicker pads. Using the outer pad, gently push the caliper pistons back. Do not do this with a screwdriver, as it may damage the rotor or other delicate parts. Using needle-nose pliers, remove the pins. Make sure to place them in a safe place so as not to lose them. *Jeff Sangeorge*

3

Remove the clip from the brake pin. *Jeff Sangeorge*

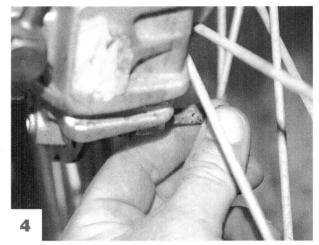

4

Remove the brake pin by pushing the end and pulling it through. *Jeff Sangeorge*

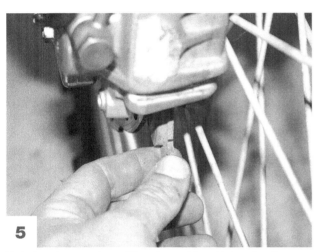

5

The brake pads are now free; pull them down and they will release from the upper retaining clip. *Jeff Sangeorge*

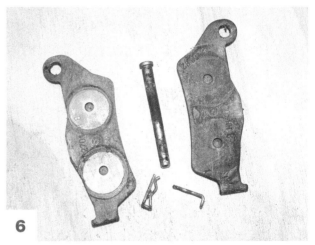

6

These are the removed parts. Notice the ears on the brake pads. They slip into the upper retaining clip in the caliper. At this point inspect the brake pin for excessive corrosion and wear. If the pin is grooved and worn, it's time to replace it. The pin allows the pads to float and if it's grooved, they won't float as well. *Jeff Sangeorge*

7

Clean your pin with a rag and some light solvent. Do not grease your pin; it's not needed and will attract dirt and grit, prematurely wearing your pin out. *Jeff Sangeorge*

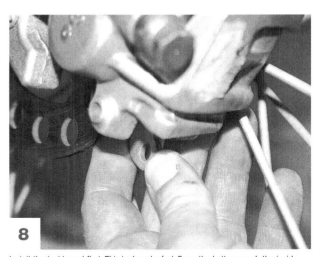

8

Install the inside pad first. This is done by feel. From the bottom, push the inside pad up until it clips in the upper retainer. *Jeff Sangeorge*

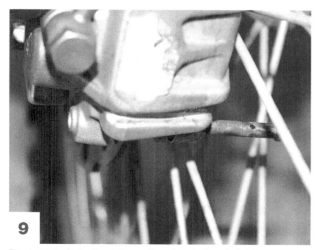

9 Then install the brake pin until it goes through the inside pad. *Jeff Sangeorge*

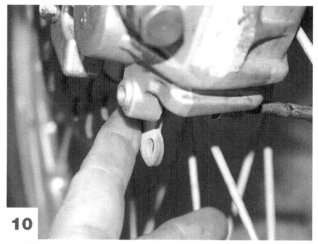

10 Install the outer pad just like the inner, making sure the pad clips in the upper retainer clip. *Jeff Sangeorge*

11 Push the brake pin in the rest of the way, making sure it went through the pad eye. *Jeff Sangeorge*

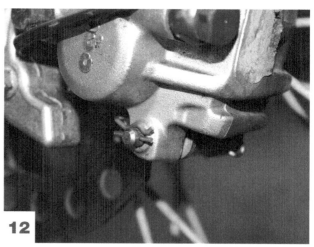

12 Once the brake pin is installed, install the retaining clips as before and you're done. Now squeeze the front brake until the pads have come back up and the lever feel is achieved. The first time you use the new brakes, you need to seat them to the rotors. While moving, gently drag the brakes for the first 5 to 10 minutes of riding. *Jeff Sangeorge*

PROJECT 9
How to Change Rear Brake Pads

 Time: 30 minutes

 Cost: $$

Tools: Basic mechanics tools and stand, bleeder wrench, clear plastic hose, brake bleeding tool is a nice extra

Parts: New brake pads, brake fluid

 Experience: 2

Carry a spare set of pads in your tool box with you when you go out to ride. It's not uncommon to chew up a set of rear pads during a muddy enduro or long trail ride. You'll need to learn how to change them in the field with the tools you carry.

Check your pads before each ride. If they are more then two-thirds worn, replace them. As the pads wear, they become less efficient, which means you're stopping distance increases.

Drag your brakes a bit after you install new ones. This allows them to seat to your worn rotor. This will insure maximum stopping power when needed.

When cleaning your bike, never use solvents or soap on or near your brakes. The solvents can damage vital rubber parts and the soaps can leave a film on the rotor that can increase your stopping distance. To clean your rotor, spray brake cleaner in a rag and apply to the rotor. Make sure the rotor is cool; they get really hot during use.

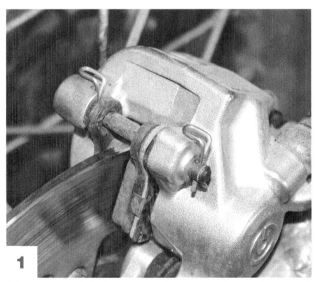

1

Before you remove the brakes, make sure this area is free of excess dirt, mud, and muck. If they are full of dirt, spray them off with a hose. Changing the brakes can be done when they are wet, so this will not slow your progress. This model of bike uses two clips to hold the brake pin. Other models use a screw-type brake pin. Either way, they are usually located at the rear of the caliper.

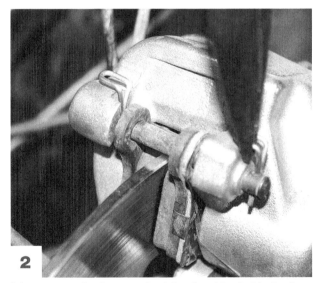

2

Before you remove the clips, you must push the caliper pistons back to allow for the thicker pads. Using the outer pad, gently push the caliper pistons back. Do not do this with a screwdriver, as it may damage the rotor or other delicate parts. Using needle-nose pliers, remove the pins. Make sure to place them in a safe place so as not to lose them.

3

Remove the brake pin by pushing the end and pulling it through.

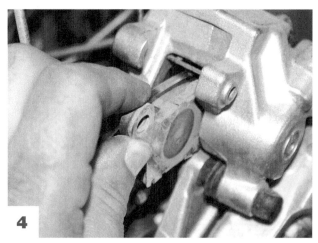

4

The brake pads are now free. Pull them back and they will release from the front retaining clip.

5

These are the removed parts. Notice the ears on the brake pads. They slip into the upper retaining clip in the caliper. Also notice the addition of an insulator pad and a stainless-steel buffer plate. These are used to keep excessive heat from transferring from the brake pad to the caliper. At this point, inspect the brake pin for excessive corrosion and wear. If the pin is grooved and worn, it's time to replace it. The pin allows the pads to float, and if it's grooved, they won't float as well.

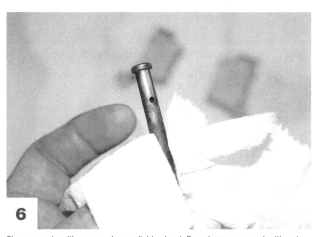

6

Clean your pin with a rag and some light solvent. Do not grease your pin; it's not needed and will attract dirt and grit, prematurely wearing your pin out.

7

Install the inside pad first. This is done by feel. From the back, push the inside pad up until it clips in the front retainer.

8

Install the outer pad by pushing it into the front retaining clip.

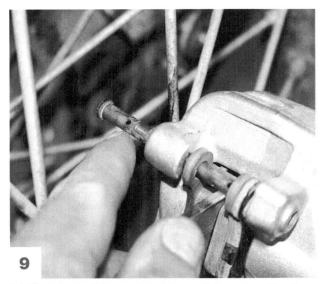

9

Install the brake pin with the cross holes facing you. Make sure it goes through both of the brake pad eyes.

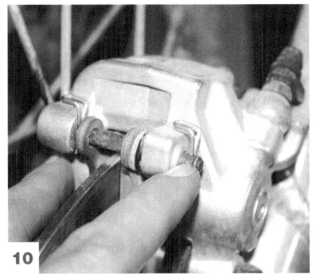

10

Install the retaining clips as shown. Now press the rear brake until the pads have come back up and the lever feel is achieved. The first time you use the new brakes you need to seat them to the rotors. While moving, gently drag the brakes for the first 5 to 10 minutes of riding. Check the brakes for proper function and you're done.

HOW TO REPLACE A BRAKE PAD PIN

1

Remove the existing brake pin clips and brake pin and set aside. Install the Moose KTM Rear Brake Pin as shown.

2

Swing the pin over until it touches the pre-clipped position as shown.

3

Using a hammer, gently tap the brake pin into the clipped position. NOTE: It is crucial that the pin clip be fully seated. If it is not seated, you run the risk of losing the pin and damaging the bike or hurting yourself.

4

Note the fully clipped position.

5

To remove the pin, simply push from behind with a flathead screwdriver. This brake pin is designed to use over and over. After each removal, inspect it for damage and wear. Replace if worn.

THE BRAKES

Chapter 9
The Suspension

Pity suspension—always working, seldom praised. If Hollywood made a show about a motorcycle factory, people would shoot most of it in styling. "Look at this decal, Brett!" "Nice paint scheme, Rhonda!" Pshaw. That's not work that wins races (though it might sell bikes). What separates winners from the rest of the pack is what separates them from the dirt itself, their bike's suspension. Even if our friend Rat Bike Johnson were the top rider in a competitive field, he could not win on a hard-slamming course if his suspension were shot, or far out of tune.

Suspension is where the rubber hits the dirt—or not, on a clapped out or poorly set-up bike. It has an upside and a downside, always, and they're equally important. On the upside, suspension supports the rider, absorbing bumps, ruts, whoops, and hard landings, keeping him upright and free of cracked teeth and compression fractures. On the downside, the suspension works just as hard, pushing the tires onto the dirt so that braking, throttle, and steering inputs get executed. Diminish these capacities and you can see how a great racer could lose. Rather than smoothing chaos so the rider stays poised, a junk suspension bucks and bounces and slams; it fights the rider instead of helping him eat up terrain.

Let's look at ways to make suspension work for you. We'll start with setup because poor adjustment for your size and weight will prevent any suspension, regardless of cost, from serving you well. We'll also discuss maintenance, repairs, and upgrades to help you get the best ride from your machine.

Whoops will test your suspension settings and condition in dramatic fashion. They are an ideal location to test different suspension settings. *KTM-Sportmotorcycle AG*

BASELINE SETTINGS

Every day, I see people send out their suspensions for expensive revalving without attempting to adjust and record the baseline settings, such as spring preload, compression, and rebound adjustments; fork tube overlap; tire pressures; and even the torque settings for the steering head, triple clamp bolts, and swingarm pivot. All of these characteristics affect the way your bike handles. In many cases, the suspension components only need to be rebuilt and set up correctly for the rider's weight and riding demands.

SETTING PRELOAD

Measure and set rear preload before measuring the front. If rear preload has to be increased, more weight will then be placed on the front end and it will sag more than normal. Here are some guidelines for measuring the sag to set spring preload:

1. First, measure the distance of the front and rear ends while fully extended on a bike stand. Measure the rear from the axle's center to a point on the bike's bodywork, muffler or, if you have an older bike, on the subframe. Measure the front from the axle's center to the bottom of the fork seal, or to the triple clamp. Be sure to measure from the same points each time. Use a metric tape measure and record the extended lengths of the front and rear ends. A metric tape measure's small increments are easier to work with than fractions of an inch.

2. Set preload after practice and refuel the bike with the normal amount of fuel you use for a race. If it's a mud race, don't scrape off the mud.

3. Wear your normal race gear.

4. Get on the bike and bounce up and down while the mechanic pushes the bike. This will help work out the friction from the suspension to allow for an accurate measurement. Coast to a stop without braking—tapping the brake will shift the bike's weight and give you a false measurement.

5. Sit in your normal racing position while someone holds the bike vertical on flat ground. Have your mechanic measure the compressed distance on the rear suspension, using the same two measurement points used for the extended distance.

6. Increase or decrease shock spring preload to set the rear sag at 90 to 105 millimeters.

7. Measure the front fork sag the same way and, if necessary, adjust the sag to 35 to 50 millimeters with 5 to 15 millimeters spring preload (measured internally).

8. Lastly, measure the unladen sag of the rear shock. Be sure to measure this after you have the sag adjusted with the rider aboard. Let the bike sink under its own weight and measure the sag. It should sag 15 to 25 millimeters if the spring rate is correct. If the sag is less than 15

Rear suspension preload is set by adjusting the two rings on the top of the spring on the rear shock. *Yamaha Motor Corporation*

millimeters, the spring is too soft for your weight. If the sag is greater than 25 millimeters, the spring is too stiff for your weight. It sounds backward, but think of it like this: If the sag is too little, then you had to preload the spring too much in order to get it to the correct race sag for your weight.

DETERMINING SPRING RATES

Measuring the unladen sag of the rear shock, after you have set preload, is a good guide for the rear spring rate. The front is more difficult; measure sag and then compare the fork spring preload. Expert riders might choose stiffer fork springs than indicated because they use the front brake hard and thus transfer more weight forward. Two main causes of

Adjusting compression and rebound damping is simplified with this set of wrenches. *Motion Pro*

head-shake are a too-soft front spring rate or too little oil in the front fork.

Spring force and valving work hand in hand. Good suspension tuners measure the spring rate before attempting revalving.

DAMPING CIRCUITS AND ADJUSTERS

The suspension circuits of the fork and shocks are the HSC (high-speed compression), HSR (high-speed rebound), MVC (mid-valve compression), LSC (low-speed compression), and LSR (low-speed rebound). The compression adjuster for the shock is located on the reservoir, and the rebound adjuster is on the clevis (bottom shock mount). The compression adjuster is located on the bottom of cartridge forks and on the top of twin tube forks. The rebound adjuster is located on the fork cap of cartridge forks and on the bottom of twin tube forks. Not all forks have rebound adjusters. Kayaba first used rebound adjusters on production cartridge forks in 1989.

LSR and LSC Circuits

The low-speed circuits work in scenarios like landing on the back sides of jumps, G-outs, and accelerating on a straight with far-spaced, shallow whoops. All Japanese dirt bikes have suspension adjusting screws that affect the low-speed circuits only. Turning the adjusting screws clockwise will increase the damping and slow/stiffen the low-speed circuit. Turning the screws counterclockwise will decrease the damping and speed up and soften the low-speed circuit.

HSC and HSR Circuits

The high-speed circuits work in two common track sections: landing from big jumps and accelerating on a straight with tightly spaced, sharp-edged whoops. In 1996, Honda was the first to introduce HSC adjusters on the rear shock of the CR models. The adjuster has an inner screw for the LSC circuit and an outer ring for the HSC circuit. This adjuster can only make a slight difference in the high-speed damping. White Power shock and fork adjusters are high-speed-only adjusters.

MVC

The mid-valve compression circuit works in three common track sections: landing from big jumps, braking bumps at the end of fast straights, and accelerating on a straight with tightly spaced, sharp-edged whoops.

BASIC TORQUE SETTINGS

There are some basic torque settings that have a dramatic effect on the handling of a bike. The torque settings of the rear end are covered later in this chapter, so we'll focus on the front end.

The crucial torque settings on the front end include the steering head, triple clamps, and axle clamps. Modern dirt bikes have tapered steering-head bearings that require a deft touch to torque correctly. Too much torque makes it difficult to steer; too little allows the fork to rock fore and aft during braking or when hitting bumps. Improper torque can also cause premature bearing wear.

A generic way to adjust the steering head tension goes like this:

1. Put the bike on a stand and elevate the front wheel.
2. Loosen the top clamp bolts and the large center nut of the steering stem's bolt.

Proper torque settings on the linkage and frame can make a dramatic difference in performance and handling. *Suzuki*

THE SUSPENSION

3. Use a steel punch and hammer to tighten the spanner nut located just below the top clamp. Turn the spanner nut 1/8 turn at a time and check the steering tension by turning the handlebars. Remember that when you tighten the large center nut on the steering stem, steering tension will increase. Steering tension is largely based on rider preference. Some mechanics use the flop test. They turn the handlebars slightly off center and the front end flops to the steering stop. Keep in mind that the steering tension will decrease with use and require periodic maintenance. When a bike is new, the tension changes quickly because the bearings and races are still in the process of seating on the frame and steering stem.

Triple-clamp bolts must be loosened and retorqued periodically to reduce the stress on the fork's internals and realign the fork in the triple clamps. If the clamp bolts are too tight, the fork will bind during wheel travel. Another important aspect of the triple clamps is the fork tube overlap. Measure the overlap distance of the tubes and make sure they are equal. Then torque the clamp bolts to specification provided in your bike's service manual.

Front-axle clamp tightening is crucial to the fork's performance. The fork tubes must remain parallel from top to bottom; otherwise, binding and premature bushing wear will occur. Here is a generic procedure for ensuring the fork tubes are parallel before you tighten the axle clamps:

1. Place the bike on a stand and elevate the front wheel.
2. Torque the axle to spec, but leave the axle clamps slightly loose.
3. Spin the front wheel with your hand and quickly grab the front brake. Repeat this procedure at least three times to help align the fork.
4. Make sure the arrows on the axle clamps are pointing up and torque the top bolts/nuts to spec, then the bottom bolts/nuts.

Tightening the swingarm pivot requires a torque wrench rated in foot-pounds because the value is in the 50-plus-ft-lb range.

SUSPENSION DATA LOG

Keep a log of suspension adjustments and settings to help you in tuning. The log should track the following data for the fork: oil weight and level; spring rates and preload; fork tube overlap; compression and rebound settings; and tire type and pressures. Keep similar logs for the shock with the addition of spring sag.

Make some spare copies of this data log and record all the pertinent information about your suspension, ideally at every track. This information is also vital for having work done on your suspension.

Personal Data
Rider's weight (with gear): _____ (pounds)
Type of riding: motocross enduro DTX
supercross desert hare scrambles
hillclimb dual-sport
Location:
Date:

Terrain
(circle conditions you encounter frequently)
Soil: sand mud rocks tree roots loam
hard clay
Elevation: big hills off-camber many jumps
square-edged bumps sand whoops

Fork
Spring rate _____ kg
Spring sag _____ mm
Unladen sag _____ mm
Spring preload _____ mm
Fork tube overlap _____ mm
Steering head tension set? _____
Compression adjuster: _____ clicks out
Rebound adjuster _____ clicks out/number of turns

Shock
Spring rate _____ kg
Spring sag _____ mm
Unladen sag _____ mm
Spring preload _____ mm
Compression adjuster: _____ clicks out
Rebound adjuster _____ clicks out/number of turns
Notes on how the bike handled, any crashes.
Be as specific as possible.

CARTRIDGE FORK SERVICE AND TUNING

More than likely, your bike uses cartridge forks. This section has tips for getting better performance out of any such fork. Some tips involve just replacing worn bushings, while other tips are difficult to perform and require specialized knowledge and tools. Some parts of the cartridge are easily damaged and expensive to replace. Before you attempt to service your bike's cartridge forks, purchase the factory service manual for details on assembly and tightening torque specs.

How a Cartridge Fork Works

The cartridge consists of two tubes with damping valves. The tubes slide together. The large tube is the damper rod and it houses the compression valves. The small tube is the piston

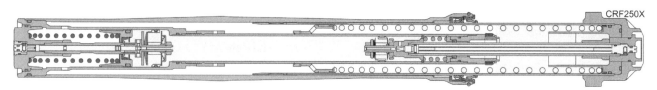

CRF250X

Completely servicing front forks requires a complete set of special tools to remove all the internals. *American Honda*

rod and it houses the rebound valves. Cartridge forks rely on several plastic and metallic bushings to keep the telescopic rods from binding as they slide back and forth.

Cartridge fork valving consists of thin washers and cylindrical pistons with tiny bleed passages and slightly larger ports for the fluid to flow through. Damping is accomplished by restricting the fluid flow. An inherent problem with cartridge forks is that debris from the bushings gets trapped between the valve washers and in the piston, thereby ruining the damping effect. This is the main reason why cartridge forks need to be cleaned and have the oil changed often (every 10 to 15 hours of riding). The twin-tube design features improvements to extend the service time between cartridge servicing and improve the high-speed tuning (resistance to hard bottoming).

Special Tools for Servicing Forks

It takes more special tools to service cartridge forks than to rebuild the motorcycle's engine. The basic tools include a damper-rod holder, a bleeder rod, and a seal driver. Race Tech offers the widest selection of suspension rebuilding tools apart from the motorcycle manufacturers. A tape measure can be used to set and measure the oil level, but a suction-type level-setting tool is more convenient.

Damper-rod holding tools are used to prevent the rod from spinning when the base valve bolt is unthreaded. These holding tools are not universal in size and flange shape because the flange shape on top of the damper rod varies by brand and model.

Bleeder rod tools thread on to the top of the piston rod. During the final air-bleeding procedure, it's necessary to stroke the piston rod through its travel to facilitate bleeding of the cartridge. At least four different sizes of bleeder rods are made to service cartridge forks.

Seal drivers are metal slugs machined to fit the outer diameter of the fork tube. There are two types of seal drivers: solid and split. Split drivers are needed for upside-down forks because they have axle clamps. Conventional cartridge forks can use solid seal drivers because the driver is installed from the top of the tube.

Servicing twin tube forks does not require a holding tool or a bleeder rod; you will need two special wrenches. One wrench holds the fork cap and the other holds the damping rod. However, you still need a seal driver to install the fork seals.

There are some general tools that you'll need as well, including a vise with soft jaws, an assortment of large-diameter six-point sockets, a plastic mallet, a flat-blade screwdriver, an oil pan, and cleaning solvents.

If you are interested in revalving the fork valves, you'll need some very special tools, such as digital calipers for measuring the shims, and drivers to remove the peened tab on the bottoming cone. The bottoming cone is located in the middle of the piston rod. By removing the bottoming cone, you can separate the piston rod from the damper rod.

Changing Fork Oil

I strongly recommend that you completely disassemble and clean your cartridge forks every 20 riding hours. However, if you are sure that the forks are in good condition and you just want to change the oil, here is a simple method.

1. Remove the fork from the bike.
2. Unscrew the jam nut on the fork cap.
3. Unscrew the fork cap.
4. Remove the plastic spacer.
5. Slide out the spring.
6. Turn the fork upside down and drain the oil.
7. Stroke the piston rod to pump the oil out of the cartridge while draining the fork.
8. Add about 4 ounces of fork oil to each tube and use it to flush out the tubes.
9. After you have drained out the flushing oil, follow the procedure listed later in this section for filling the oil and bleeding air from the cartridge.
10. Reassemble the fork and put it back on your bike, being careful to torque the pinch bolts to recommended settings.

Disassembling Fork

Simply changing the oil is fine for periodic maintenance, but if your fork hasn't been serviced in a season or more, you'll have to disassemble and clean the cartridge. Cartridge forks are especially susceptible to dirty oil, as gunk tends to accumulate around the cartridge and the fork loses damping.

1. Remove the fork and drain the oil (see above).
2. Take the nut off the very bottom of the fork, either with an air impact wrench or by holding the damper rod in place with a damper-rod holding tool.

3. Pull the cartridge out of the bottom of the fork.
4. Lay out all the parts and clean thoroughly with contact cleaner (note that at this point, the fork tube can be pulled from the fork slider to replace fork seals, etc.).
5. Replace any worn seals or bushings (see below).
6. Install the cartridge.
7. Tighten the nut on the bottom of the fork, using the special tool or an air impact wrench (be very careful with the impact wrench; you can blow the O-ring off of the cartridge and lose all damping).
8. Install the spring and spacer.
9. Follow the procedure listed later in this section for filling the forks with oil and bleeding air from the cartridge.
10. Reassemble the fork and put it back on your bike, being careful to torque the pinch bolts to recommended settings.

Replacing Bushings

The seals, wipers, and bushings should be replaced at least once a year. If you are looking for the highest level of performance, replace the bushing that fits in the head of the damper rod and supports the piston rod. The standard bushing has excess clearance that can cause the piston rod to go off-center and produce more stiction in the fork. After you have spent the time to polish the bearing surfaces of the damper and piston rods, replace the standard bushing with an accessory bushing that has tighter clearances and a low coefficient of friction.

When your fork loses rebound damping, the main cause is worn piston rod bushings. When these bushings are worn out, they allow the cartridge fluid to bypass the bushing and piston rod, thereby losing the damping effect. If your bike's cartridge fork makes a clunking sound when it extends, the piston rod bushing is worn out.

The piston rod bushing can be replaced by unthreading the head from the damper rod, where the bushing is housed. This procedure is very difficult and should only be entrusted to a professional suspension technician. The technician will heat the steel head to break the bond of the locking agent on the threads. Then, a chain clamp wrench is used to grasp the steel head and unthread it from the aluminum damper rod. After the bushing is replaced, the threads of the damper rod and head must be carefully cleaned and a permanent locking agent applied. Then, the head is tightened onto the damper rod with the chain clamp wrench.

The internals of a fork consist of springs and damping rods. *KTM-Sportmotorcycle AG*

The Teflon bushings support the fork tube to the slider. You can tell when they are worn because there will be discoloration on the load-bearing surface. These bushings are easy to replace and should be changed once a year. The slider bushing (large-diameter) falls out when you separate the two tubes. The fork tube bushing (small-diameter) is under spring tension, so it must be removed using a straight-blade screwdriver to spread the bushing at the side slit, and slide it off the end of the fork tube. When you install the large-diameter bushings, take care to seat them properly in the slider before trying to install the fork seals. You do not need to use any special oil or grease on these bushings because they are Teflon coated.

Replacing Fork Seals

Once you have the fork disassembled and the fork slider and tube separated (see previous section), the fork seals can be removed. When installing the new seals, you must be very careful not to tear them when sliding them over the fork tube. Some grease and a plastic bag are key to getting your new seals installed without tearing.

1. First, apply Teflon grease to the wiper and seal.
2. Then, place a plastic bag over the end of the fork tube.
3. Slide the seal over the plastic bag and onto the fork tube. The plastic bag covers the bushing grooves and prevents the seal from tearing as it slides over the sharp edges of the bushing grooves.

Now you can reassemble your fork and be confident that your new seals will hold.

Filling with Oil and Bleeding Air from the Cartridge

Here are some tips for filling Showa or Kayaba cartridge forks with oil and bleeding out the air:

1. During the initial filling and bleeding sequence, compress the fork tube and fill the fork to within 2 inches of the top.
2. Extend the fork, cup your hand over the end of the tube, and compress the fork. You'll feel air pressure building up under your hand. The oil is under pressure and that will help force tiny air bubbles through the shims of the compression valve and also displace the air that gets trapped between the fork tube and slider. Repeat this procedure at least four times, adding oil each time.
3. Use a stroker rod to grasp the piston rod and stroke the rod up and down until the tension through the stroke is equal. Equal tension is an indication that the air is bled from the cartridge.
4. To set the oil level, remove the spring and compress the fork. Use a thin ruler (preferably metric) to measure the distance between the top of the tube and the top of the

oil. An oil level setting tool (or a large syringe with a bit of hose attached) is the quickest way to set your oil level. Make sure there is an excess amount of oil in the fork so the oil level setting tool can suck out oil to set the proper level.

5. The oil level should be set with the spring removed and the fork tube bottomed. Kawasaki recommends setting the oil level 10 millimeters higher than the spec to compensate for the small amount of air trapped between the slider and tube. That bit of air works its way out when the bike is ridden.

TWIN TUBE MAINTENANCE AND TUNING

The twin tube cartridge forks are essentially cartridges that don't recirculate the oil into the outer tubes. The twin tube fork doesn't require as much maintenance because the internal cartridge is sealed from the outer tubes, and the sliding interface between the two outer fork tubes is the source of the metallic contamination that ruins the performance of a cartridge fork. Twin tube forks also don't require special tools to service the cartridge. Some companies, such as Motion Pro and Race Tech, make dedicated wrench sets for the top cap and the cartridge rod; you can use standard wrenches to do the same job. This is a generic procedure for servicing a twin tube fork:

1. Loosen the fork cap with a six-point box wrench. It's best to hold the fork tube in the bike's triple clamp; just be sure to loosen the top clamp bolts. If the fork is separate from the bike, you can use soft jaws in a vise; take care not to clamp the vise so tight that you crush the fork tube.
2. Loosen the bolt at the bottom of the fork until it separates from the bottom fork tube.
3. Depress the fork cap until the cartridge rod extends out the bottom of the fork far enough to expose the wrench flats. Use an open-end wrench to hold the cartridge rod and unthread the bottom bolt completely. Take care when removing the bolt because the telescopic rebound adjuster tube will fall out of the bottom of the cartridge.
4. Remove the cartridge from the fork tubes by pulling it out from the top.
5. Use a straight-bladed screwdriver to remove the wiper, and then remove the circlip that retains the fork seal.
6. Use a propane torch to heat the area around the seal to break the bond of the bushing.
7. Grasp the fork tubes with both hands and yank them apart several times rapidly until the tubes separate.
8. Carefully inspect the bushings inside and outside to look for wear marks. Normally, you should replace the bushings and seals every time you change the fork oil, or about every 50 riding hours. That will ensure that

THE SUSPENSION

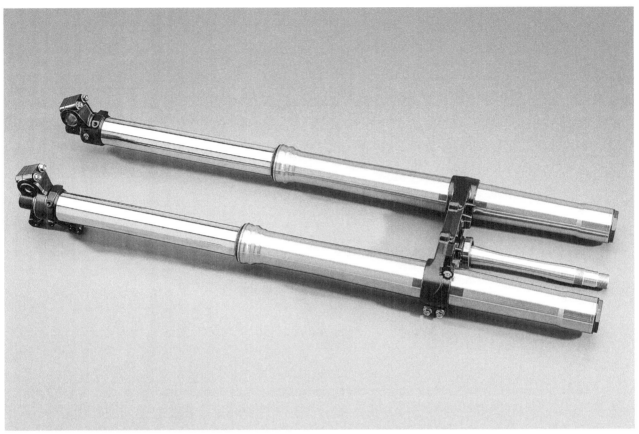

Regular oil changes will make your forks perform their best. Revalving kits can be installed at home, but this is a task best left to professionals.
Yamaha Motor Corporation

the expensive aluminum fork slider doesn't wear out prematurely. Installing new bushings and seals is the same for normal cartridge forks.

9. Disassemble the compression valve and clean any debris from the piston ports and between the shims by spraying brake cleaner on the parts.

10. To assemble the fork, start by filling the inside of the cartridge to the level specified by the manufacturer. Usually that is a ledge where the compression valve fits.

11. Bleed the cartridge of air in the normal way by slowly stroking the cartridge rod through its full travel. Do this until the rod moves smoothly. Smooth travel indicates that the air is bled to the top of the cartridge.

12. Put the cartridge in the top of the fork, insert the telescopic rebound rod, and tighten the bottom bolt.

13. Fill the outer tubes with a measured volume of oil based on the manufacturer's specification.

14. Thread in the top cap and compression valve.

BASIC FORK REVALVING

A recent design rage for cartridge forks is to increase the diameter of the compression and rebound pistons and separate the compression valving into low-, medium-, and high-speed damping modes. For our tuning tips discussion, we refer to the two states of compression valving as passive (slow speed) and active (mid speed).

Circulating Controversy

The main difference between the popular models of cartridge forks is the circulation paths of the oil. Twin tube forks are noncirculating, whereas most other cartridge forks are circulating. Twin tube forks utilize the oil in a sealed cartridge. The theory is that the main sources of contamination in a fork are the wear between the spring, interface of the fork tube and slider, and the bushings. The metallic debris generated from these moving parts contaminates the oil and forms deposits in crucial areas like the pistons and valve stacks. Aftermarket tuning companies, such as Pro Circuit, offer services to convert circulating cartridge forks to noncirculating types. They don't convert it to a twin tube fork, but rather a hybrid design. Other tuners, such as Terry Davis of Terry Cable, manufacture aftermarket fork kits that increase circulation in non-twin tube forks. The theory is that in desert racing the vehicle speeds are so fast that when you ride over a section of washboard terrain, the cartridge doesn't have the ability to replenish with oil. The oil is pumped into the outer tubes and the damping fails because of air lock.

Forks come from the factory tuned to for an average rider. If you are taking big hits on a supercross track, or riding through tight, heavily rutted trails in the woods, you may want to have your suspension revalved by a pro to finely tune the machine to your performance needs.
KTM-Sportmotorcycle AG

THE SUSPENSION

Passive and Active Valving

On a twin-tube cartridge fork, the piston mounted on the cartridge rod is bidirectional and controls the rebound and active compression damping. The compression adjusting screw located in the fork cap controls the passive damping. Different types of pistons and shim valves can separate the compression damping circuits. The compression valve and adjusting screw are mounted on one end of the fork, usually at the top on twin tube forks or to the bottom of recirculating cartridge forks. The rebound adjuster is mounted in the bottom of the fork on twin tube forks and to the fork caps on recirculating forks. It doubles as the bolt that fastens the cartridge tube to the lower fork leg, thereby holding the fork together.

The compression valve is mounted in a column of fluid (fork oil) inside the cartridge. The type of damping that the compression valve absorbs is passive in nature because the valve doesn't move through the oil. The oil is forced through the compression valve by the displacement action of the moving rebound piston.

The shim valves mounted on the top side of the cartridge rod piston are called the mid-valves and control the active damping of compression. When the fork compresses, the cartridge rod and piston accelerate through the column of fluid inside the cartridge. The mid-valves have a huge effect on the damping of the fork for most riding situations. The mid-valves are like the jet needle in a carburetor. In order to modify the mid-valve, you have to disassemble the cartridge, including removing the head from the damper rod. That is a difficult procedure that should be entrusted only to a professional suspension technician.

PROBLEMS THAT MIMIC POOR TUNING

Mechanical problems, such as worn parts, can cause your fork to act as if it is poorly tuned when it is not. Before you spend a lot of money on revalving or other fork tuning, make sure there is not a mechanical cause for your problems. The following is a list of potential trouble spots to check on your fork:

94

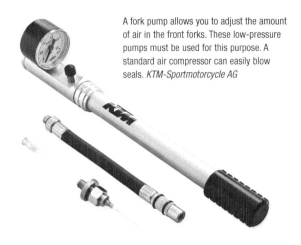
A fork pump allows you to adjust the amount of air in the front forks. These low-pressure pumps must be used for this purpose. A standard air compressor can easily blow seals. *KTM-Sportmotorcycle AG*

1. Oil breakdown can make the damping seem too fast or soft, especially when the fork oil gets hot. Debris can also accumulate in the valving to hinder the damping. Fix by cleaning the fork and changing the fork oil.
2. Blown oil seals cause a lack of damping and a number of other catastrophic problems, such as worn bushings. Replace the seals.
3. Worn rebound piston rings. Most bikes use a plastic seamless band for a rebound piston ring. If your fork seems to rebound too quickly, the oil may be bypassing the rebound piston and shim valving. Unfortunately, this seal band cannot be replaced; you must buy the entire piston rod assembly.
4. Sacked fork springs. Fork springs become shorter in length with use, which can cause headshake or wobbling at high speeds. Plan on replacing fork springs every season. Check to make sure they are even in length as a set.
5. Dented aluminum sliders. The sliders are made from thin-walled aluminum tubing, so the rocky roost from other bikes can easily dent the sliders. These dents can cause the fork to bind, making fork damping harsh. Replace the sliders when they get dented, and install plastic rock guards to prevent rock dents.
6. Worn bushing for the piston rod to damper rod. This bushing is located in the head of the damper rod and supports the piston rod. If your fork appears to have lost rebound damping, this bushing is probably worn and must be replaced.

TUNING WITH OIL VISCOSITY

There are two ways to rate suspension fluids: the Society of Automotive Engineers (SAE) weight and the viscosity index number. The SAE determines the weight number with a standard test that measures oil flow through a fixed orifice at a certain temperature in a 30-minute period. The viscosity index number is a measurement of the oil's flow rate through a fixed orifice over a specific temperature range in a set time

period. The fluid velocities through the tiny steel shim valving and pistons of the cartridge forks are much greater than in the old-style forks, which used drilled jet passages.

Be sure to use cartridge fork oil when you replace the oil, and the weight, in reality, is not that important. Cartridge fork oil is available from about 2 1/2 to 7 weight and any of those work well. In general, as the weight gets higher, you'll get an incremental increase in compression and rebound damping, but most riders wouldn't be able to notice the difference.

In general, raise the oil level when you're bottoming hard. Increased oil will help the last third of the stroke only.

FORK OIL BREAKDOWN

The fork oil breaks down when its additives are depleted and it is contaminated with aluminum and steel debris. The additives that give the oil a low flow-resistance are polymer particles, and they eventually accumulate as a varnish-like coating on the inside of the fork tubes. Consequently, the oil in new-style cartridge forks should be changed every 15 or 20 rides to maintain the best performance.

The main source of debris in the oil is spring flaking. Eibach aftermarket springs are coated with a flexible polymer that resists flaking. The aluminum damper rods and sliders, along with the plastic and bronze high-wear bearing parts, also slowly break down during use and contaminate the oil. Further debris is produced when steel preload cones rub against the springs. Modern aluminum preload cones, such as those produced by Pro-Action, greatly reduce the amount of debris produced by the cones rubbing on the springs.

FORK SPRING PRELOAD TUNING

Before you try to measure and set the preload, measure the length of both springs and compare the measurements to the manufacturer's spec for minimum length. If the springs are too short, it means they are sacked out and need to be replaced. When you purchase new springs, make sure you get the proper spring rate for your bike and rider weight. The Japanese manufacturers have recommendations listed in the service manual for the best spring rate based on rider weight. If you are an expert rider and use the front brake hard or ride on tracks with big jumps, you should select the next stiffer spring rate from the one recommended in the service manual.

Here is how to measure and set the spring preload: Disassemble the fork. Let the fork tube bottom and extend the piston rod. Slide the spring over the piston rod. With the rod extended, measure the distance between the end of the spring and the point where the spring retaining collet clips into the rod. That gives you the preload measurement. Normally, the preload should be 5 to 15 millimeters. The only way for you to vary the preload is to adjust the jam nut height on the piston rod to set the correct preload.

White Power and Ohlins fork springs are available in a wide variety of spring rates and are the proper length to replace extra-long Japanese springs that have too much

Common problems with front suspension include improper rebound and compression settings, blown fork seals, and springs that are too stiff or too soft. *Yamaha Motor Corporation*

preload. Tru Tech sells aftermarket fork caps that feature an adjusting screw to vary the spring preload. This is an excellent product but requires frequent maintenance. If you purchase a set of these fork caps, be sure to pick up a spare set of seals for the caps.

REAR SHOCK SERVICING

This section is a general overview for single shock servicing. You'll see what you can clean and inspect yourself and how a professional service technician would service a shock. This section is also intended to give a thorough understanding of how suspension works and tell you all the things they leave out of the service manual. You can become a more informed consumer by learning when to have your shock serviced and how to shop for suspension services.

Total shock service with cleaning and oil changing should be performed every 15 to 20 riding hours. Servicing suspension components is a specialized task that requires knowledge, experience, and access to special tools and replacement parts. If you lack any of these important things, don't attempt to service your suspension components yourself. Trust revalving to a suspension technician.

Also, you should regularly clean, inspect, and grease your rear linkage. See the section Servicing Rear Suspension Linkage later in this chapter for more details.

Your bike's shock is constantly subjected to internal and external torture. Inside the shock, the bronze piston ring scrapes up against the hard-anodized aluminum shock body walls in oil that reaches temperatures of 450 degrees Fahrenheit. The bronze and aluminum particles quickly contaminate the small volume of shock oil, causing the oil to break down.

To make matters worse, the outside of the shock is constantly subjected to dirt particles being rammed into the shock seal by the foam bumper and the high-strength detergents from the spray of a pressure washer.

External elements can cause the wiper and seal to fail. Small quantities of oil flow past the seal and you hardly notice until most of the oil is lost and the shock shaft turns blue from overheating. It's easy to forget about the shock because it's bolted into the center of the bike, but it's hard to forget about the replacement cost of a shock if it fails.

BASIC CLEANING

This procedure should be performed every five riding hours:

1. Power-wash the shock. You want the dirt off the outside of the shock before you do the detail cleaning. Take care not to spray directly at the shock seal. Also, be sure to spray clean the fine threads on the shock body.
2. Spray penetrating oil on the threads and wait 15 minutes before you try to unthread the spring retaining nut. Unthread the nut to remove the spring collet and the spring so you can remove the seal cap. There are two types of spring collets. One has an open slot and the other is a solid disc with a circlip. The circlip must be removed before you can remove the spring.
3. Use a plastic mallet and punch to rock the seal cap back and forth until the cap pops loose from the shock body. Notice how much dirt and debris is under the seal cap, jammed up against the seal wiper. It's very important to carefully clean under the foam bumper and the seal cap with detergent and water.
4. Check the seal wiper for oil seepage. Seepage indicates that the seal is worn and needs to be replaced.
5. Check the shock shaft for deep scratches and a blue color. The blue indicates that the shock severely overheated, probably from the loss of oil at the seal. The shaft can be replated or replaced if it is discolored or deeply scored.
6. Your factory service manual lists a minimum free length for the shock spring. Measure it to make sure it hasn't sacked out.

The rear shock is accessed by removing the rear subframe. Compression and rebound adjustments are found on the shock reservoir, and are accessible without subframe removal. *American Honda*

7. Remove the seals from the top shock mount and clean the dirt and old grease from the seals and spherical bearing. The bearing doesn't require lube, but you should pack the seals with grease to prevent dirt and water from reaching the bearing.

8. Check the lower shock-mount clevis for cracks at the bolt hole.

SHOCK DISASSEMBLY

The following is a typical disassembly procedure that a professional service technician would follow when servicing a shock:

1. Depressurize the gas bladder, noting any oil mist escaping with the gas, which would indicate a perforated bladder that needs to be replaced.

2. Remove the compression adjuster bolt and let the oil drain. Take care when removing the compression

adjuster bolt. You must use a tiny drill bit to drill down the center of the three center-punch points, where the threads of the shock body and the compression adjuster are threaded together. Drill into center punch points about 0.03 inch—just enough to drill through the points. The compression adjuster can then be unthreaded without the threat of damaging the fine threads.

3. Use a bladder cap–removing T-handle to depress the bladder cap enough to remove the circlip. Now, the bladder cap can be removed.

4. Remove the shock shaft by popping up the seal cap, depressing the seal pack assembly with two drift rods, and removing the circlip that holds the seal pack in place. Use a scraper to remove the burr left by the circlip because this burr could prevent the seal pack from lifting out of the shock body. Remove the shaft assembly from the shock body.

5. Clean all the shock parts thoroughly in mineral spirits solvent, but never in fuel. Fuels are explosive and will damage the rubber seal and foam bumper.

6. Smart technicians measure the inside bore of the shock body for excessive out-of-round wear. Although the shock bodies are hard-anodized, they can still wear out and let oil bypass the piston and shim valves, thereby reducing the damping effect. Those shock bodies wear out in a few seasons of riding. Some manufacturers don't offer the bodies through spare parts, but there is a way to repair worn-out shock bodies. The body is rebuilt by honing it straight and electroplating it with nickel silicon carbide and then diamond-honing to size.

7. Other high-wear parts of the shock include the seal pack and piston ring. The seal pack has a bushing built inside, along with the seal and wiper. When the wiper fails, the seal and bushing wear out quickly. They should be replaced as a set. The best way to install the seal packs on the shock shaft without damaging the seal is to wrap a piece of Teflon tape over the end of the shaft threads. Piston rings are made of either bronze or plastic. The bronze ones wear fast and should be replaced every time you have the oil changed.

8. If the shock shaft is bent, blue, or deeply scratched, repair or replace it if you can find the part. Some companies offer rechroming and polishing services for shock shafts. The best method of shaft plating is hard chrome. Companies such as Race Tech and Pro-Action offer these services, but turnaround time is about three weeks. Works Performance offers complete shaft assemblies for late-model Japanese dirt bikes. These items come with the shaft, clevis, seal pack, and bumper. You have to swap over your piston and valve stack. The Works Performance product is an inexpensive alternative to buying a new shock.

Suspension set-up and tuning is just as vital off-road as it is soaking up harsh landings on the motocross track. A well set-up off-road suspension will eat up rocks and roots and let the rider stay in control. *KTM-Sportmotorcycle AG*

NOTES ON WHITE POWER AND OHLINS PDS SHOCKS

PDS is an acronym for position damping sensitive and is the type of rear shock used on modern motorcycles that mounts directly to the swingarm without a rising-rate linkage setup. PDS shocks are extremely difficult to rebuild unless you have a bevy of special tools, including a bleeder pump machine.

Installation Tips

Check the shock linkage and steering head bearings for wear and grease. Also, be sure to reset the race sag on the back end. On full-size bikes, the rear race sag should be 90 to 105 millimeters with unladen sag of 17 to 25 millimeters. Always check race sag with your full riding gear on, the fuel tank at race volume, and your feet on the pegs. If you go to a mud race, set the rear race sag after the bike gets muddy in practice. You'll be surprised how much it varies from when the bike is clean.

VIDEO SUSPENSION TUNING

Suspension tuning can be a mystery for both the rider and mechanic. As a rider on race day, you go out for your practice session and your suspension nearly kills you. You come back to the pits and your mechanic asks you if the high-speed rebound feels too fast. You haven't got a clue because for the last 20 minutes you struggled to keep your motorcycle on two wheels. After riding and tuning motorcycles for years, I still cannot diagnose suspension problems by riding or watching the bike on a racetrack.

The best suspension tuners in the world have a well-developed sense of high-speed vision. They can watch a bike and rider on various sections of the track to determine how well the four different suspension circuits are working. Some suspension tuners are starting to encourage riders to make video samples for review.

You can acquire that same sense of high-speed vision with the help of a video camera. After videotaping the rider attacking various sections of the track, you can replay the tape one frame at a time and see exactly how the four different suspension circuits damp the impacts of jumps, whoops, and other track irregularities.

This section tells you how to use videotape to tune your suspension. First, you'll learn the four suspension circuits and the track sections that help isolate each circuit. At the end of this section is a troubleshooting chart that will help you to identify problems with each circuit. A suspension data

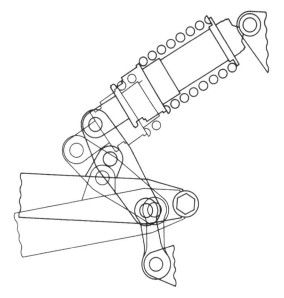

Rear suspension linkage provides a progressive rate of shock travel. This allows suspension designers to fine-tune how your bike responds. *American Honda*

log sheet is also provided so you can record all the pertinent information on your bike and have the data reviewed by a suspension tuning expert. The data log will help you to develop a mental framework for setting up your suspension properly. Lastly, you'll learn what changes suspension tuners make during revalving. A warning though: Do not try to revalve your own suspension. One small mistake can put you over the bars.

First, set up your suspension with the proper springs, settings, oil heights, and so on. If you still need revalving performed, at least then you will know exactly what your suspension needs are. Too many people have their suspension parts revalved without first trying to set up the bike properly.

TUNING WITH THE DAMPING CIRCUITS

As previously mentioned, the four suspension circuits of the forks and shock are the high-speed compression (HSC), high-speed rebound (HSR), low-speed compression (LSC), and low-speed rebound (LSR). Your main objective in video suspension tuning is to make video samples of the rider on sections of the track that best isolate two of these circuits at a time. Before you start riding and taping, change the suspension fluids, grease the linkage, and have the proper spring rates and sag settings on the shock and fork.

Low-Speed Compression (LSC) and Low-Speed Rebound (LSR) Tuning

The low-speed circuits work in two common track scenarios: braking for tight turns and accelerating on a straight with far-spaced, shallow whoops. When taping a rider, be sure to have the whole bike and part of the ground in the film frame. Stand far enough back from the track section and pan with the rider for at least 25 yards. Replay the tape one frame at a

White Power shocks are used on a number of popular brands of motorcycles, and are well-made high-quality units. *KTM-Sportmotorcycle AG*

time and pay attention to how the wheel follows the ground as the bike hits the bumps. The wheel shouldn't compress quickly or rebound abruptly. All Japanese dirt bikes have suspension-adjusting screws that affect the low-speed circuits only. Turning the adjusting screws clockwise will increase the damping and slow/stiffen the low-speed circuit. Turning the screws counterclockwise will decrease damping and speed up/soften the low-speed circuit.

High-Speed Compression (HSC) and High-Speed Rebound (HSR) Tuning

The high-speed circuits work under two common track maneuvers: landing from big jumps and accelerating on a straight with tightly spaced, sharp-edged whoops. Video a rider as he lands from a big jump and continue taping for about 15 yards after he lands because there are usually many small bumps in the landing path after a big jump. Replay the tape one frame at a time and watch to see how equally both the front and rear suspension compress and rebound. If the rear shock rebounds too fast, the rear end may spring up so fast that it loads the fork. If both ends rebound too fast, the whole bike may spring up off the ground. That can be hazardous if there is a turn after the jump.

When taping in whoop sections, try to pan with the rider in as much of the section as possible. Watch how the suspension reacts to the sharp-edged whoops at speed. The rear wheel shouldn't pack up. Packing is caused when the HSC and HSR are too slow to react to the terrain.

If that's the case, the wheel will stay compressed as it hits the next whoop. Eventually, the rider loses control and must slow down. Taping in whoops also helps the rider; if the bike is reacting properly, he may gain enough confidence to go faster through the section.

If the videotape indicates that you need to change the high-speed circuits, you must take the suspension to an expert in revalving because there are no external adjustments that you can make to the high-speed circuits.

SUSPENSION REVALVING
How Damping Works

Suspension fluid (oil) flows through the ports of the piston and up against the shims. The shims pose a resistance to the oil flow, which provides a damping effect. The damping effect is directly related to the diameter and the thickness of the shim. The shims act as a series of tiny springs, flexing to increase the flow area for the oil. The greater the flow area, the greater the oil flow and the less the damping effect. The first shims that the oil encounters are the ones that affect the low-speed damping. These shims are large in diameter and thin in thickness. The oil deflects these shims easily because of their large surface area, and the relatively thin steel poses low spring tension. The shim stack or valving is arranged in a taper shape. The large-diameter low-speed shims are positioned closest to the piston, and the small-

diameter high-speed shims are positioned farthest away from the piston. The low-, mid-, and high-speed circuit shims are separated by transition shims. Think of the valve stack as gears in a transmission and the transition shims as shift forks. The more tapered the valve stacks, and the thinner the transition shims, the plusher the suspension becomes in its handling. Less plush suspension is typically too stiff to absorb the small bumps on acceleration and too soft for square-edged bumps at speed. Much of the problem has to do with a mismatch between the piston's port arrangement and the overall valve stack.

Why Revalve?

The term revalving is often tossed around in the dirt bike magazines, but have you ever wondered what suspension tuners do to revalve a fork or a shock? The answer ranges from not much to a whole lot. Some unscrupulous tuners just power-wash the outside of the components, turn the clickers, and charge you a lot of money. Other tuners replace the pistons and valve stacks, carefully crafting the arrangement of the valve shims to suit your riding demands and compensate for the idiosyncrasies of your model bike. Tuners need information about you and the way you ride in order to revalve your suspension. If they don't give you a survey form or interview you, be suspicious about the work they are asking to be paid to perform. Revalving can be defined as the removal, repositioning, or replacement of shims in the valve stacks of the compression and rebound pistons of a cartridge fork or rear shock. Revalving should be performed when you've exhausted the basics, such as setting the sag, making sure your bike has the right springs, and checking that the fork and shock have fresh oil, seals, and bushings. Only then can you determine whether your bike needs revalving to make it handle better. The main reasons why you need good handling suspension on a dirt bike are:

- To keep the wheels in contact with the ground to provide traction and drive for the rear wheel and steering for the front wheel
- To minimize the impacts and vibration on the motorcycle
- To minimize the stress loads on the rider and prevent fatigue and injuries.

The rear wheel must stay in contact with the ground to provide driving force. The front wheel needs to stay in contact with the ground to provide steering control. Impacts on the motorcycle can cause all sorts of problems, including loose bolts, foaming of the fuel in the carb's float bowl, long-term damage to the bearings that support the suspension components, and long-term damage to the electrical components.

The chronic problems caused to a rider by a poor handling bike are much more obvious. Forearm pump-up

The twin-spar aluminum frame, aluminum swingarm, and single rear shock is the standard design on modern off-road bikes. The combination provides a low center of gravity and tremendous rigidity. *American Honda*

is probably the most common. Long-term damage to a rider's neck and spine may take years to manifest, but some people might be immediately sensitive to pain. Having a professional suspension tuner revalve your suspension might seem expensive, but what price do you put on pain?

The main things that affect a suspension system are changes in the sprung mass from moving up and down and changes in motion, such as acceleration, braking, and turning.

The sprung mass of a moving dirt bike can be hard to define because the entire motorcycle leaves the ground. Technically, the sprung mass includes everything but the wheels, swingarm, lower fork tubes, and rear shock. Those parts are considered unsprung mass. Because dirt bikes are capable of jumping, gravity and the weight of the rider affect the sprung mass. The movement of a motorcycle's suspension going up is termed rebound and the movement down is compression.

Changes in the motion of a motorcycle can cause it to roll, pitch, yaw, or any combination thereof. When a motorcycle accelerates, the bike pitches backward. The driving chain forces try to wrap the swingarm underneath the bike. That cannot occur because the shock is a finite length and connects the swingarm to the frame, but it causes a transfer of force. The rear wheel pushes down into the ground, transferring force up the swingarm and causing the front end to lift. The natural tendency of the rear wheel is to hop because the damping isn't enough to compensate for the spring force. When a motorcycle brakes for a turn, the bike pitches forward, shifting the weight to the front. The rear end tends to kick because of the torque reaction of the brake caliper on the swingarm and the weight shift.

When a motorcycle is turned, it rolls, pitches, and yaws at the apex of the turn—complicated motion! The front end is forced to either compress and change the fork angle or extend and plow out of the turn. Meanwhile, the rear end tries to make a radial motion without losing traction and spinning out.

INTERNAL AND EXTERNAL ADJUSTMENTS

Suspension dampers can be adjusted internally and externally. External adjustments are limited to the riding circumstances and the adjustment range on the compression and rebound clickers. Internal adjustments are virtually unlimited because they encompass revalving and replacing the damper piston and valve-shim stack.

The external adjusters, low-speed compression and rebound, can only effect minor changes in handling. Typical low-speed compression or rebound riding situations might include far-spaced shallow whoops, tabletop jumps, and braking and accelerating around tight turns. All compression and rebound clicker adjusters are marked S and H, meaning soft and hard. That can also be interpreted as soft-fast and hard-stiff.

A professional suspension tuner's work revolves around internal adjustments. When a suspension component is revalved, it is also rebuilt, meaning that the bushings and seals are checked for replacement and the oil is changed.

Revalving is the discipline of repositioning, removing, or replacing valve shims in such an order as to improve the damper's performance.

AFTERMARKET PISTON KITS

The latest recent trend is to combine a piston design with a valve shim pack so as to effect a greater change. There are three main types of piston/shim systems. The main difference between the three is the port design of the piston. Race Tech has a setup that relies on a high-flow piston with a large series of shims that can be rearranged in set patterns to adapt to the needs of a set number of rider profiles. Pro-Action's setup relies on a piston with smaller ports and a multistage shim arrangement that separates the circuits of passive and active to give the damper a wider tuning range. The piston works at the edge of the spectrum and provides a hydraulic lock capability during riding situations where all the suspension travel is used quickly. The MX-Tech design uses a unique piston port arrangement and a DLC (diamond-like coating)

A set of special tools allows you to press out rear suspension bushings and bearings. *Motion Pro*

to prevent the piston ring from seizing and premature failure of sealing.

The Race Tech Gold Valve is simple and can be installed by inexperienced technicians. The support provided by Race Tech is excellent. The kits come with detailed instructions, an optional video, and training seminars geared toward amateur race tuners and home-based mechanics. The MX-Tech and Pro-Action 3-Stage incremental valve aren't available over the counter. Only company technicians can install them. The reason is that the valving must be set up for the individual, and there is a wide variety of valving patterns to suit virtually any rider profile. The Pro-Action approach also relies on matching the proper spring to the valving. MX-Tech and Pro-Action's setups are more expensive than a typical revalving job, but they are more comprehensive and produce a truly custom result.

HOW INCREMENTAL VALVING WORKS

The rear shock valve stack is comprised of a series of steel washers with a variety of outer diameters and thicknesses, mounted on two sides of a piston. This is called a bidirectional valve. One side handles the compression damping and the other handles the rebound damping. The valve shim stacks have different arrangement patterns because the compression stack aids the spring and the rebound stack controls the stored energy release of the spring. As to shim sizing, the larger the diameter and the thinner the thickness, the more easily the shim will bend and increase oil flow through the piston. The faster the oil flow, the less the damping. Stock Japanese dampers use high-flow pistons with a complicated series of shims that aren't very sensitive at slow shaft speeds. The shims don't open at slow shaft speeds and the clickers primarily control the damping—this can cause potential handling problems when the rider accelerates out of turns. The bike is riding at a point on the rear spring where the clickers don't provide enough damping and the piston valving isn't in the response range, so the bike chatters.

Incremental valving addresses such issues by separating the three main damping phases: low, mid, and high. They do this by using a special piston and a valve stack with transition shims to separate the three circuits. The incremental valve stack is more sensitive at low shaft speeds so the clickers don't have to carry the damping load. The mid-speed valve helps make the transition from low- to high-speed damping modes to give a plush ride, especially under an acceleration load. The piston has smaller ports too which provide a hydraulic lock effect at high shaft speeds, which reduces the load on the nitrogen-charged gas bladder and the elastomer foam bumper.

THE SHOCK DYNO

A shock dyno is a computer-controlled, electro-hydraulic machine that measures the damping characteristics of dampers (rear shock or front fork). A shock dyno is comprised of an electric motor, a hydraulic ram, a mounting guide, and a load cell (pressure transducer). A shock dyno quantifies how much resistance (force in pounds) the damper produces at different shaft speeds (velocity in inches/second) and stroke lengths (displacement/travel in inches).

The load cell is connected to a PC program that plots the damping of the compression and rebound over a range of shaft speeds. The two basic types of graphic plots that a shock dyno provides are force-versus-velocity and force-versus-displacement. There is an optimum profile for the plots, so a suspension technician can use the results of the plots to see if there is an obvious problem with a shock or fork. The force-versus-displacement plots can show how smoothly valve shims are opening, whether there is air trapped in the shock, the condition of the seals and bushings, and the condition of the oil with regard to fading over time. The shock dyno can also test the condition of the adjusters, the gas bladder, and the bearing on the top mount. In auto sports, it's routine to test shocks before and after servicing. It enables the professional suspension technician to test and verify his work.

SUSPENSION TUNING FOR UNIQUELY SIZED PEOPLE

The thing that most frustrates me about dirt bikes is that they're all the same size. Riders are made in all different sizes, but dirt bikes are made for skinny guys who are 5 foot 10 inches tall. Without a thick wallet and the engineering and fabrication expertise to resize the whole bike, riders who deviate from the manufacturer's hypothetical everyrider proportions can make important suspension changes for a better-fitting bike.

Shortening Suspension for Rider Comfort

Ever wonder why dirt bikes are built with 12 inches of travel when 4 inches of it is sag? Why don't the manufacturers provide a kit to give a bike 8 good inches of travel? Perhaps they will after they read this book!

Suspension tuners can shorten forks and shocks. FMF's contractive suspension utilizes springs fitted to the rebound side of the shock shaft or fork damper rods. When the bike tops out its suspension, it relies on the springs to contract to the sag point (8 inches). A magazine tested some prototype bikes and raved about the handling through turns but criticized the bike for its vulnerability at getting grounded in deep ruts.

Jeremy Wilkey of MX-Tech, a suspension tuner outside Chicago, specializes in all sorts of suspension tuning, but especially shortening suspension for DTX (dirt track) and other off-road applications. When performing such modifications, many factors have to be considered because each change to a suspension component affects several other things.

A suspension component can be shortened a few different ways. For a rear shock, a spacer can be turned on a lathe and fitted between the rebound stop washer and the seal pack. A 1-inch-long spacer will shorten the rear travel by 4 inches because of the linkage system. Most shocks have enough threads on the shock body to accommodate adjustment of the spring. If they don't, the spring must be shortened. When a spring is shortened, it becomes effectively stiffer. When the spring is stiffer, the rebound damping must be increased to compensate for the additional potential stored energy of the stiffer spring. Generally speaking, if you are a heavy person, shortening the travel will adjust the spring to your weight, but the shock will still need to be revalved. If you are a lightweight person, you may need to switch to a progressive shock spring. Obviously, by changing the ride height of the bike, the rising rate of the linkage system is going to be narrowed.

One product that is available to adjust the linkage ratio is the DeVol Link. The mounts of this product are fitted with adjustable lugs. For modifications to the front fork, it may be possible to just shorten the spring and place the cutoff section of spring on the rebound rod in place of the top-out spring. I did that on my XR600 to make contractive suspension. Some types of cartridge forks don't have the space for a spring, but a plastic or elastomer foam rubber spacer can be made to shorten the fork travel. Like the rear shock, the spring rate is the biggest factor. You don't have to shorten the front travel as much as the rear because you can still adjust the fork at the triple clamps. Normally, a bike with shortened travel will be better suited for low-speed riding. Consideration will need to be given when jumping or riding through deep ruts because the lowered ground clearance will make the bike more prone to grounding out.

Modifications for Big Guys

Big guys face the same problems as the vertically challenged. Dirt bikes aren't designed for them either. A lot of big guys adjust their bikes by revalving the suspension and installing a stiffer set of springs. Tall guys have the added problem of leverage. When they stand up and lean forward or backward, they can easily change the pitch of the bike and drastically affect the handling. That's why stiff springs are important.

Some popular mods that big guys perform to customize dirt bikes are a taller seat using special seat foam and covers manufactured by GUTS, handlebars with a higher rise, forward-offset handlebar clamps, extended shift and brake levers, and wider footpegs by Fastway. These mods are done to adjust the ergonomics of the bike but may compromise the handling.

FRAME MAINTENANCE

Most people think of the frame as the thing the rest of the mororcycle parts bolt to. That is true in a sense, but a frame can also be a tunable component of the suspension system. The stiffness of the frame is one thing that distinguishes a new bike from an old bike. A stiff frame gives you confidence that you can bottom the bike from jumps or stuff it into a berm without losing control.

Let's think about what makes a frame feel worn out and twitchy. The front fork, shock linkage, and swingarm are fastened to the frame with large bolts that pivot on bearings. When the bolts loosen up, the bearings lose the side tension needed to keep the components in alignment. If the bearings are worn on the linkage, dangerous side forces will be applied to the shock as it compresses, increasing rear shock friction, reducing responsiveness, and causing a handling problem, or, worse, a bent shock shaft. Also, the tapered roller bearings that support the triple clamp assembly loosen up over time, and too little tension will allow the fork assembly to rock back and forth when the bike hits bumps and when braking for turns. Slop in the steering head bearings is the major reason for side-to-side shaking of the front end.

Inspecting the Frame

The hammering dirt bikes experience at riders' hands takes its toll over time. Parts loosen up, wear, and bend. The frame, supporting all parts and the rider, absorbs much punishment. Metal fatigue can affect a frame when the engine mount bolts or pivot bolts get loose. Excessive vibration from the engine and flex forces from the swingarm and steering head can cause frame cracks. Check for frame cracks where the neck is welded to the top and down tubes. Also check the engine mount sleeve flanges that are welded on each side of the tube because cracks can form around the circumference of the tube. This is a common failure on early KX perimeter frames. Some bikes have thin plates for engine mounts. The manufacturer doesn't weld along the entire seam of the plate and frame tube; they only spot-weld the plate at key places. Look for cracks on the spot welds. The frame can crack at both the motor mounts and the top shock-mounting plate. Also, if the bottom frame tubes aren't covered with a skid plate, they may be susceptible to water corrosion, so inspect the bottom of the frame too.

Frames become sprung with use, the most common evidence of which is a widening of the engine cradle. That's why you often hear a cracking noise and see gaps open up between the mounts and the engine when you loosen the engine mounts.

Linkage Maintenance

To gain access to the linkage bearings, place the bike on a stand, remove the linkage bolts, and elevate the rear wheel.

To service the linkage, start with the most overlooked part—the spherical bearing of the top shock mount. Removing the shock makes it easier to service the linkage. The basic linkage setup is two pull rods, three pivot bolts, and a link.

Place the parts in a container and wash off the dirt and grease in mineral spirits solvent. Linkage bearings are full-

complement, meaning that they don't have retaining cages. Be aware that all the individual needle bearings will fall out when you clean the linkage.

TIGHTENING PIVOT BOLTS

The torque on the pivot bolts is crucial. If it is too high, the swingarm and linkage will bind. If the torque is too low, the swingarm and linkage will twist when the suspension is bottomed, making the bike twitchy. See your service manual for correct torque figures.

Shimming the mounts is as important as tightening the bolts to the proper torque. As mentioned earlier, frames tend to spread out near the engine cradle, which results in gaps between the mounts and the engine, the swingarm, or the top shock mounting plate that bolts to the mounts. If you tighten the bolts on perimeter frames without shimming these gaps, you put the frame under considerable stress, and the stress may cause the frame to crack faster than normal. Kawasaki makes thin engine-mount shims (8 millimeters and 10 millimeters inside diameter) that can be inserted between the engine and frame to take up the excess clearance and reduce the stress on the frame. These shims fit the motor mounts of any Japanese dirt bike.

LINKAGE SERVICE
Servicing Rear Suspension Linkage

Remove the link bolt that fastens the linkage to the swingarm and elevate the rear wheel with a 10-inch block. This allows greater access to the shock bolt and other link pivot bolts. Take care when removing the links because some bikes use thin shim washers between the linkages. The linkage consists of two main parts: the frame-mounted link arms and the swingarm-mounted link bar.

Remove the rubber seals from the ends of the pivot bushings. Push the bushings halfway out and use degreaser and a shop towel to remove the old grease and dirt buildup. If the needle bearings are dry or corroded, the seals are leaking and the bearings and seals should be replaced. If the bearings still have grease on them, use a small brush to apply new grease to the bearings. Take care not to displace any of the needle bearings because they don't have a race cage to hold them in place. Repeat this procedure for the bearings on the other side of the linkage.

Some linkage bearings are retained by circlips. Remove the clips before attempting to remove the bearing races or you could break the linkage.

If you have to change the bearing races, use a hydraulic press and a couple of sockets—one with a diameter bigger than the bearing on the bottom and one socket with a slightly smaller diameter than the race to press down from the top.

To grease the swingarm pivots, you'll have to remove the swingarm pivot bolt. You may have to remove the brake pedal to remove the pivot bolt, and you should grease the brake pivot too. Remove the chain or you won't be able to extend the swingarm back far enough to reach the pivot bearings. The pivot bolt may be difficult to remove, so use a brass drift rod and a hammer to drive the bolt out. The brass rod is softer than the pivot bolt and won't damage the threads. If the bolt is still very difficult to remove, loosen the engine mounting bolts. Clean and grease the bearings and bushings the same way you did for the linkage parts.

Quick Link Lubing

Follow these steps to quickly lubricate the rear suspension link:

1. Place the bike on a stand and remove the linkage pivot bolt that goes through the swingarm.
2. Elevate the rear wheel with a 6-inch tall block.
3. Unbolt the link stay bars from the frame.
4. Clean the old grease and dirt from the seals and bearings with a rag and regrease the bearings with wheel-bearing grease.
5. Reinstall the parts and torque the linkage pivots to factory specs.

SUSPENSION TERMINOLOGY

Have you ever read a magazine test on a new bike and been confused by the words used to describe the bike's handling? Suspension terminology is a mixture of engineering and slang words. Read this section before you read any of the sections on suspension servicing.

Angular Motions

Pitch—a motion fore or aft when the front end dives or when the rear end squats.

Roll—a motion where the motorcycle leans left or right from straight-up riding.

Yaw—a motion which veers left or right from the motorcycle's heading angle.

General Terms

Active damping—when a piston and shim valve accelerate through the column of fluid in a fork or shock.

Air spring—the volume of the air space at the top of the fork, working with the suspension fluid, provides cushion effect when the fork is bottomed out.

Air tanks—a closed-end cylinder with a connection line to the fork cap and controlled with an adjustable needle valve. Air tanks give a wider range of operation to the air spring.

Anti-squat ratio—a formula that calculates the relation between the drive sprocket, the rear tire contact patch, the swingarm pivot height, and the chain force lines to determine the rear suspension's resistance to squatting under acceleration.

Arm pump—when the muscles in a rider's forearms tense up to the point that handgrip is weakened or uncontrollable.

Axle—the axis about which a wheel spins.

Baseline settings—a series of standard settings performed to the chassis in order to establish a known base of information. Settings items include race sag, unladen sag, compression and rebound clicker positions, tire pressure, and chain tension.

Base valve—the compression piston and valving that fits onto the compression bolt assembly.

Bladder—a closed-end, thick rubber, cylindrical-shaped piece that contains the nitrogen gas in a rear shock.

Bottoming—a riding situation in which all the suspension travel is used.

Bumper—a tapered, dense foam piece that fits on the shock shaft and provides last-ditch resistance to bottoming.

Bushing—a bronze or plastic ring used as a load-bearing surface in forks or shocks.

Center of gravity/mass center—the center point of the motorcycle's mass, normally located somewhere behind the cylinder and below the carburetor of a dirt bike.

Chassis—the frame, swingarm, suspension, and wheels of a motorcycle.

Clevis—a fork-shaped piece of aluminum used as the bottom mount for most shocks.

Clickers—the screws or knobs used to fine-tune the low-speed damping on forks or shocks.

Compression bolt assembly—a large-diameter bolt that houses the LSC adjusting screw and the compression valve assembly.

Compression damping—the damping circuit that absorbs the energy of compression forces on the damper.

Countersteering—when the rider applies steering pressure in the opposite direction of the turn.

Damper—a fluid chamber with a means of regulating the fluid flow to restrain the speed of the moving end of the damper during the compression or rebound strokes.

Damper assembly—the parts of a shock comprised of the clevis, shaft, bumper, piston, and shims.

Damper rod—the large-diameter aluminum tube in the lower legs of a telescopic fork.

Damper speed—the relative speed at which the moving end of a damper compresses or rebounds. The two different speeds are high and low.

Damping—the process of absorbing the energy of impacts transmitted through the fork or rear shock on the compression stroke and the process of absorbing the energy of the spring on the rebound stroke.

Damping circuits—-There are normally four damping circuits that affect the damper's speed: low-speed compression (LSC), high-speed compression (HSC), low-speed rebound (LSR), and high-speed rebound (HSR).

Flicking—the action of putting the bike into a full lean position quickly.

Front-end diving—bike motion when the front fork compresses quickly. It usually occurs when braking for turns.

Handling—the quality of response from the chassis of a motorcycle while riding through turns, jumps, hills, whoops, and bumps.

Harshness—an undesirable quality of the damping that results in sharp shocks being transferred through the suspension to the chassis.

Headshaking—the high-speed oscillation of the fork as a result of losing self-steering. Headshaking occurs on acceleration when the front end starts to wheelie and there isn't enough downward pressure from the fork to make it self-steer. Headshaking occurs when decelerating with the front brake, compressing the fork, and changing the pitch of the bike. The fork angle changes to produce less trail, causing a loss of self-steering.

High side—the outside of a turn.

Hopping—when the tire bounces up off the ground due to a reaction from a bump.

HSC—the high-speed compression circuit is affected most when riding fast over square-edged bumps.

HSR—the high-speed rebound circuit is affected in the same riding circumstances as HSC.

Kicking—describes both pogoing and packing.

Low side—the inside of a turn.

LSC—the low-speed compression circuit is affected most when riding through turns.

LSR—the low-speed rebound circuit is affected in the same riding circumstances as LSC.

Mid-turn wobble—when the bike wobbles or weaves near the apex of a turn.

Mid-valves—on a twin tube fork, at the top of the cartridge rod, a piston-port and shim valve control the active compression damping.

Nitrogen—an inert gas used to pressurize the bladder or reservoir of shocks.

Packing—when the rear shock is compressed by the wheel hitting one bump and cannot rebound quickly enough to absorb the impact of the second or third bump.

Passive damping—a piston and shim valve mounted with a displacement volume of suspension fluid flowing through it.

PDS—"position damping sensitive" is the type of rear shock design that is used on modern dirt bikes where one end of the shock is mounted directly to the swingarm.

Piston—a cylindrical piece of steel with several ports arranged around the periphery so as to direct oil toward the face of shocks.

Piston ring—a ring that fits around the piston and prevents oil from bypassing the piston and shims.

Piston rod—a small-diameter steel rod that fits into the upper legs of a cartridge fork. It fastens to the fork cap on one end and holds the rebound piston and shims on the other end.

Pivot—a fixed point about which a lever rotates. Examples: swingarm or suspension linkage.

Pogoing—when the rear shock rebounds so quickly that the rear wheel leaves the ground.

Preload—tension applied to the fork and shock springs to bring the bike to the proper ride height or race sag

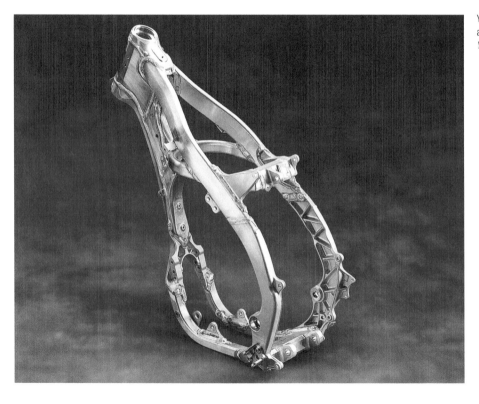

Your frame requires some care, mostly lubing and proper torque settings on the bolts.
Yamaha Motor Corporation

THE SUSPENSION

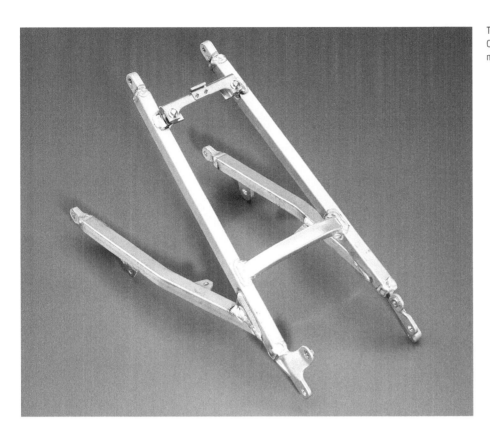

The subframe can easily crack and bend. Check it regularly for splits in the metal and nasty dings. *Yamaha Motor Corporation*

dimension. The preload can be biased to change the bike's steering geometry. For example, high preload/less sag in the front fork will make the steering heavy/slow and more stable at high speed.

Race sag—the number of millimeters that the fork or shock sags with the rider on the bike in full riding gear. This is essential to proper suspension tuning but is often overlooked or adjusted incorrectly.

Rake—the angle between the steering axis and a vertical line.

Rear end squatting—compression of the rear suspension on acceleration.

Rebound damping—the damping circuit that restrains the release of the stored energy in the compressed spring to reduce the rebounding speed of the damper.

Reservoir—a cylindrical device that contains suspension fluid and nitrogen gas, with a floating piston separating the fluid from the gas.

Revalving—altering the compression and rebound shims in order to fine-tune damping characteristics.

Seal—a rubber or plastic cylindrical piece that prevents oil from being lost from the damper.

Shaft—the chrome-plated rod on the rear shock that has a clevis on one end and the piston and shims fastened to the other end.

Shim—a circular flat washer of thin steel, used to exert resistance on the oil flow through a piston; a series of shims (valve stack or valving) with varying outer diameters and thicknesses arranged in sequence to provide a damping effect.

Shock body—the aluminum cylinder that contains the damper assembly.

Shock dyno—a machine that cycles a shock absorber at different damper speeds and measures the resistance posed by the four damping circuits.

Shock fade—When the shock oil becomes so hot that the damping effect is reduced, so the shock compresses easily and rebounds quickly.

Speed wobble—when a motorcycle wavers back and forth rapidly at high speeds.

Spiking—how the fork works when the damping is too stiff/slow. This is also associated with arm pump (defined above).

Spring—a steel wire that is wound into a coil shape and tempered to provide resistance to compression forces and store energy for expansion to the extended position.

Steering angle—the angle of the handlebars as you rotate them left or right about the steering axis.

Steering axis—the axis about which the fork rotates.

Stiction—a combination of the words "static" and "friction" used to describe the drag exerted on the moving damper parts by the stationary parts, such as the bushings, seals, and wipers. Low stiction is desirable because it results in more responsive suspension.

Stiff/slow or soft/fast—the damping characteristics of the fork or shock. With regard to the clickers, these

SUSPENSION TROUBLESHOOTING

FRONT FORKS: PROBLEM (P), CAUSE (C), AND ACTION (A) SUGGESTIONS

P) Front end bottoms after big jumps.
C) Fork springs too soft; fork oil level too low; mid-valve compression damping too soft.
A) Install stiffer springs; raise fork oil level 10 millimeters; revalve HSC for more damping.

P) Fork makes clunking sound on bottoming.
C) Fork oil level too low; bottoming cone needs more aggressive angle or length.
A) Raise oil level; install aftermarket bottoming cone or air tanks.

P) Fork makes clunking sound when topping out.
C) Fork rebounds too fast.
A) Check bushing in the top of damper rod head; check top-out spring or stop.

P) Fork shudders when riding downhill over bumps.
C) Fork tubes unbalanced.
A) Service fork; check spring lengths; carefully set axle clamp, and triple clamp torque.

P) Headshaking occurs on deceleration.
C) Front tire pressure too low or sidewalls are shot; fork springs too soft or not enough preload; fork oil level too low; fork compressed.
A) Increase tire pressure to 15 psi, check for cracks in tire's sidewall; change to stiffer springs or add preload spacers; raise fork oil level 5 millimeters; install a steering damper.

P) Fork dives excessively during braking.
C) Fork springs too soft or worn out; fork oil level too low or fork oil contaminated; compression valve stuck open from trapped debris; damper bushing worn out; LSC too soft.
A) Replace fork springs with the correct rate; service fork; turn LSC adjuster in three clicks.

P) Front end climbs out of ruts.
C) LSC too stiff; springs have too much preload.
A) Turn compression clicker out three clicks; set spring preload to 5 to 10 millimeters.

P) Front end oversteers and washes out in turns.
C) Fork springs too stiff; LSC too stiff; fork tubes do not overlap enough.
A) Install softer springs; turn out compression adjuster three clicks; increase fork tube overlap 5 millimeters.

P) Front end understeers and high sides in turns.
C) Fork tube-to-clamp overlap too great; fork springs too soft; LSC too soft.
A) Reduce fork tube overlap; install stiffer springs; turn in compression adjuster three clicks.

P) Fork compresses with inconsistent feel.
C) Fork clamps at axle out of alignment; lower triple clamp bolts too tight.
A) Realign front axle clamps; loosen and retorque triple clamp bolts.

P) Fork locks when riding up the face of a steep jump at speed or when landing into the face of a jump.
C) Mid-speed valves are too stiff.
A) Revalve mid-valve for softer damping.

P) Fork sag reduced after riding in hot weather.
C) Fork bushings worn, allowing aeration and pressure buildup in forks; fork oil contaminated.
A) Service fork; let fork cool down, fully extend, and bleed off air pressure through fork caps.

P) Front end rattles and shakes fore and aft when riding or braking over bumps.
C) Steering head bearings loose or worn.
A) Check steering head bearings and preload torque.

P) Front end self-centers and steering feels notchy.
C) Steering head bearings worn.
A) Replace steering head bearings and races.

P) Race sag more than 2 inches.
C) Fork springs worn out or spring rate too soft.
A) Install stiffer springs.

P) Fork seals are chronic leakers.
C) Fork tubes scratched; bushings worn out; seals not installed properly.
A) Check tube for scratches; replace bushings, seals, and wipers; wrap a plastic bag around seals on installation and use Teflon grease on the seals and wipers.

---

words refer to the direction of rotation that you will turn the clickers in order to improve the damping. Turning the clickers clockwise will make the damping stiff/slow. Turning the clickers counterclockwise will make the damping soft/fast.

Stinkbug—a term that refers to a dirt bike's pitch forward and the damping characteristics front to back. A dirt bike with the back end set high compared to the front end.

Swapping—when the rear end of the bike skips from side to side very quickly.

Swingarm—the rear fork that connects the rear wheel to the frame.

Swingarm angle—the angle of rotational motion about the swingarm pivot axis.

Swingarm pivot axis—the point where the swingarm mounts to the frame and about which the swingarm rotates.

Tank slapper—when the fork rotates from stop to stop rapidly and the rider's arms and body slap back and forth against the motorcycle's gas tank.

Trail—on the front end, the horizontal distance between the point where the steering axis reaches the road surface and the center of the front tire's contact patch. Generally, forks with offset axles have more trail than forks with straight-through axles.

Transition shims—these are shims with very small outer diameters used to separate the normal shims of the low- and high-speed valve stacks.

Transmitability—the suspension oil's ability to transmit shock loads. As the oil's temperature rises, the transmitabiliry falls. For example, with every increase in temperature of 18 degrees Fahrenheit, the transmitability of the oil falls 50 percent.

REAR SHOCK: PROBLEM (P), CAUSE (C), AND ACTION (A) SUGGESTIONS

P) Bike has too much sag.
C) Spring needs more preload.
A) Tighten the spanner ring on the shock to reduce sag, tighten jam nut.

P) Bike has too little sag.
C) Spring needs less preload.
A) Loosen the spanner ring on the shock to increase sag, tighten jam nut.

P) Bike has too much unladen sag when the race sag is correct.
C) Spring rate is too stiff for the rider's weight.
A) Install the next lower-rate spring.

P) Bike has too little unladen sag when the race sag is correct.
C) Spring rate is too soft for the rider's weight.
A) Install the next higher-rate spring.

P) Rear end kicks over braking bumps.
C) LSR is too soft/fast.
A) Turn in the LSR adjuster three clicks.

P) Rear end chatters under acceleration out of turns.
C) LSC too soft; LSR too stiff.
A) Turn in LSC adjuster three clicks; turn LSR adjuster out two clicks.

P) Rear end packs while riding over whoops.
C) LSC too stiff; LSR too soft.
A) Turn out LSC adjuster two clicks; turn in LSR adjuster two clicks.

P) Rear end pogos when hitting small square-edged bumps.
C) Mid-speed rebound valving too soft/fast.
A) Revalve shock or increase rear sag and turn in LSR adjuster three clicks.

P) Rear end bottoms out hard when landing from big jumps.
C) HSC too soft.
A) Reduce rear sag; increase spring rate; revalve shock.

P) Rear end hardly compresses when landing from big jumps.
C) HSC too stiff.
A) Revalve shock.

P) Damping performance becomes noticeably softer after riding for 20 minutes.
C) Oil is contaminated.
A) Service shock.

P) Rear end wants to swing around when cornering.
C) Wheel alignment incorrect; rear axle loose; oversteering.
A) Check wheel alignment; reduce fork tube overlap.

P) Bike pitches back as if in a wheelie.
C) Spring bias incorrect.
A) Check front versus rear spring sag; reduce rear sag; increase LSC.

P) Bike pitches forward as if in an endo.
C) Spring bias incorrect.
A) Check front versus rear sag; increase rear sag; increase LSC; increase fork spring preload.

P) No unladen sag after shock gets hot.
C) Air trapped in shock; gas bladder punctured.
A) Service shock and check bladder.

P) Shock leaks oil.
C) Seal pack worn; perforated bladder; shaft's chrome worn down; shaft scratched.
A) Rebuild shock and examine shaft for wear.

Trapped air space—the height of the air space that forms in the top of the fork tube between the fork cap and the oil.

Triple clamp assembly—includes the steering stem, bottom clamp, and top clamp. The triple clamp assembly connects the fork to the frame.

Unladen sag—the number of millimeters that the bike sags under its own weight without a rider.

Unsprung/sprung weight—the unsprung weight of the motorcycle comprises many parts, including the wheels, brakes, swingarm and suspension linkage, and the lower front fork legs, the weight of which does not bear down on the fork and shock springs. The sprung weight is all the parts of the motorcycle that are supported by the suspension.

Valves—refers to a series of shims either for the compression or the rebound damping.

Viscosity—a rating system for oil that measures the oil's flow rate through a fixed orifice at a certain temperature. Also known as the oil's weight, as in 30-weight oil.

Viscosity index (VI)—the flow rate characteristic of the oil over a range of temperatures. The VI rating of an oil is directly linked to the oil's transmitabiliry. Cartridge fork oil has a VI number of 115. Shock oil normally has a much higher average operating temperature so its VI number is 300.

Washout—a term used to describe what happens when the bike's tires lose traction and slide to the outside of a turn, causing the bike and rider to fall to the inside of a turn.

Weight bias—the amount of weight on each wheel of the motorcycle, also called weight distribution.

Wheelbase—the distance between the front and rear axle centers.

Wheelie—a motorcycle in motion with the front wheel off the ground.

PROJECT 10
How to Set Your Suspension Sag

 Time: 30 minutes

 Cost: 0

 Tools: Two assistants (or bike lift with wheel clamp), riding gear, and a metric tape measure

 Parts: None

 Experience: 1

The most important thing to set—before you do any modifications to your bike—is the setting of your suspension sag. Get this right, and your bike will be well on its way to handling as well as it can. Proper sag fulfills two goals. First, a suspension unit needs a certain amount of room within its travel to work properly. (If you have too little sag, your bike will be prone to topping out the suspension as it extends to its limit. Similarly, too much sag allows you to experience the jolt of bottoming out much more frequently.) Second, once your sag is set, you will be able to determine whether your spring rate is correct for your weight and size. All of the information below is based on techniques developed by Paul Thede of Race Tech (www.racetech.com).

The calculations required to discover the free sag (the amount of sag of the bike under its own weight) and the static sage (the sag with the rider and all gear on board) are fairly simple if you keep clear notes. First, measure the length of the suspension (front and rear) with the bike on a stand and the wheels off the ground. Then measure the static sag as described below. The static sag should be within the ranges of 65 to 75 millimeters front and 95 to 100 millimeters rear. If you don't get these numbers, you'll need to adjust the suspension preload to achieve these numbers.

Lastly, measure the length of the front and rear suspension with the bike's wheels on the ground supporting just the weight of the bike. Subtract the measurement from the fully extended measurement, and you'll know your free sag. Ideally, this will be about 15 to 25 millimeters. If it is less, your spring is too stiff for your weight. If the free sag is longer, your spring is too soft. You'll need to get different springs.

1 Begin with the bike up on a work stand with the suspension fully extended. Measure the front and rear suspension to determine their full length. *Evans Brasfield*

2 Now get the rider in full gear and in proper riding position on the bike, supported by an assistant or a clamp on a bike lift. *Evans Brasfield*

3

Slowly lift the front end until the suspension is fully extended and then let it settle back down under the rider's weight. Measure from a fixed object (like the beginning of the slider) to where it enters the fork wiper. Take three different readings and average them. Subtract this number from the fully extended measurement and you have your static sag. *Evans Brasfield*

4

When you don't have a convenient mark to measure the rear suspension, a piece of tape with a line on it will do in a pinch. Just make sure it is directly above the axle. *Evans Brasfield*

5

Since we're dealing in millimeters, you need to be meticulous with your measurements. Double-check them. *Evans Brasfield*

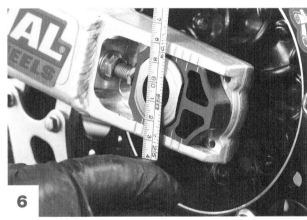

6

Don't just eyeball for the center of the axle. You can vary quite a bit depending on the angle you look at it. Instead, choose the top inside edge of a hollow axle. *Evans Brasfield*

7

When adjusting the preload, remember that more preload lessens the static sag. Notice how the locking ring has been loosened from the adjusting ring. The black mark will make it easy to keep track of how far the ring has been turned. *Evans Brasfield*

8

Keeping track of the number of turns on the fork is vital so that you can adjust both legs the same amount. *Evans Brasfield*

Chapter 10
The Cooling System

Dirt bike design underwent considerable evolution and refinement before liquid-cooled engines became popular. As a result, the cooling system often has a retrofitted sensibility—like parts tacked on at the last minute, after the crucial form and function decisions had been made. Because of the need for good airflow, radiators nearly always reside at the front of a vehicle. Something on the fork would get the most air, but the weight would affect steering and handling.

What's left is the location behind the front wheel, a spot pinched side to side by a dirt bike's narrow esthetic and chased up from the ground to avoid the debris thrown back by the front tire. Sure as the new day comes, Rat Bike Johnson's radiator is plugged with dirt, dinged by rocks and sticks, low on coolant, and not delivering the cooling his engine requires to perform at its peak. His bike is running too hot, making less power, and leaving Rat Bike ranting against his luck as other racers disappear ahead of him.

Keeping a bike engine cool for maximum performance takes some routine maintenance—and sometimes some quick fixes!

SOFT TOOLS

Several excellent products are invaluable when you need to repair your cooling system. Duro Master Mend epoxy can make temporary repairs to the outside of the radiator. Alumaseal can make temporary repairs to the inside of the system, and it works great for chronic head-gasket leaks. Use radiator cleaner to flush out the cooling system on a yearly basis because corrosion, debris, and waste products from combustion gases collecting in the coolant can accumulate

Sand puts heavy strain on cooling systems. The engine is running hard turning the tire through the thick ground. On hot days racing in deep sand, your cooling system will be taxed heavily. *KTM-Sportmotorcycle AG*

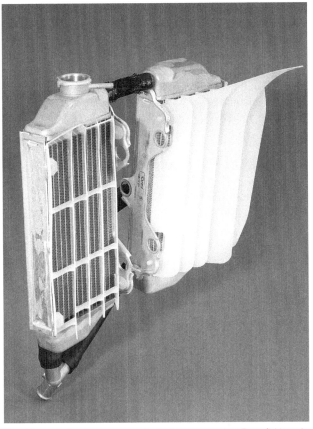

One of the easiest performance upgrades is aftermarket coolant. These fluids work quite well at reducing engine temperature, and are reasonably priced. Moose Juice, Engine Ice, and Spectro coolant all offer similar performance gains.
Yamaha Motor Corporation

in the tiny channels of the radiator and reduce the cooling efficiency.

Enginekool, Moose Juice, Engine Ice, or Spectro coolant products are surfactants that enable better flow through the water jackets of the engine. These products are available from most auto parts stores or your local dirt bike shop.

BASIC CLEANING AND INSPECTION

A dirt bike's cooling system should be flushed and changed once a year. Before you drain the cooling system, add 4 ounces of an aluminum radiator flushing fluid. Several companies make the product, and it is available from any auto parts store. Run the engine for about 10 minutes and then drain the cooling system. Take care when disposing of the old fluid, which is regulated by environmental laws and often poisonous to humans, pets, and wildlife. Call your local auto repair garage and ask if it has a drum for used coolant. Nontoxic, biodegradable coolants are available. They should be disposed of in the same way as any other coolant because they will be contaminated by the same pollutants during use.

Remove the water pump cover and check for corrosion and debris. Check the water pump's bearings by grasping the water impeller with your fingers and trying to move it up and down. If you feel any movement, the water pump bearings and seals need to be replaced. If you see oil leaking into the water pump housing, it is a sign that the seals and bearings are worn too. Sometimes, the bearings will be so worn that they cut a groove in the water pump shaft. In most cases, when the water pump seals and bearings are worn, so is the shaft. It's best to replace the parts as a set because they aren't that expensive. The water pump is gear-driven by the crankshaft. Some bikes use gears made of plastic; other bikes use metal gears. Metal gears are more durable but are very noisy. Plastic gears are vulnerable to melting, especially when the gearbox oil is low and at very high temperatures.

FILLING AND BLEEDING TIPS

Some bikes have bolts on top of the cylinder head or water spigot that are used to bleed trapped air in the cooling system. If the air isn't bled from the system, the air pocket will prevent the coolant from circulating and the temperature will rise until the radiator cap releases. The proper way to bleed the trapped air is to fill the system to the top of the radiator, leave the cap off, and loosen the bolt until coolant streams out. Then tighten the bolt, top off the radiator, install the cap, and run the engine for 10 minutes before checking the coolant level. **CAUTION:** Let the engine cool down before turning the radiator cap to avoid releasing scalding coolant, which will rush out of a hot radiator as soon as you break the seal.

Troubleshooting the Cooling System

Here are a few common cooling-system problems (P), along with the likely cause (C) and and the action (A) for addressing it.

P: Coolant overflows into the hose below the radiator cap.

C1: Radiator cap faulty, thus releasing coolant improperly, or coolant level too high.

C2: Water pump impeller stripped from the shaft.

C3: Head gasket blown, allowing high-pressure combustion gases to enter the water jackets.

A1: Pressure test the cap and, if necessary, lower the coolant level to just above the core.

A2: Check impeller by observing flow just under the radiator cap with the engine idling. The fluid should circulate rapidly with an increase in engine rpm.

A3: Replace the head gasket and lap-flat the sealing surfaces of the head and cylinder to remove warpage.

P: Coolant dribbles out of the bottom of the water pump cover through a tiny hole.

C: The water pump shaft, bearings, and seals are worn out. The tiny hole is located between the two seals to channel the leaking coolant away from the transmission.

A: Replace water pump shaft, bearing, and both seals.

DAMAGE CONTROL

Dirt bike radiators seem to mysteriously attract rocks and branches. Crashing a bike can damage the radiators too. Radiators and exhaust pipes are like bumpers for dirt bikes, so chances are you will have to perform emergency repairs on your bike's cooling system. It may be at a race, on the trail, or in the wilderness several miles from any roads. Every trail rider should carry epoxy in a tool bag.

Any type of quick-setting epoxy works great for radiator repairs. Epoxy isn't an adhesive in that it isn't sticky. Epoxy bonds when it can wrap around the edges of surfaces. It's easy to get epoxy to bond on a radiator because there are so many edges on the cores and the surrounding fins, but the area affected must be cleaned before the epoxy is applied.

Quick-setting epoxies need only about 30 minutes drying time when air temperatures are over 75 degrees Fahrenheit—longer in colder weather.

Epoxy radiator repairs are only temporary fixes. Don't rely on them beyond the time you need to get the damaged cooling system home. Replace the damaged radiator or have it heli-arc welded by one of the many companies that specialize in radiator repair, such as Myler's in Utah or Fontana Radiator Works in California.

PROTECTION FOR RADIATORS

Radiators can be protected on the front and the sides. Aluminum bars protect the sides of the radiator from damage if the bike is dropped on its side. Screens are used in place of

Radiator guards offer some additional gusseting for protection in crashes or even when off-road riders bounce off of trees. If your bike doesn't come from the factory with these, you can find plenty of aftermarket radiator guards. *KTM-Sportmotorcycle AG*

High-performance coolant has been shown to lower engine operating temperature signficantly. *Engine Ice*

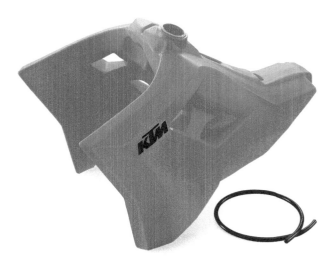

Some fuel tanks use the radiator shroud area to carry gasoline. This adds range to the bike and protects the radiators. *KTM-Sportmotorcycle AG*

This cutaway of a YZ450F shows how the water pump is driven. You can also see the path the coolant takes to the head. *Yamaha Motor Corporation*

the plastic louvers in front to protect the radiator cores from being punctured by tree branches. This protection comes at a cost, however—the cooling system will not work as efficiently when the louvers are removed and replaced with screens. The louvers serve to collect and channel air at high velocity into the cores. DeVol Racing makes radiator guards for many popular bikes.

IMPROVING THE COOLING SYSTEM

There are three things that you can do to improve the efficiency of the cooling system: raise the pressure, improve the flow, and add capacity. Switching to a radiator cap marked 1.6 will raise the pop-off pressure point in the radiator and raise its boiling point. Installing a Boyesen Engineering aluminum impeller and water pump spigot will improve the flow. Most stock impellers are made of plastic and can actually melt. The Boyesen product features vanes with a cup shape to increase coolant flow. The outer spigots are designed with a shape to accommodate the larger, more efficient impellers. Lengthening the hoses or installing a larger afrermarket radiator can increase the capacity of the cooling system.

PROJECT 11
How to Change Engine Coolant

 Time: 30 minutes

 Cost: $

 Tools: Sockets, ratchet, torque wrench (inch-pounds), rags, drain pan, container to transport coolant

 Parts: Engine coolant, new copper drain-plug washer

 Experience: 1

Coolant is vital to the health of your engine. Unfortunately, when many riders think of coolant, they only think of antifreeze. Although protecting your engine from freezing during winter storage is important, coolant performs several other important duties. The aluminum internals to your engine are prone to oxidizing. Coolant forms a protective coating over the bare aluminum, keeping it from eroding at high-heat areas and from corrosion building up on cooler locations, which would reduce the efficiency of the cooling system. Coolant also lubricates the water pump and prevents foaming. Lastly, coolant raises the boiling point above that of straight water—which is a good thing in the high temperature environment of a performance four-stroke dirt bike.

Changing your coolant every two years is the minimum you should consider, since the materials in coolant do break down over time. However, checking the coolant periodically will give you an idea of the condition of your cooling system. If it looks like Mountain Dew, it's probably OK. Other colors, such as rust (red-brown) or oil (black) residue, may signal engine problems. Tools are available for testing your coolant's freeze-prevention qualities. Prestone makes clever throwaway test strips that you dip into the coolant, read the color, and then toss into the trash. You can also use a testing tool that measures the specific gravity of the solution and displays the results with floating balls or a needle. Consider these if your bike winters in an unheated garage.

1 Only change your coolant when the engine is cold. When hot, the system is under pressure, and opening the spout or drain plug will send hot coolant everywhere.

2 Make sure you have a large container to catch the coolant. You'd be surprised at how far it jumps from the bike. Immediately put the used coolant in a sealed container for transportation to your nearest recycling center. Coolant is toxic and, for some strange reason, quite attractive to children and animals. *Evans Brasfield*

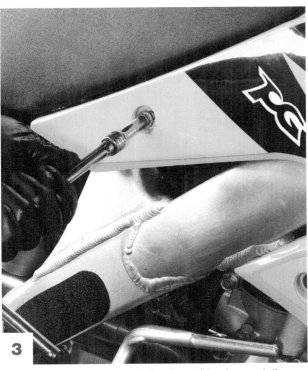

3

Although you can probably bend your bodywork enough to gain access to the radiator fill cap, take the couple of minutes required to remove the plastic. Prior to filling the system, be sure to torque the drain plug to the factory specification. *Evans Brasfield*

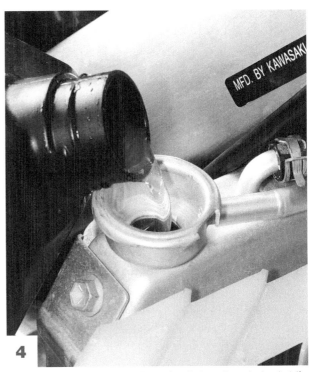

4

When filling the system with coolant, it's much easier to used premixed coolant. If you only have coolant that needs to be diluted to a 50/50 mix, make sure you use distilled water to prevent the addition of minerals to the cooling system. *Evans Brasfield*

5

Don't forget to rock your bike side to side to burp any bubbles from the system. Leave some breathing room in the top of the radiator. As the coolant heats up, it expands. If you fill the system to the brim, you'll just be dumping more coolant out of the overflow and into the environment. *Evans Brasfield*

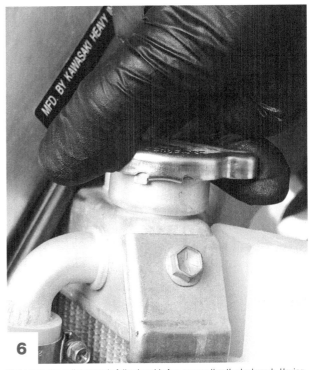

6

Make sure the radiator cap is fully closed before remounting the bodywork. Having the cap fall off when you're miles from the nearest road would be a very bad thing. *Evans Brasfield*

Chapter 11
The Basic Principles of Four-stroke Engines

BY KEVIN CAMERON

Before you can truly understand performance, you need to understand how your engine works. Internal combustion (IC) engines are based on a simple sequence of events:

1. A rising piston compresses a cylinder full of air.
2. That compressed air is heated by burning fuel in it.
3. Heating the air raises its pressure.
4. This pressure drives the piston forcibly back downward.
5. A crank mechanism links this piston motion to a rotating shaft.
6. During all this, the inertia of a flywheel keeps everything turning, even when the piston is not producing power.

All the rest of the IC engine's complexity is just housekeeping, concerned with emptying out the burned gases, refilling the cylinder with fresh air/fuel mixture, and protecting the parts from breaking, seizing, or melting. The basic idea is simple. The housekeeping is complicated.

In the currently dominant four-stroke engine, it takes four end-to-end strokes of a piston to complete the engine cycle (hence the name, four-stroke). We call the maximum-volume piston position bottom dead center (BDC) and the minimum-volume position top dead center (TDC).

INTAKE (1)

The first stroke is intake. Intake valves open as the piston moves from TDC to BDC, drawing in a fresh charge of air and fuel.

COMPRESSION (2)

As the intake valves close, the piston begins the compression stroke, moving from BDC to TDC. This compression raises cylinder pressure from atmospheric (about 15 psi) to something like 175 to 200 psi. Just before

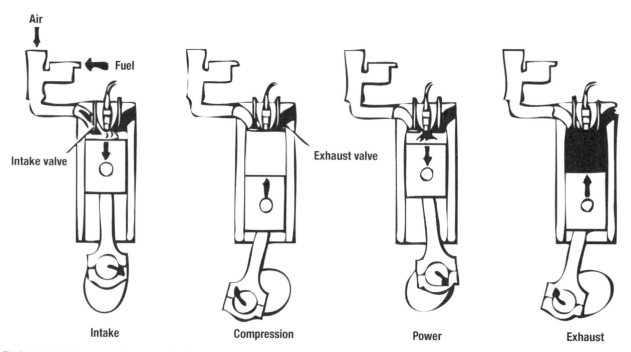

The four basic engine cycles are the fundamental steps that power your motorcycle. *Amsoil*

TDC, the compressed air-fuel charge is ignited and quickly burns in 30 to 70 crank degrees, raising gas temperature thousands of degrees. With this comes a 5:1 or 6:1 rise in cylinder pressure. Peak pressure in a well-designed engine at full throttle is, as a rule of thumb, 100 times the compression ratio and can easily be 1,000 psi or more. It is typically reached at 14 degrees after TDC (ATDC).

POWER (3)

The crank rotates farther and the piston begins the power stroke, going from just after TDC and maybe 1,000 psi, down toward BDC and an end-of-stroke cylinder pressure of 100 psi or less. Near the end of the power stroke, the exhaust valves begin to open, giving the exhaust process a useful head start.

EXHAUST (4)

The crank turns farther (driven by energy stored in its flywheel mass), driving the piston up again from BDC toward TDC on the exhaust stroke and chasing out remaining burned gases. The exhaust valves close as the intakes open again, and the cycle repeats with another intake stroke.

WHY FOUR-STROKE?

The reason the four-stroke system is now dominant is that it gives a good combination of power and economy, and it can be made to meet emissions standards relatively easily. The separation of its strokes is the basis of these qualities. The intake stroke draws in pure fresh charge (good for power), yet there is little chance of any fresh charge going to waste out an open exhaust port (good for emissions and efficiency) because the exhaust port is open only during the exhaust stroke.

EFFICIENCY—WHERE THE ENERGY GOES

A well-designed spark-ignition engine converts 25 percent of its fuel energy into useful work at the crankshaft. The rest is wasted as heat. This is like lighting four stove burners to make tea on just one. The largest part of the waste heat is left in the exhaust gas, whose pressure is too low for the piston to extract any further energy from it. Further energy can, however, be extracted from exhaust gas by fancy devices, such as turbochargers, steam bottoming cycles, etc.

The next big slice of waste heat appears in the coolant—the fluid (water, antifreeze, oil) used to carry away heat from hot parts to prevent lubricant failure, melting, or seizing. This includes waste heat generated as friction. Well-designed engines typically have mechanical efficiencies of about 85 percent. This means that, of the total power delivered by expanding combustion gas against piston domes, only 85 percent makes it to the output shaft as net power.

The rest does the job of overcoming the various sources of friction. Piston and piston-ring friction, together with pumping loss, are the largest losses, followed by crank and rod bearings, valve mechanism, and all the internal thrashing of oil and air by the moving parts. The higher an engine revs,

the greater its internal loads and the greater the friction loss. This is why recent, higher-revving sportbike engines have such light pistons and con rods.

FUEL MIXING

At 10,000 rpm, it takes about a hundredth of a second for the fuel to leave the injector or carburetor, travel down the intake port into the cylinder, and then be compressed. During this time, enough of the fuel must evaporate to form an ignitable mixture. Not all air-gasoline mixtures are spark-ignitable; mixtures richer than about 10:1 (1 part fuel to 10 parts air), or leaner than about 18:1 (1 part fuel to 18 parts air), cannot be ignited by a normal spark. Even with a correct mixture of about 14.8:1, if a significant part of the gasoline supplied fails to vaporize, the resulting droplet/vapor mixture can still be *effectively* too lean to be ignited. A spark can't ignite big, cold fuel droplets.

Rapid evaporation requires a highly volatile fuel—in this case, gasoline. Any serious loss of fuel volatility has prompt effects on engine performance, causing poor throttle response and worse. Engines run poorly when they are cold because the engine's metal parts are too cold to evaporate much of the fuel. The vapor part of the mixture is therefore lean, and the result is nonstarting or the dreaded start-and-stall. To make a cold engine start, therefore, the mixture must be enriched in some way. Recent electronic fuel injection does this automatically, but older engines have chokes for cold starting.

IGNITION

The ignition system quickly builds up a voltage difference across the spark plug electrodes. Any stray electrons in the gap are violently accelerated by this voltage difference, and they slam into atoms in their way, liberating more electrons. This is gap ionization, which provides enough conduction electrons in the gap to make it conductive. Almost instantly, a shower of electrons develops and becomes a considerable electric current across the gap. Bombarded by these conduction electrons, whatever is in the gap is highly heated. This breaks up chemical compounds, allowing atoms from fuel and air to recombine in the energy-releasing process called combustion. The spark is small and doesn't last long, so the sample of air-fuel mixture that it zaps is crucial. If the mixture in the plug gap is correct, ignition will be prompt with a maximum chance that the tiny flame kernel will swell into rapid combustion. If the sample is rich or lean, the flame kernel may take longer to get going, or may fizzle out, causing a misfire.

This model also explains why plug gaps for automobiles have grown so large. Many years ago they were at 0.024 inch, then 0.032, then 0.040, and now they are at 0.060 inch or more. This was done to counteract the misfire-producing effects of leaner mixtures adopted for emissions reasons. The bigger the gap, the bigger the sample of charge through

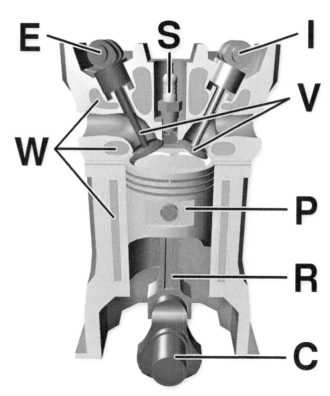

E S I

V

W

P

R

C

This diagram shows how a simple two-valve four-stroke engine flows air-fuel mixture through the combustion chamber.

which the spark jumps, and the greater the chance of hitting some correct mixture instead of a rich or lean zone.

One engineer friend of mine says, "One can tell approximately how much combustion pressure an engine makes by the kind of plug caps the owner has had to put on it." What this means is that the denser the charge, the more powerful the ignition must be to ionize and fire the gap and the more elaborate the insulation has to be as a result. As the ignition system fires, it must build up voltage across the plug gap faster than it can leak away across any accidental high-resistance pathways, such as along carbon on the plug's insulator nose or up a salty fingerprint on the external insulator surface. Such fast rise-time ignitions can create the opposite problem—that of popping right through the plug cap or along the insulator surface beneath its grip. This has been a problem with some racing ignitions, and one fix is to carefully degrease both the plug insulator and the plug cap (checking for a close fit between) during assembly. Even a fingerprint is sometimes a culprit here. Degrease with alcohol, contact cleaner, or lacquer thinner.

COMBUSTION AND TURBULENCE

From the instant of the spark until measurable pressure rise occurs in the cylinder takes 10 or more crank degrees. This is called the ignition delay period, and it exists because the flame kernel, being small, has a small initial growth rate. Fifty or sixty more degrees are required for the flame to burn all of the mixture.

It's important to understand that normal combustion is not in any sense an explosion. In an explosion, combustion spreads at or above the local speed of sound. This would produce a violent rate of pressure rise that would destroy an engine. Even in a gun, propellant combustion is not an explosion for the same reason. Normal flame velocity in piston engines is a few tens of feet per second, giving a survivable rate of pressure rise and is seldom as much as 40 psi per crank degree.

Combustion is largely symmetrical around top dead center. If the best-torque ignition point is, say, 36 degrees before TDC (BTDC), then combustion will end roughly 36 degrees ATDC. Thus, ignition and combustion will take 1/6 to 1/5 of a turn of the crank, or in round numbers, again at our example of 10,000 rpm, a thousandth of a second. This is quick and is only made possible by the nature of turbulent flames. If you mix gasoline and air in chemically correct proportions, let the mix become still, and then ignite it, it burns quite slowly—only a few inches per second. This is too slow to make a high-rpm engine possible. But if you stir up the mixture so it is swirling, tumbling, and eddying, the flame moves much faster. How? A turbulent flame front becomes so wrinkled and shredded that it gains huge surface area. This big area, multiplied times the modest local flame speed, quickly consumes the mixture. How quickly? Measure the distance from spark plug to the farthest part of the chamber; this is the maximum flame travel distance. Divide that distance by the combustion time in our example—a thousandth of a second. For a 70-millimeter-bore engine with a central spark plug, the flame travel distance is 70/2 = 35 millimeters, or 1.38 inches, so flame speed in our example is 1.38/0.001 = 1,380 inches per second, or 1,380/12 = 115 feet per second. That's brisk, yet this speed is completely dependent upon turbulence.

And where does the turbulence come from? Most of it comes from the fast inrush of intake flow into the cylinder. At peak revs, intake velocity may play footsie with the speed of sound; all it takes to reach the speed of sound is a 0.53:1 pressure ratio across the orifice. Some turbulence is also generated by the piston near TDC, as it comes locally close to the cylinder head, squeezing mixture out from between in high-speed jets. Such turbulence-generating areas of close approach are termed squish areas.

THE NEED FOR TURBULENCE

Lack of adequate combustion chamber turbulence is a major reason for soggy midrange in high-rpm engines. In the big ports these engines often have, midrange intake air velocity is low, so the engine lacks the turbulence to burn quickly and efficiently. In engines with very large bores, short strokes, and high compression ratios, the space above the piston near TDC may be too tight for air motion to continue. In such engines, turbulence dies away as the piston nears the head, leading to slow combustion and poor performance. This is a major problem for race engine designers. Some modern four-valve auto engines operate on only one intake valve up to a certain rpm and then switch to both. This generates useful turbulence at lower revs by effectively doubling intake velocity.

This need for turbulence drives the current, progressive trend toward smaller ports for sports and racing engines. Big ports look impressive, but they drop dead in the midrange for the reason given. Better to have smaller, carefully streamlined ports that keep velocity and turbulence up—and still deliver enough air for top-end power. The higher the intake velocity, the greater the in-cylinder turbulence it generates.

TYPES OF CHARGE MOTION

Turbulence is necessary for rapid combustion, but in-cylinder air motion can take different forms. In the 1930s, it was found that *axial swirl* was a good way to store intake motion until the piston neared TDC and the ignition point. Axial swirl is air motion around the cylinder axis and is typically generated by offsetting a single intake port, so its flow enters the cylinder more on a tangent than on a diameter. Near TDC, this systematic swirl motion can break up into the small-scale turbulence that leads to high flame speed. Swirl design can be seen in Kawasaki's venerable two-valve Z1. It can also be generated by oriented squish areas in the cylinder head.

Tumble is air motion in the same sense as crank rotation; air enters the cylinder, flows across the head, down the far cylinder wall, and loops across the piston crown and up again. This type of motion is favored in four-valve engines and was conceived by the late Keith Duckworth. The degree of tumble produced is controlled by the downdraft angle of the intake ports; high ports flow well but produce less tumble, while lower ports sacrifice some flow to boost tumble. Race engines, which run at higher rpm all the time, need less tumble than street engines, which must deliver usable low and midrange power. As with swirl, tumble is just a way to momentarily store the energy of the intake process while the piston rises on compression, to ensure that there will still be vigorous motion during combustion. Near TDC, the tumble motion breaks up into smaller scale motions.

Turbulence is destroyed by two mechanisms. One is the rise in gas viscosity as the cylinder pressure rises during the compression stroke. The other is friction and disturbance caused by features in the combustion chamber valves and their matching piston cutouts, sharp edges, etc. A smooth combustion chamber performs better than one full of machined edges and angles.

FLAME PROPAGATION

As the piston nears TDC, axial swirl or tumble breaks up into smaller turbulence cells, and textbooks picture this process as if these cells were a train of gears. The spark plug lights the charge in one turbulence cell, let's say, and the flame reaches the next cell when the first cell rotates far enough to bring flame to it. Then the second cell must also rotate to bring flame to the third, and so on. From this simple model, it is easy to see why a wide, thin combustion chamber burns more slowly than a more compact, thicker one of equal volume. The thin chamber is filled by a train of many small gears (bigger ones won't fit the space), so many rotations are required to carry the flame to the cylinder wall. The compact chamber can be filled with fewer, bigger gears, so the flame is not delayed by as many rotations having to take place.

The combustion space is not, therefore, of equal thickness over the whole bore area. Instead, it is made into squish—as thin as mechanical considerations allow—everywhere but over the area occupied by the valves. This four-leaf clover area is the real combustion space, and it may be located in the head or, as Kawasaki has done it, in the piston itself. This helps combustion speed too because a chamber smaller than the bore shortens the flame path.

The mixture forced into squish areas probably does not burn very well, so the volume of charge in squish is made as small as possible by making the piston come as close as possible to these areas. How do you know how close to set it? By getting it too close and seeing the bright areas that indicate piston-to-head contact! The great tuners stand head and shoulders above the others because of the size of the piles of broken parts upon which they are standing.

In highly developed racing two-valve engines, the chamber is reduced to a sort of spectacles area that includes the two valves and their reliefs cut into the piston crown and the single or twin spark plug(s). The rest is squish. Regardless of the number of valves, the game is to put as much of the charge as possible, as close as possible, to the ignition source(s).

Recently, motorcycle engine design has been forced to move on from its long hold at a bore/stroke ratio of 1.5. Engines with even higher ratios are becoming dependent upon squish to generate turbulence in their very tight combustion chambers.

PEAK PRESSURE

With the best-power ignition timing, regardless of whether that be early or late, peak combustion pressure is reached at about 14 degrees ATDC. Why this relationship? Put a dial gauge on a piston near TDC, and watch it read off piston travel as you swing the crank past TDC. The piston is pretty much motionless for the 30 degrees centered on TDC, but begins significant downward motion around 14 degrees ATDC. If peak pressure comes earlier, there will be heat losses as the hot combustion gas waits for piston motion. If it comes later, expansion by the piston will dramatically reduce peak pressure. Either way, power will drop.

The piston and con rod have zero leverage on the crankshaft at or near TDC, increasing to maximum at about 78 degrees ATDC (when the con rod and crank arm

This cutaway YZ450F shows off the straightened intake and exhaust ports and the razor thin piston. *Yamaha Motor Corporation*

are at right angles to each other). It would be nice to have peak pressure later in the cycle, when leverage is greater, but combustion pressure falls very fast as piston motion expands the combustion gas. Thus, 80 percent of the recoverable energy in the combustion gas is delivered on the piston in the first half of the expansion stroke. This is fortunate because it allows us to use the last part of the expansion stroke for early opening of the exhaust valves, giving a valuable head start on the exhaust process—without wasting significant power.

EXHAUST

Reading through the four separate strokes, it appears that the piston must push the exhaust out of the cylinder. This is sometimes true, but it is more desirable to let the exhaust's own energy do most of the work, rather than take energy from the crank to *force* it out. For this reason, the exhaust valve(s) begin to open some time before BDC on the power stroke, allowing exhaust expansion to push itself out.

About half the heat rejected to coolant is transferred to the head through the walls of the exhaust ports. This is because velocity and turbulence are highest here. To avoid as much of this heat load as possible, exhaust ports are made as short and straight as practical, with the head pipes often extending deep into the cylinder head. In some cases, cylinder heads have been designed to fit in existing chassis, forcing an ugly exhaust port with a sharp turn in it to be used.

It has been discovered recently that well-designed but smaller-than-stock exhaust ports and valves can flow more exhaust gas than many stock-sized items. In extensive modifications, this can sometimes make room for larger intake valves. Small is beautiful; small valves suffer less heat distress (shortened heat path), and small exhaust ports introduce less heat and distortion into cylinder heads.

COOLING

The compressed charge in the cylinder of an engine on full throttle jumps up more than 4,700 degrees Fahrenheit in temperature during combustion. That's higher than the melting point of any metal in the engine. How do the parts survive? There are three basic answers to this.

Cooling Is Provided (1)

Air traveling between cooling fins, or water/antifreeze circulating through cooling passages cast into the engine, carries away heat from the hot parts fast enough to hold their temperatures at survivable levels.

Combustion Is Intermittent (2)

Combustion takes about 1/6 of a crank revolution and doesn't occur in that cylinder again for another 1 5/6 revolutions. This means the heat is on less than 10 percent of the time, with the other 90-plus percent available for the hottest parts to cool by giving up their heat to cooler parts. Thus, glowing

The Red Bull KTM factory race bikes use this unusual expansion chamber.
KTM-Sportmotorcycle AG

hot exhaust valves transfer heat to their valve seat rings, heat flows from the hot centers of piston crowns and outward toward the cooled cylinder walls, and so on. Heating and cooling are cyclical; combustion blasts temperatures up, but there is time for it to leak away to oil and coolant before the next heat shot.

Natural Insulation (3)

In a storm window, two layers of glass sandwich a layer of stagnant air between. That still air is an excellent insulator because of its low density and its stagnant state. Inside an engine, despite the turbulent entry of intake gas, the mad swirl of combustion, and the scouring exit of exhaust, there is a layer of essentially stagnant gas that clings to all the parts. This so-called boundary layer is stagnant because it is more under the influence of the nearby surface than of the moving gas a few molecules away. A good thing, too! This "natural storm window" does a great job of limiting the amount of heat transferred from hot gas to engine parts. Without it, engines would (and regularly do, when conditions destroy the boundary layer) fail within seconds.

This is not to say that it's been easy. It took decades for adequate valve materials that did not melt, erode, crack, or stretch to be developed. It took a long time to develop the engine designer's body of useful knowledge about how cool is cool enough for each part.

Lubrication

Metal rubbing on metal is bad news because, unless something prevents it, the surfaces will micro-weld at their myriad tiny points of real contact, tear, generate wear particles that make it all worse, heat up, and eventually seize. Lubrication prevents this nastiness and makes machines possible.

Three forms of lubrication exist: hydrodynamic, boundary, and mixed.

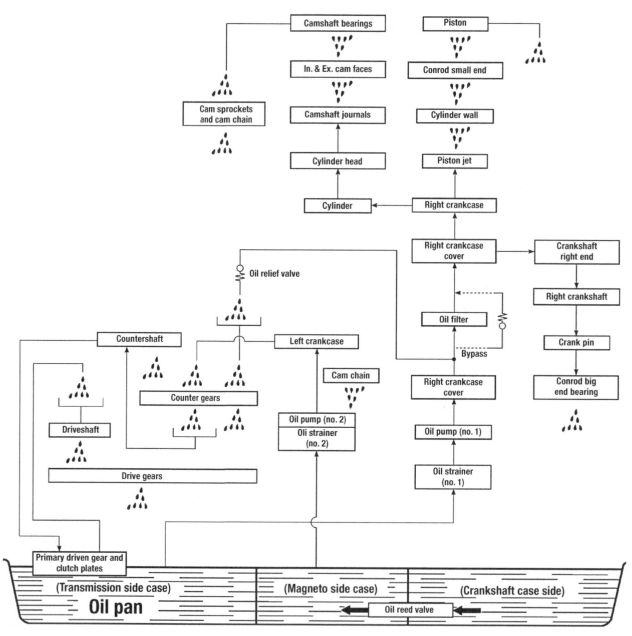

The oil path for the Suzuki RMZ450. Note the twin oil pumps and interesting oil reed valve in the pan. *Suzuki*

Hydrodynamic (1)

This fancy word just means "fluid in action," and it describes the case in which a wedge of fluid—oil in our case—is encouraged to develop between the moving parts. The motion of the parts drags the oil into the wedge, where very high pressures may be generated toward the thin end to separate the parts. Think of it as a kind of mechanical surfing, or as flight in extremely low-altitude ground-effect. Machines lubricated entirely in this mode (thrust bearings of large vertical hydroelectric turbines, for example) have run without shutdown for decades, showing zero wear and original tool marks when finally scrapped. This type of lubrication exists

in running crank bearings and between pistons, rings, and cylinder walls over much of their travel. If we could keep all parts operating in hydrodynamic lube mode, they'd never wear out because they'd never touch each other.

Boundary (2)

This is what happens between cam and tappet as you start your engine. Most of the oil has drained away, so hydrodynamic lubrication can't occur until the oil pump summons the healing fluid from the sump or tank. What is left to carry the load is some combination of *(a)* oil molecules adhering to metal surfaces via short-range forces and *(b)* oil additives that

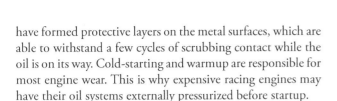

have formed protective layers on the metal surfaces, which are able to withstand a few cycles of scrubbing contact while the oil is on its way. Cold-starting and warmup are responsible for most engine wear. This is why expensive racing engines may have their oil systems externally pressurized before startup.

Mixed (3)

This is a combination of 1) and 2) and occurs wherever sliding speed is low. An example is piston-ring-to-cylinder wall friction near TDC or BDC, where piston velocity is very low, or between cam lobes and tappets at idle speed. In mixed lubrication, the moving part is moving too slowly to fly on a full oil film, carrying the load that it does. Think of it as incipient oil film stall. Some support comes from hydro, some from boundary. This is why additives are important, making false the old-timers' claim that "oil is oil."

Crank and con rods in modern engines run on so-called plain bearings. These are split shells, lined with layers of soft bearing metal that face the rotating journal itself. Various types of bearing materials are made for different duty levels. The housing of each main and rod bearing is itself split, with a cap retained by bolts or studs and nuts. Each pair of bearing shells is slightly too big for its bearing housing. This provides crush, or installation preload, that will hold the bearing in place and prevent its spinning. Each bearing shell has an installation tab or other lineup device to ensure it is installed properly.

The oil pressure that supports the rotating parts results from the viscous sweeping action of the moving surfaces, carrying oil into the loaded zone of the bearing. Pressure here can peak as high as several thousand psi. Naturally, as the bearing rotates, oil is being continually squeezed out at the edges, but more is being swept into the loaded zone to make good this loss and support the load. The oil swept in is provided by the pump continually pushing oil into the bearing's unloaded zone. The high-pressure flow of oil within the loaded zone generates heat that would soon destroy the oil's viscosity and load-carrying ability. This is prevented by flowing excess oil through the bearing simply as coolant.

Oil is picked up from the sump or tank and delivered to a main oil gallery, parallel with the crankshaft. From this gallery, drillings carry oil to the upper (less loaded) shell of each main bearing. The lower main bearing shells are normally ungrooved to maximize their load-carrying ability, but each upper shell has a groove that receives oil from the main gallery. Corresponding with this groove is a hole, or holes, in the crank journal, whose purpose is to collect oil from the groove and carry it to the adjacent con-rod bearing through drillings in the crank itself.

Sometimes this oil-delivery scheme is not enough. Note that oil must follow a tortuous path into the grooved upper main shell, around the groove, into the oil hole(s) in the crank journal, and inward against centrifugal force. Then it flows through the drilled passages to the nearby crankpin and, finally, out through its oil hole into the rod bearing. As the crank is whirling, this oil supply can become intermittent, and the oil delivered to the rod bearings can become marginal. Higher oil pressure sometimes helps, sometimes not. Engine designers sometimes resort to a different scheme—end feed—in which oil is fed into the center of the crank from one or both ends. This way, it no longer has to be pumped inward against centrifugal force, and every crankpin receives oil continuously—not just when a drilled passage happens to line up with a groove in an upper main bearing shell.

Many high-performance four-stroke motorcycles use different oil in the engine and gearbox. This is ideal because gears do best with aggressive, extreme pressure (EP) additives, so gears must be designed a bit oversized to last in non-EP engine oils. In new, shared-oil designs, both shafts are supplied with oil pressure, from which drillings lubricate the free-spinning gears on the shafts. There may also be an overhead oilway, from which downward-directed jets spray onto each of the five or six gear pairs. At high speed, this probably saves a horsepower or two.

Primary gears are the fastest-moving gears in the engine and so have the largest potential for wasting power through excessive oil churning. Oil from the pressurized shaft center emerges into the clutch, from which it is flung to create what is really the best condition for the lubrication of high-speed gears: air-oil mist.

Oil pumps are of two general types. In one, two meshing gears sweep oil around inside a tight-fitting case from intake to delivery. In the other, often called a gerotor pump, there is a gear within a gear, which draws in oil at one point and delivers it at another. There is always a relief valve in any oil system, intended to prevent pump damage when cold startup would otherwise force the pump to do the impossible: pump stiff, cold oil at warmed-up rates of flow. To ensure adequate lubrication at idle and low speed, oil systems may produce excess flow at high speed, which is why some F1 engines now have two-speed oil pumps.

Oil makers like their products to run no hotter than a bulk temperature (meaning the oil temp in the sump or tank) of 180 degrees Fahrenheit. Bulk temps of up to 300 degrees are said to be routine in family cars towing trailers across Kansas in August, but this causes excessive viscosity loss and accelerates deterioration of some additives. Run an oil cooler if you find excessive temperatures. Otherwise, a cooler is just another fashion accessory!

Another source of friction in engines is so-called windage, which I would prefer to call oilage because oil is 600 times denser than air and is the primary source of this kind of loss. As the crank spins, oil is constantly thrown from its main and rod bearings. This constitutes a power loss if the crank is flinging this oil off at high speed. In GP car engines, there are slingers at each main bearing to deflect emerging oil away from the crank, so it can just drop to the sump without being accelerated along a crank cheek, robbing valuable momentum from crank motion.

A worse problem existed in early sportbike engines, whose oil sump levels were not sufficiently far below the bottom of the cranks. During braking or other maneuvering, oil could slosh up to the crank where it could be gathered up in large volume and whirled and flung everywhere, causing a several-horsepower loss and great oil heating. (Think of each horsepower as 746 watts, which is about what a red-hot toaster draws. Therefore, a 5-horsepower oil-churning loss can be thought of as five toasters heating your oil.) Crank windage trays, and oil deflectors and scrapers, were conceived to prevent this loss.

Carburetion

Previously, I mentioned that gasoline vapor and air can be spark-ignited only within a certain range of mixture strength. Even within that range, the energy released varies with mixture strength. This is why engine tuners put so much effort into getting carburetion right; the right mixture gives maximum power, all others give less. You'll occasionally hear people reason as follows: "Fuel is power, so the more fuel I can make my engine burn, the more power it'll make." This sounds good, but it ignores the real nature of burning.

Air is roughly 80 percent inert nitrogen, 20 percent oxygen. To convert the chemical energy of fuel into heat, we have to rearrange which molecules are attached to which partners. To begin, we have to take apart the fuel and oxygen molecules. Gasoline is called a hydrocarbon because it is made up of chains or rings of carbon atoms, each one joined to one or more hydrogen atoms. Oxygen in the air is in the form of two-atom molecules. It takes some energy to knock all these structures apart so they can go back together in new arrangements that release heat in the process. This is why we have to add heat (a match, a spark) to start a fire. But when two molecules of hydrogen and a single molecule of oxygen rush violently together to form a water molecule, a definite, known amount of energy is released. If there is no oxygen, there is no energy release. When two molecules of oxygen rush to bond with a single molecule of carbon to form carbon dioxide, another definite quantity of energy is released. The reason air-fuel mixture is important is that maximum heat release occurs when the proportions cause every hydrogen, carbon, and oxygen atom in the original mixture to find a reaction partner and release energy. All this violent rushing together sets the collection of molecules into vigorous motion—and the average intensity of this motion is defined as temperature.

If there is too much fuel (rich condition), some carbon and hydrogen molecules will not find oxygen molecules and so will not react to release heat. The extra, unburned fuel cools combustion like throwing cold stones into a campfire—it absorbs heat from combustion and contributes nothing. If there is too little fuel (lean condition), there is oxygen left

Straightening the intake path is a quest of most major manufacturers. Honda accomplished this nicely on the CRF250F. *American Honda*

over after combustion that could have generated more energy if there had been enough fuel to combine with it.

In the latest emissions-controlled motorcycle engines, electronic fuel injection operates with an exhaust oxygen sensor (or lambda probe), enabling a correct mixture to be delivered at all times. This is **closed-loop** operation. Somewhat less sophisticated and effective is the earlier **open-loop** system, which uses data from atmospheric temperature and pressure sensors to enable the electronic control unit (ECU) to deliver an estimated correct mixture.

Because fuel evaporation and mixing are never perfect, because combustion near the cool chamber walls is partly quenched, and because some late combustion is terminated while incomplete by piston expansion, combustion is never quite perfect. Even at best maximum-power mixture, exhaust gas contains about 4 percent carbon *mono*xide and the telltale stink of other products of partial combustion—aldehydes and ketones. Engines making peak power also generate sharp-smelling peroxides. This complex exhaust smell is what Soichiro Honda found so exotic about the first automobile he ever saw, causing him to run after it, filled with dreams of a new world.

The ideal is an engine whose combustion is fast enough that all of it can be completed with the piston very close to the cylinder head, at or near maximum compression. This gives the highest possible peak pressure. The slower combustion is, the earlier you have to light the flame, and the longer it burns after TDC. Both of these processes are wasteful: The first because it is negative work, the second because late burn occurs at a lower effective compression ratio, making a reduced contribution to peak pressure.

ENGINE MIXTURE REQUIREMENTS

The ideal mixture that allows every fuel molecule to be completely burned—all hydrogen and carbon atoms finding just enough oxygen for complete combustion—is called a *chemically correct mixture*. You may also see this referred to as a *stoichiometric mixture*.

It would be dandy if all we had to do was give an engine this mixture all the time to get perfect performance. But problems with fuel evaporation change things in particular conditions. Gasoline is not a pure substance but a mixture of a hundred or so different varieties of hydrocarbon, some heavier, some lighter, each with its own volatility. At low temperature, only the most volatile hydrocarbons can form a vapor, while the rest remain liquid. Benzene, an excellent though carcinogenic fuel, actually freezes into a solid in cold winter temperatures.

To cold-start, engines require an extremely rich mixture of 4:1 or so. In a cold engine, only the most volatile parts of the fuel will form vapor, and to make this vapor rich enough to ignite, huge amounts of fuel must be dumped in. The large part of the fuel that doesn't vaporize just dribbles through the cold engine, unburned or partially burned (stinky black smoke). A choke or other enrichment system supplies this special rich mixture. As the engine warms up, its rising temperature begins to evaporate more of the fuel supplied, making the vapor a fraction richer. Therefore, the rider of a carbureted machine gradually leans the mixture as the engine warms by moving the choke lever toward "off."

Husaberg took a more radical approach to straightening exhaust and intake paths. *KTM-Sportmotorcycle AG*

The latest electronic fuel injection systems perform this function automatically.

Engines idle on a very rich mixture of about 10 to 11:1. This is necessary because vaporization conditions are poor at idle, when intake air velocity is low and mixing is poor. Consequently, low-volatility parts of the fuel remain liquid, creeping along the intake pipe walls, and do not burn. More fuel must be added to deliver a combustible vapor fraction.

Engines cruise on a chemically correct mixture (14.8:1) or even a bit leaner. This produces maximum economy and minimum emissions (with plenty of oxygen available, unburned hydrocarbons are minimized—every dancer has a partner).

Maximum power is achieved with a somewhat richer-than-correct mixture in the 12 to 13:1 range. The extra fuel gives the combustion gas a slightly larger specific volume, based upon a larger number of reaction product molecules. Adding more fuel than this reduces power.

The carburetors or fuel injection system must accurately deliver the right mixture for conditions. Maladjusted carburetors or injectors cause power loss, poor throttle response, stumbling, and so on. Mixture control—carburetion or the mapping of fuel injection—is therefore an art worth learning.

A current promising development is four-stroke gasoline direct injection (GDI). It uses fine-particle-size injectors originally developed for direct-injection two-strokes. When fuel particle size is 10 microns or less (0.0004 inch), the resulting mist burns just as it would with full evaporation. Also called dry injection, GDI needs less enrichment during cold starting, acceleration, and so on. This is good for both emissions and performance. Fuel particle size for conventional wet fuel injection is somewhat larger than for carburetors, being in the 50 to 150 micron range. As of April 2008, GDI had not yet arrived in motorcycle engines.

FLAME SPEED AND TURBULENCE

For best torque, any engine must burn to peak pressure at about 14 degrees ATDC. There is some combustion after this, but peak pressure at this position gives maximum torque. This is because the piston is essentially stopped for 11 to 15 degrees after TDC, but after that, it accelerates downward rapidly. This puts peak pressure just at the beginning of significant downward movement.

Flame speed varies with conditions: The denser and more turbulent the mixture, the higher the flame speed. As the mixture becomes either rich or lean, combustion slows. Thus on full throttle, flame speed is brisk, but slows as the throttle is closed. Where the exhaust pipe is helping the engine, the charge is denser so less advance is needed. Where the pipe produces a flat spot, cylinder filling sags and so does flame speed, thus requiring more advance. In effect, the ignition advance curve is the inverse of the torque curve. Research done by Honda in the early 1960s shows that in-cylinder

turbulence and flame speed grow pretty much in step with rpm—even out to 27,000 rpm. This is why an engine does not require more and more ignition advance as it revs up.

A prime misconception is that more advance is better. Even the words we use conspire to make us feel this way. Would you rather be thought of as, *advanced* or *retarded*? The truth here is otherwise. The most highly developed engines require the least timing because their combustion has been worked over to make it fast and efficient. Engineers refer to the optimum ignition setting as Minimum for Best Torque (MBT). If your modified engine makes best power with *less* timing than stock, you should be happy because this shows that you have achieved faster combustion. Slow combustion requires you to light the fire long before TDC (a disgraceful 45 degrees in the case of the old Yamaha FZ750), so that the piston must compress burning gases that have already generated some pressure. This is *negative work* that cuts your output. The longer combustion takes, the more time there is for heat loss. And not least, the longer combustion takes, the more likely detonation becomes. Therefore, designers and tuners try to speed combustion in any way they can by doing the following:

1. raising intake velocity to create turbulence;
2. providing tight squish areas between piston and cylinder head;
3. shaping the piston crown to push every possible bit of charge in close to the spark plug, to occupy a combustion chamber that is vertically roomy enough to allow turbulence to continue even when the piston nears TDC on compression. For equal volume, a hockey puck is a better combustion chamber shape than is a pancake or a CD.

Cosworth, builders of Formula One car racing engines, was able to get best power from its 85.7-millimeter-bore double four-valve (DFV) engine with ignition at only 27 degrees BTDC. This was achieved by narrowing the valve angle to create a more compact combustion chamber and filling it with tumble charge motion. The builders of National Association for Stock Car Racing (NASCAR) stock car engines regularly get their 100-millimeter-bore V-8s down to less than 30 degrees BTDC ignition timing. These chambers are also small, filled with vigorous charge motion. These concepts remain the basis of efficient combustion—a compact chamber that does not suppress charge motion near TDC.

The reverse side of this coin is exemplified by the terrible combustion chambers of the classic air-cooled racers of the 1960s, such as the Honda fours and sixes, and the Benelli fours, which need 55 or more degrees of ignition lead for peak power. Why such slow combustion? The traditional excuse is their high rpm (17,000 for Honda's 250 six), but current 600 sportbike engines rev nearly as high, yet make their power with much less ignition lead. The classic

The KTM450SXF uses a 2429-gram Elko piston. These ultra-light, ultra-thin pistons were pioneered on Formula 1 racing engines. The KTM units are expensive and extremely durable. *KTM-Sportmotorcycle AG*

machines of the 1960s had large valve-included angles and tall piston domes, so their combustion spaces resembled the peel of half an orange—thin and very spread out. Being so thin yet of large area, they had no room for flame-speeding turbulence to persist near TDC.

A useful concept is *combustion efficiency*, which is the ratio of the heat value of the fuel supplied, divided into the actual heat generated. As you'd expect, it's easier to think about this than to measure it, but here's where the losses occur. Some of the mixture is quenched—extinguished—by being too close to cooler metal surfaces. There is a layer of incomplete combustion next to the metal walls of the combustion chamber, and there is some volume of gas trapped in squish zones and in piston-ring crevice spaces that doesn't burn at all, or burns so late in the cycle that it doesn't contribute to peak pressure. Then, too, the mixture is never perfectly accurate or completely evaporated or mixed. This means that part of the fuel doesn't burn even if it isn't quenched—it's like the eligible bachelor who somehow never finds his mate.

Evidence of incomplete combustion is the strong smell of exhaust, containing sharp aldehydes and ketones, which are products of incomplete oxidation. Modern tuners may use an onboard exhaust gas analyzer.

SEALING

A major element in a successful engine is sealing. You can flow lots of air, compress the daylights out of it, and burn it in a chamber, but it's all for nothing if you have leaking valves or piston rings. They make performance soggy. Good builders keep track of the condition of their engines with a leak-down tester. With it, you pressurize a cylinder to a given air pressure with its piston held at TDC and then measure the percentage

Pre-1998 four-stroke off-road motorcycle engines were simply too large and heavy to provide competitive performance. The modern versions are extremely compact. This comparison of 2009 and 2005 Honda CRF450R heads shows how much things have progressed even in the past few years. *American Honda*

of loss in a given time period. When the leak-down percentage exceeds some amount (20 percent is a number you'll often hear in this connection), the engine needs to be freshened up. This means giving it a valve job and new piston rings, with honing of the cylinders to give a fresh surface for break-in. Drag racers cudgel their brains to push their new-engine leak-downs to tiny figures like 2 to 3 percent, but such numbers are irrelevant for engines that go for miles and miles.

A leak-down tester is not trivially cheap, but its results are interesting. If the state of your engine's sealing is very important to you, this is the way to know.

For any engine, there is a characteristic curve of power versus hours of operation. When a fresh engine is started, its power is somewhat low at first because break-in has not yet taken place. Sealing is imperfect and there is extra friction. Power rises through break-in, reaches a peak that may last a while, and then begins to drop as the valves accumulate underhead deposits, warp, and begin to leak, piston rings become soggy, and bores wear. In production racing classes, the winning teams are often those which keep their engines up nearest this peak through constant maintenance. Much of the work involved in racing is dirty dishes labor of this kind—just keeping things in their best possible condition.

Now consider how piston rings work. Their springiness pushes them out against the cylinder wall, but the real sealing force is compression or combustion pressure. It enters the space above and behind the piston ring in its groove, pushing the ring outward to seal against the cylinder wall and downward to seal against the bottom of the groove (you can always tell which face of a used ring goes downward because it is the shiny one). But as the piston rises on its compression stroke, two forces are acting on the ring. Compression and then combustion pressure is pushing it down, but as the piston decelerates sharply near TDC, the ring's inertia is tending to lift it off the bottom of the groove. If it does lift off, the gas pressure behind it vents below the ring, and without pressure behind it, the ring stops sealing.

Well, you may reasonably propose, why not just make the groove tighter? A tight groove prevents gas pressure from getting behind the ring, leading to nonsealing at speed. A typical up-and-down clearance for piston rings is over 0.001 inch. Therefore, rings in high-speed engines have been made thinner and thinner over time to reduce the near-TDC inertia force tending to jerk them upward, off the bottoms of their grooves. In some types of drag racing, rings are run in tight grooves to prevent their being broken by ultra-high accelerations, as engines run to very high revs. These rings are inflated by combustion pressure fed behind them through small holes, drilled down from the piston dome. This is not a universal remedy, as it is also possible to have **too much** gas pressure behind the rings—enough to cause extra friction and premature wear in the near-TDC region.

Another interesting piston ring technique used in racing is crankcase evacuation. Racers have found that if crankcase pressure is kept negative by various means, lighter-pressure oil rings can be used. Their lower friction sets free useful power. Case evacuation is handled by some combination of intake vacuum, vacuum piped from the header-pipe junction, timed breathers, or, in the case of F1 engines, actual pumps.

COMPRESSION RATIO

IC engines work by allowing hot, high-pressure gas to expand against a piston. Igniting a mixture at atmospheric pressure generates a moderate pressure rise of maybe 7 atmospheres (7 x 15 psi = 95 psi), but compressing the mixture first increases the pressure rise a lot (peak pressure in a nonsupercharged race engine can be 1,000 to 1,200 psi). This is why the mixture is compressed before it is ignited. The ratio of the volume above the piston at BDC (full expansion) to the volume above the piston at TDC (full compression) is arbitrarily called the compression ratio, but we could just as accurately call it the expansion ratio. It is both.

MAKING THINGS HARD TO UNDERSTAND— THERMODYNAMICS

In heat engines, efficiency is governed by the difference between the maximum and minimum cycle temperatures: The bigger the difference, the higher the efficiency. This means that the higher the compression ratio (CR), the higher the efficiency and the more the air/fuel charge is heated by compression, and to this temperature is added the more than 4,700 degrees Fahrenheit that comes from combustion of a healthy charge. This is the maximum cycle temperature, and raising the CR does, indeed, raise it. The minimum cycle temperature is that of the exhaust gas when the exhaust valve opens. Viewed from the power stroke, the higher the CR, the more the gas will be expanded, and the cooler it will be at the moment of exhaust. Thus, again, a higher CR also lowers the minimum cycle temperature. (One non-intuitive result of this is: The higher the CR, the cooler the exhaust valves run.)

A major reason diesel engines deliver higher efficiency than do spark-ignition engines is their higher CRs of between 17 and 23:1. If you run an engine on an instrumented dyno, you will see the effects of changing to a higher compression ratio. Brake-specific fuel consumption will fall as the CR is pushed higher.

BRAKE MEAN EFFECTIVE PRESSURE (BMEP)

BMEP is that constant net pressure that, if it acted on the piston throughout the power stroke, would produce the same power as the actual, varying pressure during combustion and expansion. BMEP is the *effect* of many things acting together: cylinder filling, combustion efficiency, heat loss, friction, and compression ratio. BMEP is the profit left after all the engine's internal bills have been paid. To raise BMEP, go after those losses in detail.

A higher compression ratio, better cylinder filling, lower heat loss or friction, or higher combustion efficiency tend to raise BMEP. Unsupercharged engines with exceptional breathing and combustion may reach a BMEP of 230 psi at peak torque. Well-developed sportbike engines are currently around the 190 psi mark.

DETONATION SETS THE LIMIT OF POWER

When higher CRs were tried in the early years, the result was delightful: more power *and* greater economy. But theory often collides with practice. When engine CRs were raised sufficiently, strange knocking noises were heard as engines overheated and parts broke. This was the phenomenon of *engine knock* or *detonation*. High-speed photographs, made through transparent cylinder heads, showed what was happening. The spark ignited the mixture and the flame front expanded, compressing and heating the unburned charge ahead of the flame. When the flame nearly reached the farthest bits of unburned mixture out near the cylinder wall, bright flashes appeared in that unburned mixture. This was auto-ignition of the so-called end-gas, or last charge to burn, and it truly exploded, burning at sonic speed. The resulting shockwave caused the knocking sound and the destructive effects.

This process—detonation—is caused by heat acting on the unburned charge. Heat effects begin during compression and speed up greatly once the charge is ignited. The expanding ball of burned gas compresses and heats the remaining unburned charge ahead of it. Heat breaks down some of the fuel molecules into active fragments that are really an explosive, and if this process goes far enough, this chemically changed charge goes off by itself. To avoid this, early engines had to run inefficient low CRs, like the *3:1* of the Model T Ford. The discovery of the effective anti-detonant tetraethyl lead in 1923 allowed CR to rise to 5:1 or 6:1.

Intensive development of fuels for supercharged aircraft engines during World War II pushed fuel octane number up over 100, allowing a sharp rise in postwar automotive CRs.

SENSE AND NONSENSE ABOUT COMPRESSION

Raising the CR increases the compression heating of the charge and thereby raises peak flame temperature. This dumps more heat into your engine's cooling system. You can tolerate a lot of compression for a short time without knock, but as the parts heat up, the hot engine begins to knock and soon destroys itself. This is how drag racers can get away with 16:1 compression ratios. This extra compression gives extra torque to get those big slicks turning in the crucial first 50 feet, but the engine is run as cold as possible, which is what lets it survive. A World Superbike road race engine may have 13 to 14:1 compression, but you'll notice the huge radiators they carry to deal with all the heat this compression pushes into their coolant. When the goal is all-out power, builders get the best fuel they can find and push compression up until

Water cooling provides consistent engine operating temperatures, which allow the ultra-tight tolerances present in modern four-stroke engines. *Beta*

they find the edge of detonation—and they operate there, barely on the safe side. A street-ridden engine needs more margin of safety than this; pump fuel quality varies and lower-rpm operation allows more time for detonation to develop, so lower compression ratios are safer. Honda engineers have a term they use for this margin of safety that separates normal operation from detonation: They call it "combustion toughness." Others call it simply "detonation margin."

The bigger the cylinder, the less compression-tolerant an engine is. This is partly because the bigger chamber takes longer to burn and partly because heat must flow farther from the hot centers of the pistons, outward to the cooled cylinder walls. Higher piston temperature pushes the end-gas closer to detonation. Where a small-bore (70-millimeter) street sports engine may have a 13:1 compression ratio, it's normal for a big-bore engine (90 to 100 millimeters) to be between 12:1 and 10:1.

ADVANTAGES OF WATER COOLING

Water-cooled engines have heat toughness in the form of three strong defenses:

1. If the engine generates more heat, the thermostat opens a bit more, sending more of the coolant stream through the radiator and less directly back into the engine
2. Even after the thermostat is fully open, water has a very high specific heat (it takes a lot of heat energy to raise its temperature—1 calorie per gram, per degree Centigrade, which is 3 times higher than that of aluminum, and 9 to 10 times that of steel). This puts the brakes on further temperature rise.

3. If *that* fails, there is the fact that it takes a *fortune* in energy to actually *boil* water—a whopping 540 calories per gram to convert water at 100 degrees Centigrade, into steam at the same temperature. This protects the engine from local hot spotting, for example near hot valve seats.

By contrast, an air-cooled engine has no such reserves—the only way it can dissipate more heat is to get hotter. Because of this, air-coolers must be run a bit on the conservative side in the compression department. Many, many races have been won by air-cooled engines with no more than 10.5:1 compression.

The limit on compression is indicated in either of two ways:

1. The engine begins to detonate; or
2. The power gained from more compression can't keep up with the extra heat lost into the cooling system. More compression, even with a non-detonating fuel, is then pointless. The curve of *theoretical* benefit from increased compression ratio goes up steeply at first—that's why Model T Ford–based racers got such a boost from going to 5:1 from the stock 3:1. Then the curve gets pretty flat after 12:1.

Always remember that the higher the compression, the smaller and tighter the combustion chamber becomes. To retain mixture turbulence all the way to TDC, the chamber must contain some fairly open volume in which the charge can move. Otherwise, combustion speed is reduced. Because of this, the best compression ratio is often determined by the needs of combustion (lower CR gives more room for turbulence) rather than pure thermodynamics (higher CR is better). Lots of builders go nuts on compression because it has done wonders for their drag engines. Then they wonder why it won't do the same for their road-race or street engines. Fact is, very high compression works off the line when the engine is revving lower, maybe even below its torque peak, but such an engine is too tight in the combustion chamber to burn fast enough to top-end well. In drag racing, winning in the first 50 feet is super important. Speed out in the lights is secondary. For a sports/road-race engine, the compromise has to be different because there is no first 50 feet.

AIRFLOW IN AND OUT

Airflow in engines is not as simple as it seems. In a simple view, the intake valve would open at TDC and the piston would draw in a cylinder full of mixture as it moves to BDC. Then the intake valve would close so compression could begin. But in real life, no valve can open or close instantly. That would require infinite acceleration/deceleration forces, which would destroy the valve and its mechanism (as well as being impossible anyway). Therefore, real valves take

significant time to open and close. That being so, and since we need to have the valve substantially open when the piston is moving fastest near 78 degrees ATDC (this is where con rod and crank arm are at right angles to each other), we have to start the intake valve opening process early—*before* TDC.

Even though we give intake this early start, at higher rpm the cylinder-filling process is not complete by the time the piston reaches BDC. This is because air has inertia, and when the intake begins opening and the piston pulls down on its intake stroke, it takes some time for the air to accelerate and follow the moving piston. The higher the engine revs, the more the intake process lags behind piston motion.

When we look at a graph of cylinder pressure versus piston position taken from an engine running at high revs, we first see a steep pressure drop as the piston pulls a vacuum in the cylinder. Then we see the pressure rise smoothly back up as the mixture in the intake port accelerates toward the cylinder and begins delivering high-speed airflow. If we closed the intake valve at BDC, we would be wasting the ability of this high speed flow to keep charging into the cylinder—*even after the piston has started back on its compression upstroke.* It is to take advantage of this inrush of air that we leave the intake valve open *after* BDC. In a racy two-valve engine, intake closing might be as much as 80 degrees ABDC. Four-valve engines don't need as much timing because they have more flow area, but they may close their intakes 50 to 60 degrees ABDC.

This is a stinky compromise because by leaving the intake open past BDC to improve cylinder filling at high rpm, we are *degrading* cylinder filling at lower revs. This is because at lower revs, intake velocity is too low to continue its inrush after BDC. When the piston starts back up on compression, it will stop this slower moving intake flow, then reverse it, pumping charge *back out of the cylinder.* The result will be less charge trapped in the cylinder, so less torque will be produced. Such backflow may also blow fuel mixture back into the airbox, where it then makes the next cylinder's intake stroke too rich.

In other words, cam timing that works best at peak revs and works poorly at lower revs. As a result, cam timing is *always* a compromise: not enough timing for best power on top, but too much timing for good power off the bottom.

EXHAUST

Now consider the exhaust. It takes power to push exhaust out of the engine, but we have other uses for that power (fun! total victory!). Therefore, instead of opening the exhaust valve close to BDC, we open it early, allowing exhaust pressure to begin the work of emptying the cylinder. At first this seems wrong because early exhaust valve opening appears to shorten the power stroke. But as noted before, 80 percent of the available energy in the combustion gas has done its work in the first half of the power stroke. This is because combustion pressure peaks at about 14 degrees ATDC and falls quickly as the piston moves away from TDC on its power stroke.

Therefore, early exhaust opening is wasting very little *useful* power stroke. As the exhaust valve begins to open 50 to 70 degrees BBDC, hot gas rushes out from its own pressure at or above the speed of sound. If this process is right, very little exhaust will then have to be *forced* out of the cylinder by the piston, during the formal exhaust upstroke. And that means little power will be wasted.

OVERLAP AND EXHAUST PIPE ACTION

Now we come to the period called *overlap*, which is the time around TDC at the end of the exhaust stroke when the intake valve is beginning to open, yet the exhaust valve has not yet completely closed. This is a crucial period in the valve cycle because it can potentially allow direct energy exchange between the pressure waves in the exhaust pipe and the intake process that is about to begin.

As the exhaust valve opens, a positive pressure pulse is discharged into the exhaust pipe. It travels to the end of the pipe (or its junction with a collector, megaphone, etc.) and expands there, reflecting back toward the engine with its sign reversed; that is, the positive wave has now become a negative one, or a suction pulse. If the pipe length and engine rpm are about right, this suction pulse will reach the engine during overlap, and it will travel into the cylinder through the still-open exhausts to help pump out the exhaust residuals still present in the combustion space. Because the intake valve is just beginning to open, this suction wave also travels out to the intake system, causing flow toward the cylinder to begin. These two actions—extra cylinder scavenging and giving an early start to the intake process—result in *improved* cylinder filling and increased torque.

Now as you can see, if we increase the overlap period, we create a wider window through which exhaust pipe action can assist cylinder filling, and torque at this speed range increases. That's the good news.

But at some lower engine rpm, the negative exhaust pipe wave reaches the cylinder too soon, and it is the next wave

Honda's Unicam design uses a single overhead cam, which is lighter and more compact than double-overhead cam setups. *American Honda*

in the pipe—a positive one (they alternate, positive-negative-positive, and so on, indefinitely)—that hits during overlap. The positive wave stuffs exhaust gas from the pipe back into the cylinder and may even blow some back through the intake valve and port. By contaminating the cylinder with extra exhaust and delaying the intake stroke, this positive wave *reduces* torque. And—you guessed it—when we widen the overlap period to get more torque up at design rpm, we also get less torque at lower rpm. It's as though the act of pulling the torque curve *up* at higher revs simultaneously pulls it *down* into a big hole at lower revs. Compromise.

COMPROMISE BREAKING

The four-valve engine breaks out of this by providing what the engine needs (prompt airflow) without imposing its own needs on the process (the two-valve engine's need for longer timings in which to complete the valve cycle).

The squared-cubed law says that as parts are made smaller, they lose weight faster than they lose area. Thus, two smaller intake valves can be made lighter in relation to their flow area than can a single larger valve. With less valve mass in relation to stem cross-section, they can be accelerated harder. This is the mechanical basis for the switch to four valves per cylinder.

ABOUT FIVE VALVES

When Yamaha introduced its Genesis engine family in 1985, there was much interest in the possible advantages of five, six, or even seven valves per cylinder. The low-lift flow advantage of a four-valve is present in even greater degree in engines with five or more valves, and this should make them able to run even shorter cam timing and deliver even wider powerbands.

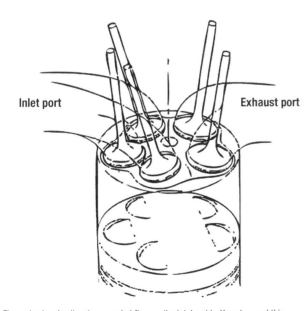

Inlet port   Exhaust port

Five-valve heads allow increased airflow on the intake side. Yamaha used this technology in the mid-1980s on street bikes, and brought it to their off-road lined nearly three decades later. *WFO Graphic Design*

But the road to success proved rocky. The resulting combustion chamber was tight and compromised. If you wanted acceleration, you had to do without top-end because the high compression chamber was too tight to burn quickly at higher revs (it had too little headroom for turbulent charge motion). The early Genesis engines ran as much as 45 degrees of spark lead—a clear indication of combustion problems. To run on top, compression had to be dropped, resulting in soggier acceleration. The later engines were improved by Jim Leonard and others and have won their share of Daytona 200s. In MotoGP, Yamaha switched from five valves to four just before the 2004 season.

Ferrari's experience with five valves ran straight into the classic problem of valve seat distortion. As early as World War I, engineers understood that the more holes you put into the head, the more it tends to distort from heat (especially if the engine is air cooled), leading to valve leakage. Ferrari's five-valve endurance-racing engines were sometimes unable to restart after pit stops. The advantages that beckon so invitingly from a sheet of calculations cannot always be realized.

LOSING OUR MINDS—AIRFLOW

Besides the dyno, the most frequently used tool of the engine developer is the flow bench. This is a glorified vacuum cleaner/blower to push or pull air through the port under study, equipped with some type of orifice meter for measuring airflow. It costs a moderate $1,500 to $2,000 to get into this game and begin testing at a pressure of 10 to 15 inches of water. An inch of water is the pressure it takes to lift a column of water 1 inch. Atmospheric pressure is about 32 *feet* of water, so 1 inch is $1/(32 \times 12) = 0.002604$ atmosphere, or 0.0383 psi.

If you listen, you will hear rumors that NASCAR teams are testing flow at much higher pressures and may foster the belief that since this must be better, testing at lower pressures must be useless. Not true at all! Lots of good work goes on at 10 to 15 inches—work that produces solid power gains. The reason for testing at higher pressures, I believe, is that big engines with small valves and ports reach intake velocities near the speed of sound. This can produce local shocks and other effects that would be invisible in low-pressure flow testing.

In flow testing, your cylinder head is attached to a dummy cylinder of the same bore as your engine. This is done to accurately model any valve masking or other effects caused by the presence of the cylinder wall. This dummy cylinder is then attached to the flow bench. A device is used to hold open the valve(s) of the port under test by any desired amount. It's usual to test at 0.050 inch, 0.100 inch, 0.150 inch, and so on to the maximum lift of the cam to be used. Then a curve is drawn, connecting the test points to produce a graph of flow versus lift.

Airflow changes with temperature, and on the popular Superflow flow benches, the blower motor is cooled by the

Yamaha pioneered the use of five-valve heads with their FZ750 in the mid-1980s. They also used the design in their off-road motorcycle engines, but have recently phased that out in favor of four-valve heads. *Yamaha Motor Corporation*

airflow, which therefore heats up as the bench runs. This must be compensated for with arithmetic, as must the changes in barometric pressure. It is all very tedious to end up with apples to compare with apples to be sure you really know what you are doing. Naturally, there are computer programs to make this easier. No end of procedural errors is possible in flow testing. Many are the red faces that have been caused by air leaks between parts or by the simple error of leaving out the spark plug from the cylinder head under test. Wow! That last tweak really did the job! Oops, guess I'd better redo that run.

Hearing protectors will keep you in a better mood as the hours of testing flow by. The flow bench is a serious research tool, and research rewards only the careful and methodical. The airflow researcher who gets the decimals right and tests without prejudice is the one who smokes 'em.

The trend in port development is to get more air through stock-sized (or even smaller) ports and valves. The advantage is that as intake velocity rises, there is more and more energy in the inflowing stream of charge at BDC. This energy is (as old Newton taught us) velocity squared, times the mass of what is in motion. Ports are designed to have only part of the intake charge at really high velocity, to avoid unnecessary flow losses. Typically, a part of the port just behind the valve, equal to 20 to 25 percent of the cylinder volume, is made small to generate this velocity. As the piston sits still at BDC, this intake energy spends itself in supercharging the cylinder, continuing to rush in until it is used up in compressing the

charge in the cylinder. Then, ideally, the intake valve is just closing, trapping this extra pressure.

Thinking from this model: it's easy to see why we should push intake velocity higher with smaller ports, not lower it by hogging out the ports. Velocity squared is a powerful relationship. If we raise intake velocity by 10 percent, we are raising the BDC intake energy by 1.1 x 1.1=1.21, or 21 percent. But if we *drop* intake velocity by that same 10 percent, we have 0.9 x 0.9 = 0.81, or a 19 percent *loss* in BDC intake energy.

Getting power out of higher BDC intake energy is not always as simple as just making everything smaller (in some cases it's just that simple) because at a sufficiently high velocity, flow friction eats up the gains. Always remember that above an orifice pressure ratio of about 0.53, a shock will form somewhere in the duct. After that, the piston can suck as hard as it likes, but there will be no further increase in flow because no pressure signal can flow upstream through a shock. This is sonic choking. The velocity game is to raise velocity and airflow at the same time, and that calls for subtle streamlining. Some distinctly non-intuitive things are learned along the way.

Be prepared, if you venture into airflow work or begin a collaboration with an airflow specialist, to see some ugly ports that flow massive air and some beautiful-looking ports that mysteriously act like they're full of rocks.

A great deal of the magic in porting occurs at or very near the choke point, which is the valve seat. Its shape and

dimensions are, therefore, crucial. This is why a five-angle or blend valve job is basic to Supersport-level performance.

Intake testing should be performed either with the engine's complete intake tract in place (rubber manifold, carb, and bell mouth, if any) or with some standard, smooth bell mouth attached to the head. Otherwise, the air will not enter the port in a realistic way.

Likewise, blowing air out through an exhaust port will produce wacky results unless you use either the engine's proper exhaust system or a piece of pipe or a cone that is the same in all tests. This is because there is a large expansion loss as the air exits the head into the atmosphere. Just holding a crude paper cone up to the port can magically increase flow by an apparent 30 percent.

A DANGEROUS AIRFLOW MYTH TO AVOID

The concept of energy exchange is basic to all flow work. The piston drops on the intake stroke, pulling a sudden vacuum in the cylinder. This vacuum creates a pressure difference across the intake duct, accelerating the air in it and converting that pressure difference into the rising kinetic energy of motion in the accelerating intake gas. After BDC, that kinetic energy is transformed back into pressure, supercharging the cylinder to some degree. Each time an energy exchange like this is performed, there is some loss involved because no process is 100 percent efficient.

The process of converting velocity into pressure is called diffusion, and the device that does the job is called a diffuser. A diffuser is a duct that *expands* along the flow direction. Most people believe that if they place a funnel facing large-end first in an airflow, the pressure will increase as the air crams down into the smaller end of the funnel. *This is not true!* To make efficient conversion of velocity into pressure, the airflow must be slowed down gradually. To do this, we must turn the funnel around the other way. Air at high velocity enters the *small end* of the funnel and decelerates gradually as the funnel enlarges. This process is most efficient if the included angle of the funnel is small—10 degrees or less. At larger diffuser angles, the flow tends to separate from the diffuser walls, wasting energy in the creation of eddies.

As an example, before he got his factory ride, Tom Kipp Jr. and his father did a lot of private, small-scale research. One of their projects was to create a ram airbox for their 750 five-valve Yam, with a forward-facing intake and diffuser. If the intake diffuser and box had worked at 100 percent efficiency at 160 miles per hour, the box pressure would have been about 12 inches of water, but for various reasons, only about 8 inches were obtained. This is an efficiency of 8/12, equal to 0.67 or 67 percent.

The classic airflow energy converter is the venturi—a duct that first decreases in diameter, then increases again. It is sometimes called a convergent-divergent nozzle. As air enters the duct, it must accelerate as the duct tapers down. In doing so, it *loses pressure* as Bernoulli noted so many years ago. The accelerating air is gaining velocity energy as it loses pressure energy. At the throat of the venturi (the minimum cross-section), the velocity is maximum and the pressure is minimum. As the flow expands from there, velocity smoothly decreases while pressure increases. There is practically no end-to-end pressure loss through a well-designed venturi, operating at a considerably subsonic throat velocity.

A carburetor is a venturi, and so is the intake port. In the carb, a venturi is used to create a pressure difference signal that will flow fuel. In the intake port, the airflow must accelerate to pass through the restriction between valve and seat, which is why seat and valve shapes are so important. As airflow exits from beneath the seat, there are ways to make the inside surface of the cylinder head act at least somewhat like a diffuser, reducing the sharp expansion losses that otherwise occur.

When a diffuser works well, it can be really dramatic. Back in 1978, the American Motorcycle Association (AMA) decided that the two-stroke TZ750 racers had to be slowed down, and it imposed its infamous orifice rule, Tech Bulletin 78-1, requiring all airflow to each cylinder to pass through a 23-millimeter round hole. The early attempts to make power with this little hole failed because they used a diffuser angle too steep to recover pressure efficiently after the orifice. Yamaha engineers knew their business, however, and provided a gentle 10-degree diffuser of maximum length on the engine side of the orifice, with only a short, rounded entry upstream. This recovered pressure from the high throat velocity so effectively that factory rider Kenny Roberts not only won the Daytona 200, but also set a new record in doing so. This was despite having the engine's intake area cut in half by the orifice rule.

In a sense, the rider's back and the sides of the machine are diffusers turned inside-out. Their job is to keep airflow attached, slowing it down from its maximum speed as it flows around the machine's thickest part. You can clearly see diffuser stall, or flow separation, on a tucked-in rider's back as fluttering of his jacket. If you go to the races, you'll sometimes see riders raise their butts on long, fast straightaways, making the diffuser angle of their backs less steep to prevent flow separation. Riders report they can gain 150 to 200 revs in top gear by doing this. Why do they go faster? The airflow, instead of separating into turbulent eddies, remains attached to the rider's back, its smooth pressure exerting a slight but measurable forward shove on this sloping human diffuser.

And on and on. Engines are full of simple physical phenomena, exploited in clever, often less than obvious ways. The people who make progress in these areas are of two basic kinds: energetic triers who test everything and thinkers who employ physical intuition. Experience makes everything better, because it gives you a feel for what you are working with. Engineering knowledge is useful, but it can be misused to build a box you can't get out of, so you end up not testing things you mistakenly know can't work. Keep an open mind.

Chapter 12
The Four-stroke Engine

Four-stroke engines are very reliable, but when they finally break down, there are so many engine components that problems can be hard to diagnose. A four-stroke engine has more moving parts than a two-stroke engine, especially in the top end of the engine. Components such as the valves, guides, piston, and rings wear at different rates based on service intervals and riding use. For example, if you run the engine with a dirty air filter, the piston and rings will wear faster than the valves. Conversely, if the valve-to-tappet clearance is too tight and the valves hang slightly open from the valve seats, the valves are subject to overheating from the high combustion temperature and pressure. So how are you supposed to diagnose top-end engine components without totally disassembling the engine?

The starting point is to do a leak-down test. This diagnostic test enables you to determine the condition of your top-end components.

LEAK-DOWN TESTING

A leak-down tester provides regulated, pressurized air to the cylinder through a hose threaded into the spark plug hole. A leak-down tester has two pressure gauges, one to control the test pressure and one to monitor the percent of airflow that leaks past the worn engine components. These types of testers are available from Snap-on tool dealers or auto parts stores. You will also need an air tank with 100 psi or an air compressor. Leak-down testers come with a variety of adapters that thread into any size of spark plug hole. Leak-down testers sell for $50 to $150.

If you don't have the knowledge or the specialized tools to perform a leak-down test on your bike, bring it to a motorcycle shop. A leak-down test takes about an hour and shops charge between $30 and $60 for one. A leak-down test is much less expensive to do during a tune-up because the technician will already have the valve cover removed to set

A leak-down test is the most essential way to determine your engine's health. *Evans Brasfield*

the tappet clearance. Perform a leak-down test once a year to stay informed on the condition of your bike's engine.

TYPICAL PROBLEMS OF FOUR-STROKE ENGINES

Once you have a leak-down test performed, if the results show more than a ten percent loss of pressure, you have an issue to fix. Somewhere, pressure is escaping past the components, causing a horsepower and efficiency loss. The following are some tips for diagnosing and fixing leaks for the top-end engine components.

Piston-to-Cylinder Interface

The interface between the piston and cylinder bore is critical to an engine's performance and longevity. An engine with a worn-out piston and rings will allow pressure to transfer to the crankcase, that's commonly known as blow-by. Ideally you want the pressure on top of the piston where it can generate power rather than below the piston where it generates resistance. Piston and ring life varies widely based on design and use. A KTM 640 Adventure is designed to last for 10,000 miles of desert racing whereas an average 250F runs for 10 hours of motocross racing before replacement becomes critical.

There are two types of cylinders, iron-lined and nickel-composite plated. Iron-lined refers to a thick cylinder sleeve that is thermally fitted inside an aluminum block. Nickel-composite is a thin electrolytic coating applied directly to the aluminum block. Iron-lined cylinders are heavy but durable in that they can be bored and honed in increments of .010in/.25mm Nickel-composite plated cylinders are used on racing engines because they are lightweight, provide better heat transfer to the water-jackets or cooling fins, and the plating is very hard for wear resistance. Iron-lined cylinders are inexpensive to repair at an average of $50 to bore and hone a cylinder. Nickel-composite plated cylinders are expensive to repair at an average of $250 for re-plating and honing. The only method to determine if the piston assembly and cylinder are worn is to measure the piston diameter with a micrometer and the cylinder bore with a dial-bore-gauge.

Valve-to-Valve Seat Interface

The valve-to-valve seat interface is critical to combustion chamber pressure sealing and port flow. The most common sealing problem is the accumulation of deposits on the valve and valve seat due to combustion or acid erosion from fuel additives like ethanol. There are two common types of valve and valve seat materials used on modern dirt bikes. For the valves the materials include stainless steel and titanium. For the valve seats the materials include cast

Four-stroke engines last when well-maintained. When they do finally wear out, kits like this one solve problems in expensive fashion. *KTM-Sportmotorcycle AG*

iron and nickel-bronze. Engines designed for longevity have stainless steel valves with cast iron valve seats for corrosion resistance whereas performance engines use titanium valves for lightweight with nickel-bronze valve seats for heat transfer. All valves have coatings to improve longevity. Stainless steel valves are treated with Stelite and titanium valves are plated with hard-chrome or oxides finish.

The typical wear pattern of the valve-to-valve seat is a cupped shape on the valve's sealing surface. The most common reason for wear is the lack of adjustment maintenance between the valve tappet and the camshaft. As the valve and valve seat wear, the clearance between the valve tappet and the camshaft is reduced. Eventually the camshaft prevents the valve from sealing against the valve seat and pressure losses occur with combustion deposits forming on the seat.

Repairing this type of malady isn't as simple as just re-facing the valve; in fact modern coated valves can't be re-faced because they have a wear resistant coating. Replacing the valves rarely works because the valve seat has a wear pattern. The best method for repairing a worn-out cylinder head is to replace the valves, sometimes the valve guides, and re-machine the valve seat.

CYLINDER HONING

If the cylinder bore isn't worn to the point of requiring boring and honing for iron-lined cylinders or re-plating for nickel-composite cylinders, a flex-hone can be used to de-glaze and clean the crosshatch pattern of the cylinder wall. This will help new piston rings seal. There are two types of flex hones; ball and brush. Ball hones are made of aluminum oxide and used for iron-lined cylinders. Brush hones are made of silicon carbide and used for nickel-composite cylinders. Ball hones can damage a plated cylinder and brush hones are ineffective on iron-lined cylinders. Both types of hones are available from Brush Research and distributed through companies like Wiseco and industrial supply stores.

Flex hones can be mounted in a hand-drill and lubricated with oil. Honing a cylinder involves stroking the hone up and down through the cylinder bore in an effort to produce a 45-degree crosshatch pattern. The crosshatch pattern enables the cylinder wall to retain oil to lubricate the piston.

There is another alternative method and that involves the use of rigid mandrels and diamond tooling, but the equipment is expensive and requires extensive technical training. Diamond honing services are available from performance engine builders.

Other Problems

Four-stroke engines are particularly sensitive to poor maintenance practices. Here are a number of common problems encountered with four-stroke engines as they wear. If you maintain the bike correctly, you can keep these issues at bay. If you don't, these issues will transform into catastrophic—and expensive—engine failure.

Tight Valves

If the tappet clearance is inadequate, the valves may hang open when the engine is running at peak temperatures. The exhaust valves may get so hot that they break apart, causing catastrophic engine damage. Leaky intake valves may cause a backfire that ignites unburned gas mixtures in the air boot and air box, thereby starting a fire.

Worn Spark Plug

Over time, the spark plug gap will increase due to erosion of the electrode and ground arm. The greater the spark plug gap, the greater the voltage required to arc across the gap. This raises the temperature of the electrode and ground arm, eventually causing the metal to fracture. If the spark plug's tiny ground arm breaks off, it could wedge itself between the valve and valve seat, causing the valve to break apart. Spark plugs last as long as 60,000 miles on some automobiles but only a fraction of that time in a motorcycle. Modern motorcycle engines have high-compression, high-turbulence combustion chambers that produce spark plug temperatures between 1,800 and 2,300 degrees Fahrenheit. Most manufacturers recommend changing the plugs every 1,000 miles.

Worn Piston

A worn piston has excessive clearance to the cylinder wall, which causes an increase in crankcase pressure, in turn forcing some oil out the breather vent. When too much oil is lost, the remaining oil's temperature rises, causing a breakdown in lubrication. Eventually, the piston will shatter from the vibration. The shattered fragments of the piston fall into the crankcase and can damage the crankshaft and gearbox.

Four-stroke Top-end Rebuilding

A four-stroke engine is more difficult to rebuild than a two-stroke engine because there are more moving parts in the engine's top end. Here is a guide to rebuilding the top ends of single-cylinder four-stroke engines.

Timing sprockets eventually wear out. Replacement kits are available.
KTM-Sportmotorcycle AG

Before you attempt to disassemble the engine, you need to do a pressure leak-down on the engine. This will help you determine which parts are worn. Also, you should remove the fuel tank and pressure-wash the engine. This will help prevent dirt from falling into the disassembled engine. The following section details the procedure for rebuilding the top end of a single-cylinder four-stroke engine.

TOOLS AND MATERIALS

You should have the following tools and materials before you begin: new top-end gasket kit, service manual, torque wrench, oil drain pan, spray penetrating oil, spray cleaner, plastic mallet, assorted wrenches and sockets, parts bins, clean towels, measuring caliper, Flex-Hone, and drill.

TEAR DOWN

Start the engine disassembly by removing the inspection caps from the left side. KTM engines have a manual cam chain adjuster, so the chain links must be removed and refitted whenever the cylinder head is removed. KTM makes a special tool to press a new master link on to the cam chain. The old link cannot be reused. This procedure is performed at TDC; it's easy to hold the KTM crank because there is a special bolt on the front of the engine cover. One is located in the middle of the cover to allow access to the crankshaft bolt. This bolt retains the flywheel and will be used to rotate the crankshaft to get the piston in the proper positions while rebuilding the top end and timing the camshaft. The crankshaft should only be turned in the normal direction of rotation; otherwise, the cam chain tensioner could be damaged. The other inspection cap is mounted in the front of the engine cover, and it allows you to see the TDC stamping mark on the side of the flywheel. This is an important reference mark when timing the camshaft during top-end assembly. Remove the spark plug, exhaust pipe, carburetor, cam cover, and oil lines.

CAMSHAFT REMOVAL AND REFERENCE MARKS

After removing the cam cover, rotate the crankshaft so the TDC mark on the flywheel aligns in the center of the inspection window. The camshaft should not depress the valves; if it does, rotate the crankshaft another revolution and the piston will be at TDC on the compression stroke. All Japanese single-cylinder four-stroke engines are designed for camshaft installation at this crankshaft position. Look at the reference marks on the right side of the camshaft drive sprocket. Compare the marks with the ones in the service manual or make a drawing for your own reference. Normally, there is a straight line on the sprocket that aligns with the gasket surface of the cam cover. Pay close attention to these marks—you will have to align the camshaft upon assembly and synchronize the crankshaft to the camshaft. Failure to do this properly will cause engine damage. To remove the camshaft, you may have to remove the sprocket from the camshaft, depending on your model engine. If you do remove

the sprocket, take care not to drop the sprocket alignment pin into the crankcases.

HEAD REMOVAL

Now, you can remove the cam-chain tensioner, head, and cylinder. The head and cylinder are fitted with alignment pins, so it may be difficult to remove these parts. Never use a screwdriver or chisel to split the head and cylinder apart because that will damage the gasket surfaces. Instead, use a dead-shot plastic mallet to split the engine components apart. The cam-chain guides are plastic bars that either fasten or are wedged into place. Tie a piece of wire around the cam chain to prevent it from falling into the crankcases.

Always stuff clean rags in the crankcases when attempting to remove or install circlips. If anything falls into the open crankcase, you may need to disassemble the engine unless you get lucky fishing it out with a telescopic magnet.

On all four-stroke dirt bikes, you need a special tool to remove the valve springs. Automotive tools are too big and won't fit. Kiowa makes kits with a G-clamp and several sizes of tips to fit the wide range of dirt bikes. They can be easily mounted in a bench vise to give you more control when trying to compress the spring and remove the keepers.

CLEANING AND INSPECTION

Clean the engine parts in mineral spirits solvent to remove the oil. Carbon buildup can be removed with spray oven cleaner. After cleaning, rinse the parts with detergent and water. If you don't have the proper tool to compress the valve springs, bring the head to a franchised dealer and pay them to remove the valve springs. **Warning:** Automotive valve spring compressors may not fit the tiny valve retainers of motorcycle engines and may damage the cylinder head. Take care to keep the sets of valve springs and retainers together, matched to the sides they were removed from. To check the valve-to-guide

Cylinder head removal is more complex on four-stroke engines than it is on two-strokes. Consult your factory shop manual for step-by-step instructions. *KTM-Sportmotorcycle AG*

clearance, extend the valve from the seat 10 millimeters, grasp the valve head, and try to move it side to side. If you feel excessive movement and the back side of the valve is covered with carbon deposits, the valve guide and seal are worn and must be replaced.

Next, clean the valve with a wire brush and check the valve seat for pitting, cupping, or a sharp edge. The pitting indicates that the hard coating on the valve is destroyed, and a sharp edge indicates that the engine was over-revved and the valve springs floated, causing the valve to hammer up against the seat. Valves cannot be repaired because of the hard coating. The only option is to replace the valve. Kibblewhite stainless-steel valves are the most reliable aftermarket valves. Kibblewhite also sells high-performance spring kits that prevent valve floating at high rpm.

MEASURING THE PISTON AND CYLINDER

An easy way to measure the piston and bore diameters is with a digital caliper. Calipers cost about $125 and are very accurate. Measure the piston at its widest point, near the bottom of the skirt, and compare the measurement to the minimum diameter spec listed in the service manual. Measure the bore at the bottom of the cylinder because bores tend to wear fastest at that point. Some mechanics prefer to measure the cylinder bore with a dial-bore gauge, a precision measurement device that enables you to check the out-of-round and taper of the cylinder. Most motorcycle machine shops will do this service for free in an effort to get your business for overboring. If you have the tool, it only takes 10 seconds to check the size. Measure the piston rings by inserting them into the cylinder bore evenly, then measuring the end gap with a feeler gauge. If you go to the trouble to disassemble your engine, you may as well replace the rings.

Check the piston pin and small end of the connecting rod for scouring. Four-stroke engines do not use needle bearings like two-stroke engines. The pins ride on the polished steel surface of the rod or on a bronze bushing pressed in the rod. You can see tiny bits of bronze seized to the pin between the scour marks.

If you don't have a ring compressor, you can use this simple method. Turn the cylinder upside down. Use your thumbs to squeeze the rings into the grooves and into the bore. For the older YZF and KTM cylinders that do not have skirt cutaways, grind and polish two small U shapes in the bottom of the skirt in line with the piston pin. This will make it easier to install the rings and allow room for the piston pin to protrude for easy installation.

Single-overhead-cam engines, such as the CRF and KTM, are easy to align. Make sure you apply a locking agent like Loctite Red on the threads of the two retaining bolts.

There are two ways to install the piston assembly in the cylinder. The first is to pin the piston to the rod and lower the cylinder onto the rod. You'll need a good ring compressor for the KTM and Yamaha YZF engines. However, with the

Honda CRF you can squeeze the rings like a two-stroke and slide the cylinder down on the piston. Make sure none of the piston ring gaps overlap. Position them 90 to 120 degrees apart. All markings on the compression rings should face up.

CYLINDER HONING

If the cylinder does not require boring, you should hone it before reassembling the engine. The best tool for deglazing a cylinder bore is a ball hone. The flexible aluminum-oxide balls remove burnt oil and refinish the crosshatch marks that are so important for proper ring sealing. Ball hones are available from Brush Research Company under the product name Flex-Hone. The hones work great for both two- and four-stroke engines. Cylinder honing is performed by chucking the hone in a drill, coating the cylinder with oil, and spinning the hone in the cylinder while rapidly moving it up and down in the cylinder for 30 seconds. Clean the cylinder in detergent and water, dry it, and spray it with penetrating oil.

READY FOR ASSEMBLY

There are several methods for installing the piston and rings in the cylinder. The Japanese motorcycle manufacturers make a special tool for squeezing the rings, but it is expensive and cumbersome. My method is as follows: Install the piston on the connecting rod and lock in the circlips. Align the end gaps of the rings so they don't overlap each other and cause a loss of compression or oil. Buy a hose clamp that is slightly larger than the piston diameter from an auto parts store. Clamp it snugly around the piston rings. Make sure that some part of the piston is exposed above the hose clamp. This will act as

Electric starters have added complexity—not to mention convenience—to four-stroke engines for motocross-oriented race bikes. *KTM-Sportmotorcycle AG*

a pilot to guide the piston into the bottom of the cylinder evenly so the rings don't break upon installation. Grasp the cylinder with one hand and center it above the piston. Use your other hand to support the underside of the piston. Push the cylinder down onto the piston until the hose clamp slides down past the rings. Now, remove the hose clamp. Bolt down the cylinder head and install the cam-chain guides.

TIMING THE CAMSHAFT AND CRANKSHAFT

The cam chain may have some slacking links below the sprocket on the crankshaft, so grasp the chain and pull it taut while turning the crankshaft until the TDC mark on the flywheel is centered in the inspection window of the left-side engine cover. Install the cam, paying attention to the alignment marks. The cam shouldn't depress the valves. Install the sprocket, but don't lock the tabs on the bolts yet. Install the cam-chain tensioner and release it so it tensions the chain. Now, rotate the crankshaft two revolutions and check the alignment marks. You may find that the marks are slightly off, indicating that the cam sprocket must be moved one tooth on the cam chain. The cam chain tension was likely loose when the cam sprocket was installed because the tensioner wasn't installed yet (it is impossible to get the cam sprocket onto the cam with the tensioner installed). To realign the cam chain to the sprocket in the proper position, you must remove the cam-chain tensioner and repeat the process. After the camshaft and crankshaft are aligned properly, apply a locking agent to the threads of the bolts that fasten the sprocket to the camshaft and then lock the tabs over the bolts.

CHECKING THE VALVE CLEARANCE

There are two types of valvetrains on modern four-stroke dirt bikes. The most basic is a rocker arm with a threaded adjuster bolt and nut; the more advanced high-performance system uses a shim cup arrangement. A small steel shim with a precise thickness is positioned between the valve and the cup. The cup rides against the cam.

Measure the valve clearance when the engine is cold and the cam lobe is facing away from the actuator (rocker arm or shim cup). The exhaust valves require more clearance to compensate for heat expansion since they run at a higher operating temperature than the intake valves. To measure the valve clearance, rotate the crankshaft to the TDC position on the compression stroke so both valves are closed and then measure the clearance with a feeler gauge. Modern 250cc and 400cc to 450cc engines that use shim cups require a special narrow feeler gauge set to fit in the space between cam lobes. Generally speaking, you can expect the rocker arm valvetrains to increase in valve clearance over time and the shim cup valvetrains to decrease valve clearance over time. The reason for this is simple: The rocker arm systems wear and the shim cup systems stay constant in dimension. The valve slowly wears and moves deeper into its seat, which causes the valve clearance to decrease. When an engine is

Counter-balancers keep engines running more smoothly, which extends engine life. *KTM-Sportmotorcycle AG*

constantly over-revved, the valve bounces off the seat and clearance decreases quickly. Engines with worn valve seats tend to pop on idle because gases escape past the valve seat.

Adjusting the rocker arm systems is easily accomplished using a feeler gauge and a set of wrenches. Adjusting the shim cup systems is much more difficult and requires removal of the camshaft to gain access to the shim, which is placed under the cup. Manufacturers offer a narrow range of shims of varying thickness. The original shims are on the thick side of the range to allow adjustment. When the clearance requires extremely thin shims, it is an indication that the valve is worn from bouncing. In that case, the valve will need to be replaced and the seat refinished. One caution when attempting to adjust the valve clearance of the shim cup style systems: Your local dealer probably won't have the shims in stock and will need to special order the parts. I suggest that you first measure the clearance and then remove the cams to access the shims. The shims are marked with a size number; write down the number corresponding to the valve for future reference. That way, when you periodically check the clearance, if it's tight or loose, you'll have an indication of what shim to order in advance.

BREAK-IN PROCEDURE

If you ball-honed the cylinder, no special ring break-in procedure is necessary. Just go easy on the throttle for the first ride. If the cylinder was over-bored, you will need to apply a high-detergent, straight-weight, nonsynthetic, break-in oil. Break in the engine in three separate sessions of 20 minutes each, with a 20-minute rest period between each session. In the first session, never exceed half throttle and third gear. In the second and third sessions, never exceed three-fourths throttle and fourth gear. Rev the engine up and down while shifting gears. Ride the bike on flat, hard ground (mud and sand exert too much of a load on the engine and can make it overheat easily). After an hour of running, change the crankcase oil.

PROJECT 12
How to Test Cylinder Compression and Leak-down

Time: 2 hours

Tools: Sockets, spark plug socket, ratchet, breaker bar, torque wrench (foot pounds and inch pounds), wrenches, Phillips screwdrivers, contact cleaner, rags, air compressor, compression tester, leak-down tester, work stand

Experience: 2

Cost: $$

Since we can't fit inside of an engine's cylinder to check out what kind of condition it is in, we have to find a way to deduce the status of something we can't see. Compression and leak-down testing are the tools that allow us to do this. A compression test simply measures how much a piston compresses the gases in the cylinder. All you do is attach a pressure gauge to the cylinder. What a compression test tells you—once you compare your results to your bike's factory specifications—is how tightly the piston rings and valves are sealing. High readings can give you clues as to whether you have carbon buildup. A low reading can tell you if your engine is in need of some TLC. Performing a leak-down test will tell you where the cylinder is losing pressure. All you do is fill the cylinders with pressurized air and listen for the leak.

You'll find two schools of thought about compression tests. One says that you should test the engine when it is at operating temperature. (Your factory service manual probably says this.) You'll get the maximum reading with a hot engine. All the parts are expanded, and the cylinder walls are lubricated. The second school of thought says check compression when the engine is cold so that you see the true state of the engine—particularly if it has become hard to start when cold. You decide what you think is best.

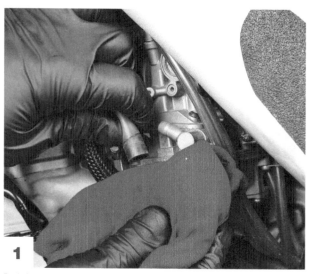

1 Begin by closing the petcock and removing the fuel line from the carburetor/throttle body. Use a rag to catch the gas that remains in the line. *Evans Brasfield*

2 Remove the sideplate bolt. *Evans Brasfield*

3 Remove the front tank mount bolts. *Evans Brasfield*

4 Remove the gas tank and set it aside. *Evans Brasfield*

5 Remove the coil (or spark plug wire) to gain access to the spark plug. *Evans Brasfield*

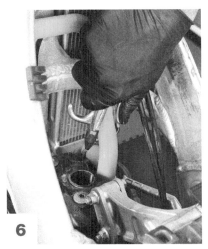

6 Use compressed air to blow any dirt and grit out of the spark plug well. If you don't, it could fall into the cylinder when you remove the spark plug. *Evans Brasfield*

7 Remove the spark plug. *Evans Brasfield*

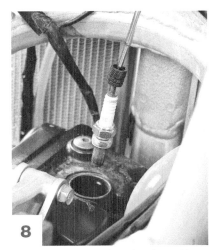

8 A magnetic tool can make it much easier to retrieve the plug from the depths of the well. *Evans Brasfield*

9 Some compression testers share a hose with the leak-down tester. Make sure that the valve is in place for the compression test and removed for the leak-down test. *Evans Brasfield*

10 Screw the hose into place, making sure it forms a tight seal. You don't want leaks giving you a false reading. *Evans Brasfield*

11 Attach the gauge and kick the starter until the needle goes no higher. Write down the reading, bleed off the pressure, and repeat a few times. Once you're confident in the accuracy, compare the number to your bike's specifications. The bike used in these photos is quite sick. *Evans Brasfield*

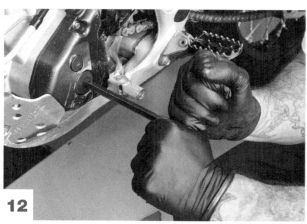

12 You'll need to perform a leak-down test on a cold engine. Remove the access plugs so that you can rotate the crank to place the piston at top dead center (TDC). *Evans Brasfield*

13 The larger hole gives you access to the crankshaft. Rotate the engine counterclockwise until you see the mark on the rotor line up with the mark on the case. *Evans Brasfield*

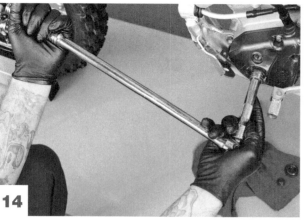

14 Have an assistant hold the crank in position while you apply the air pressure to the cylinder. It will try to turn! Follow your leak-down tester's instructions for the proper pressure. *Evans Brasfield*

15 The leak-down tester will tell you how much of the air pressure is leaking away. This engine is losing almost 70 percent of its pressure. Now, listen for the leak in the intake and exhaust ports. If you hear the hiss in them, a valve job is probably in your future (if your valve clearances are adjusted properly). Air escaping the crankcase breather means have air leaking past your piston rings, and you need to freshen your cylinder. *Evans Brasfield*

TEN TIPS TO MAKE YOUR FOUR-STROKE ENGINE LAST

Four-stroke power is addictive. Gobs of torque, a broad power curve, and terrific sounds in a lightweight package create machines that are fun and easy to ride.

These machines are incredible. The torque curves are fat down low, so you can turn on the throttle early in the turn. When the engine revs, the midrange and top-end performance of high-performance four-strokes is unparalleled.

The best off-road engines you can buy today are four-strokes. The reason for this? Technology. Modern four-stroke off-road engines are not the garden tractor engines used on the old Hondas and Yamahas. Those bikes were stone-axe reliable. And, well, slow.

Current four-strokes use high-tech tricks once reserved for Grand Prix racers. This means great things when you are on the track. The piper is paid at rebuild time. You will pay $2,000 and up for an engine rebuild, and motors can hand grenade in hours if you don't care properly for your high-technology roost-ripping masterpiece.

These engines can be reliable and long-lasting. But you have to take care of them in order to see those results! Here are a few tips to keep your motor happy, healthy, and ripping.

1. Check the oil every time you ride the bike. High-performance four-strokes use small sumps and tight tolerances. Fresh oil, and enough of it, is crucial to long life for these high-tech marvels. "About ninety percent of the failures we have seen on four-stoke motors in the last couple of years here at FMF are directly due to oil (or the lack of it)," Tom Wallace of FMF Racing said. "Every time you gas up, check the oil." Also, read your manual's section describing the proper technique for checking the oil. Most high-performance four-strokes require some running time to pump oil up into the frame before you check the level.

2. Change the crankcase oil every two to three hours you ride. The tight tolerances of four-strokes quickly take the life out of oil. Keep fresh oil in the crankcase, and change it at least as often as the manufacturer recommends. Note that this is particularly crucial with the bikes that use one sump, as the clutch and transmission debris is particularly harmful to the top end. "Oil is your best friend, but if you don't treat it right, it will become your biggest enemy," Doug Dubach of Dubach Racing said.

3. Use the right kind of oil. Pay heed to the recommendations of your manufacturer. Bikes like the Honda CRF use different kinds of oil for the crankcase and the transmission, and using the correct grade and type is crucial to engine life. As far whether to use synthetic/semisynthetic or nonsynthetic oils, that depends on your maintenance regimen. Synthetics last longer than nonsynthetic oils, but are more expensive. If you change the oil every ride, use the cheaper products. If you tend to be a bit more lax about oil changes, the extra money on the synthetics or semisynthetics may be well worth it.

4. Use an hourmeter. This is the only way to know for sure how much time is on the bike. This plays out with every type of maintenance you perform. If you know the hours on the motor, you know when to perform tasks. This really should be number one!

5. Check the valve clearances. The most common error here is checking the clearances initially at the recommended intervals, finding little change, and giving it up. Check clearances every 15 hours or so.

6. Make sure your bike is properly jetted. If the bike is running rich or lean, the tight tolerances in that high-zoot four-stroke dream ride are going to get hammered.

7. Change the oil filter regularly. Start with the suggested maintenance in your owner's manual. Don't go more than 15 hours without changing the filter. And more often will never hurt the bike.

Use the correct type of oil. Honda's CRF450 uses two separate sumps that require different types of oils. Read your manual or talk to your dealer to make sure you are using the right stuff.

8. Use paper oil filters rather than the washable stainless-steel replacement units. Paper filters are more expensive, but they stop more debris than stainless-steel washable units. If you want to save a dollar or two, consider using quality aftermarket filters. K&N and Fram both make oil filters for high-performance four-strokes.

9. Keep your air filter clean. This is no different for your four-stroke than for your two-stroke. Grit entering the motor destroys parts. Doug Dubach suggests keeping an ice cream pail or other sealed container full of filter oil and submerging the filter after cleaning it. Note that one of the easiest ways to keep a clean air filter handy is to use pre-oiled disposable filters. These don't cost much—less than $10 each—and you can toss the old one without having to wash it. Washing filters can use a lot of toxic gook—the reusable types are even moderately socially responsible (in case you care about the Earth).

10. Regularly pack the muffler. Four-strokes produce a lot of heat, and burn through the packing more quickly than two-strokes. When the packing is shot, you'll have increased sound, decreased back pressure, and a muffler that will be burned through if you don't change the packing.

PROJECT 13
How to Check and Adjust Your Valve Clearance

 Time: 2 hours

 Tools: Sockets, Allen sockets, ratchet, torque wrench (foot pounds and inch pounds), wrenches, contact cleaner, gasket sealer, rags, feeler gauge, micrometer, magnet, heavy gauge wire, or large zip tie, work stand

 Experience: 3

 Cost: $

 Parts: Replacement shims (if needed)

Now that the era of four-strokes is firmly established, dirt riders are becoming familiar with some new maintenance routines. Leading the way is the seemingly daunting valve adjustment. Although it may seem complicated on your first try, you'll find that it becomes much easier—and quicker—over time. Most importantly, as you develop your feel for measuring the clearance, the process will become much more pleasurable.

The question many two-stroke fans will have is: How often will I need to do this chore? The manual for the KX250F used in these photos states that the valve clearance needs to be checked after every six races or 15 hours of run time. If you're wondering why valves need to be adjusted, consider this: When valve clearances are too tight, they might not close completely, leading to loss of power. If the clearances are too loose, the valve may not open completely, resulting in a power loss, too. Also, when the clearances are too loose, valves tend to be slapped open by the cam lobes instead of being ramped open. This can potentially cause mushroomed valves as they slam back closed.

Remember, you're just checking the clearances every 15 hours. If everything is hunky-dory, you just button the top end back up and hit the track again. Should things need to be adjusted, factor in some more time and a little math. If you've got the right shim in your kit, the toughest part is still measuring with the feeler gauge. So, how difficult can it really be?

1 With your bike supported by a stand, remove the tank, bodywork, and ignition components that block your access to the cam cover. *Evans Brasfield*

2 Don't forget to wipe or blow off any dirt before you actually remove the cover. *Evans Brasfield*

3 You may need to remove some extra bits to be able to get the cover off. For example, the top motor mount needed to be removed to give that extra millimeter required for the cover to clear the frame. *Evans Brasfield*

4 Once the cover is off, the cam sprockets will tell you if the engine is at top dead center (TDC). Kawasaki and Suzuki have dots on the sprockets like the one shown in this photo. Honda and Yamaha have lines on the sprockets that will line up with the top edge of the head. *Evans Brasfield*

5 Since you will most likely need to rotate the crank to get the piston in TDC, remove the access plugs on the engine case and rotate the crank counter-clockwise until the marks on the cam sprockets are in the right position. *Evans Brasfield*

6 Notice how this feeler gauge is bent to make for easier access to the gap between the cam lobe and the top of the valve bucket. This helps to minimize the friction caused by bending the gauge into the tight space of the head. Angled feelers are available if you don't want to bend your own. *Evans Brasfield*

7 Slide the feeler into the space between the cam lobe and the bucket. You want just the slightest bit of friction between the feeler. Start with the tight end of the specifications. If the feeler won't fit, the clearance is too tight. Try the thickest end of the specification range, and if the feeler goes in too easily, your clearance is too loose. Otherwise, you're within spec! *Evans Brasfield*

8 To gain access to the shims, you'll need to take out the cams. Start by removing cam chain tensioner. Note how the carb is turned partially in its boot to allow room for access to the tensioner. *Evans Brasfield*

9 When removing the cams, make sure you don't drop any of the bolts or knock pins into the depths of the cam chain tunnel. Use a long zip tie to help keep the timing chain from falling into the case. *Evans Brasfield*

10 Loosen the cam cap bolts in a criss-cross pattern. Both cam covers must be removed to give enough slack. *Evans Brasfield*

11 Although you may be tempted to leave the knock pins in the head, carefully remove them to give you more room to work. Don't drop them or you may end up disassembling the whole engine! *Evans Brasfield*

12 Carefully remove the positioning ring from the cam. Note: the larger diameter goes on the exhaust side. *Evans Brasfield*

13 Take a look at this intake cam cap wear (the dark strip at the bottom of the photo), which was most likely caused by sand that worked its way past the air filter and wore through valve seal. It doesn't need to be replaced, yet. *Evans Brasfield*

14 When removing the exhaust cam, you may need to pull it a bit rearward on the engine to gain enough chain slack. Then lift the chain off the sprocket and lift it free. *Evans Brasfield*

15 Using a magnetic tool, lift the bucket off the valve you're adjusting. Now, you'll get to see the shim nestled in to its carrier atop the valve spring. Remove the shim with the magnetic tool. *Evans Brasfield*

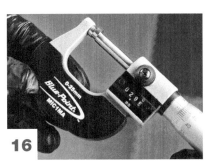

16

Measure the shim thickness with a micrometer. If the valve clearance is too tight, subtract the measured clearance from recommended clearance. Take this number and subtract it from the shim measurement to discover what shim size will be required to bring the clearance to within tolerances. (For the too-loose scenario, reverse the first equation and then add the result to the shim measurement.) *Evans Brasfield*

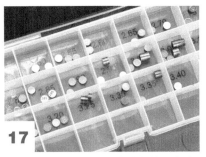

17

This is what a professional mechanic's shim selection will look like. The rest of us go to the local shop and buy them one at a time. *Evans Brasfield*

18

A happy shim about to be put to good use. *Evans Brasfield*

19

Count the cam chain links between the registration marks on the cam sprockets to make sure you maintain proper valve timing. *Evans Brasfield*

20

In order to equalize the pressures on the cam, tighten the cam cap bolts in a criss-cross pattern. Get the proper torque spec from your factory service manual. *Evans Brasfield*

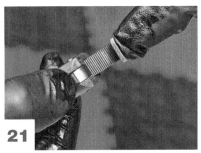

21

To reset the cam chain tensioner, press down on the lever and push the plunger into its most retracted position. *Evans Brasfield*

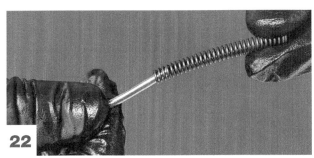

22

Slide the rod inside the spring prior to installing it into the cam chain tensioner assembly. *Evans Brasfield*

23

The fit is tight between the cap bolt and the carburetor body. *Evans Brasfield*

24

When remounting the cam cover, pay special attention to the O-ring around the spark plug well. Get them misaligned, and you'll see oil seeping out of the drain hole (at the bottom of the photo) next time you ride. *Evans Brasfield*

THE FOUR-STROKE ENGINE

149

Chapter 13
Accessories

For dirt-bike lovers such as our man Rat Bike, extra goodies can make your bike more useful. If you want to ride your motorcycle on the street, at night, or in the woods rather than on the track, read on.

LIGHTING KITS

A street-legal dirt bike must have a 12-volt battery to provide lights when the engine is shut off. Several battery manufacturers make units that can endure being tipped upside down in a crash and the constant vibration of riding off-road.

If you just want to fit lights to your MX bike to make it enduro legal, all you need is a functional head and taillight and a mirror. Companies such as Acerbis and UFO make headlight number plates and taillights built into a rear fender. These lights can be powered either by 12V DC or AC volts. The 12V DC setup requires a NiCad battery, a simple switch, and a wiring harness connecting the head and taillights. This is a total-loss system. The battery is only good for about one hour and then it has to be recharged.

An AC lighting system involves generating coils mounted near the flywheel magnets, a a voltage limiter, a switch, and

Adapting a motocross-oriented machine to off-road riding requires a host of bike accessories. Lights, guards, heavier flywheels, and gearing are the most common changes. *Kawasaki*

Heavier or rewound stators provide additional electrical power—useful if you are converting a motocross bike for off-road or dual-sport use. *KTM-Sportmotorcycle AG*

a wiring harness. There are two types of kits available for most late-model MX bikes. One setup is a simple coil that bolts on to the stator plate. The other is a more powerful system for greater headlight wattage. CRE is one company that distributes the high wattage system. The kit has an alloy side cover with a ring of several coils positioned around the outside of the flywheel magnets.

The simple lighting coil kits sell for about $80 and the deluxe kits sell for over $300. Companies such as Moose and Pro Racing sell the less expensive bolt-on coils along with other components, including wiring harnesses, voltage limiters, and switches.

FUEL TANKS

The typical range of an MX bike's fuel tank is about 30 minutes. If you intend to ride long distances, you may want to consider getting a larger fuel tank. Aftermarket companies, such as Acerbis and Clarke, make fuel tanks with capacities

A larger main fuel tank provides additional range. For extreme conditions such as riding in Baja, this 1-gallon rear-mounted tank is helpful. *Mark Frederick*

Handguards are a must-have accessory for woods riding. *Mark Frederick*

of 3.5 gallons, or about 1.5 gallons more than stock. You can also buy smaller auxiliary fuel tanks that clamp to the crossbar or fit in place of the front number plate.

DAMAGE CONTROL

If Murphy had a law for off-road riding, it would be that you will hit things, fall down, and break a component of your bike that makes it necessary for you to push it for several miles over harsh terrain. Zen law infers that if you spend the money on protection, you'll never need it.

Whether you are converting a dual-sport or MX bike for serious off-road use, you'll need to give it a shield of armor. Starting with the top of the bike and working down, the handlebars and controls are the most important area to concentrate on because that's where your hands are. Stronger handlebars are available, made with tapered wall tubing or stronger cross-braces. The standard width of an off-road handlebar is 28 inches. The Answer Pro Taper and Magura Bulge Bar are made of tapered alloy tubing that allows a certain amount of flex to prevent permanent bending upon impact. These bars also absorb some of the vibration transferred through the forks and into the bars.

If you use a traditional handlebar, you might consider filling the inside of the bar with an energy-absorbing rubber like the Bar Snake. It's a rubber rod that can be inserted through the handlebar to help absorb vibration.

Fastening guards to the ends of the handlebars is very important to protect your hands from impacts from trees and rocks. Hand guards come in a variety of designs. The two main types are aluminum flat-stock and injection-molded plastic. Fredette Racing, Moose, and Summers Racing Components make the aluminum hand guards. The Summers guard features bushings at the mounts to enable a bit of movement. Acerbis and UFO make plastic guards that are very lightweight and feature shrouds for added protection against rock roost.

Moving down to the radiators, companies such as DeVol Racing and Works Connection make aluminum guards that reduce the chance of the radiators being crushed in a fall.

Converting a motocross bike for dual-sport use creates an ultra-capable off-road machine that is legal on the street. These bikes are mostly useful for transporting between riding areas rather than serious street use. *Mark Frederick*

The bottom of the bike has some key areas that need extra protection. The frame tubes, crankcases, engine side covers, and brake and shift levers all need protection against rocks and trees. Guards for the bottom of the engine range from lightweight to heavy-duty. The lightweight guards designed for MX are usually made of aluminum or carbon fiber and are designed to streamline the bottom of the engine and make the bike less prone to grounding out on the peaks of jumps. The heavy-duty guards are huge aluminum pans that cover the bottom frame rails and extend up on the edges to protect the side covers. These guards are designed for use in conditions where there are a lot of big rocks and fallen trees. IMS specializes in heavy-duty guards because they serve the desert racing market. If you are a handy fabricator, you might want to make your own skid plate. If your bike has a steel frame, get a sheet of 1/2-inch mild steel and cut it to encompass the outer frame tubes and the bracket for the shock linkage.

Works Connection side-cover guards are also popular. These guards fasten to the engine mounting bolts and protect the side covers and the foot levers. You can also use a steel cable connected to the front edge of the levers and attached to the frame to protect the foot levers from being torn loose by ruts and trees. Buy the raw materials at the hardware store or buy cable guards from companies such as Moose, White Bros., WER, and Works Connection.

WATERPROOFING

The electrical and intake systems are two major areas of a dirt bike that need to be waterproofed. An extreme off-road adventure might require that you submerge the bike in a river all the way up to the tailpipe.

Starting with the electrical system, two materials are needed to seal wire connections: dielectric grease and electrical tape. Dielectric grease seals out water, prevents corrosion, and enables a good electrical connection. Wrap electrical tape around connectors for added assurance against moisture.

Trail Tech offers on-board computers for off-road bikes. These provide a speedometer, odometer, and other features like outside temperature and a clock. *Mark Frederick*

The intake system needs attention at the inlet and bottom drain of the airbox and the carburetor vents. Most dual-sport bikes have constricted airboxes, and the drainpipes are usually routed to a one-way check-valve chamber that allows outward flow only. MX bikes use a short rubber tube with slots that restrict airflow and enable free fluid flow out the bottom of the airbox. The Honda XR250 uses an excellent check valve that can be adapted to the airbox of most dirt bikes. The key is to enable outward flow in case water runs down the fuel tank or from the sides and seeps into the air box. If the airbox has seams on the sides, then you need to seal them with weather-strip adhesive. All carbs use vent tubes to allow air to flow in and apply atmospheric pressure to the fuel floats. The vent tubes also enable fuel to flow out of the carb when the bike is tipped over. Normally, the vent tubes exit from the bottom of the carburetor, which makes them vulnerable to drawing in water when crossing a stream. The best way to waterproof the carb's vent system is to buy 5 feet of 1/8-inch-inner-diameter tubing and replace the original vent tubes. Route the new vent tubes up into the top of the air box. That way, if the bike falls over, the fuel will spill into the airbox where it can be safely collected by the bottom drain valve.

ENGINE MODIFICATIONS
Dual-Sport Bikes

Street bikes are normally plugged up because of noise and emission considerations. There are baffles in the exhaust pipe, louvers and shrouds around the airbox, and the carburetors are jetted lean. It's not a simple matter of removing the obstructions to flow; the carb jetting may need to be compensated richer in order to get any power gains. Some aftermarket companies sell tailpipes and jetting kits as a set. These items will yield the biggest performance gains for the money, plus the aftermarket tailpipes are usually lighter in weight.

Changing the gearing usually requires a complete set of sprockets and chain. Get an O-ring chain for less maintenance. Expect to set the final drive at about 4:1, which equates to a 12-tooth sprocket on the engine and a 48-tooth sprocket on the rear wheel.

If you travel off-road, Dirt-Bagz make these sturdy panniers. They are extremely well-built, and will stay on the bike in extreme conditions. *Mark Frederick*

A GPS allows serious off-roaders to track their position. RAM mounts securely mount the unit on the bike. *Mark Frederick*

SUSPENSION MODIFICATIONS
Dual-Sport Bikes

Street bikes are usually sprung too soft for off-road riding. The heavy weight of the bike requires much stiffer springs than normally used on an MX bike. Modifying the suspension components of a dual-sport bike isn't as easy as just changing the springs. The valving must be changed to suit the harsh conditions and the stiffer springs. It's necessary to increase the damping on the compression and rebound circuits. Some of the shocks on dual-sport bikes are sealed units and cannot even be serviced, let alone revalved.

Motocross Bikes Used Off-Road

If you want to use a motocross bike for off-road racing and riding, you may want to revalve the suspension. Motocross bikes are designed with suspension valving that works best on the high end of the damping scale, meaning big jumps and square-edged bumps. That usually requires a sacrifice in damping performance for other riding conditions. You may read motorcycle magazine articles that refer to the "mid-stroke harshness" of a bike's forks or shock. That term best describes how an MX bike handles when you don't ride it hard enough. For riding off-road, you may want suspension that rides plush because you will spend more time sitting on the seat than standing in an aggressive position. You may also

Wide footpegs give additional stability when standing. These are IMS units. *Mark Frederick*

A steering stabilizer is great for woods riding, as it slows down front wheel deflection on roots. These units are vital for desert racing or other high-speed conditions. *KTM-Sportmotorcycle AG*

want the suspension to be sprung softer so you can easily shift the bike's weight and carry the front end over small obstacles. Softer springs enable the bike to sag more, which makes it easier to handle tight turns without the front end pushing to the outside of the turn.

Converting Your MX Bike for DTX or Supermoto Racing

Supermoto and dirt track racing are distinctly American sports with strong roots tracing back to the 1970s. Both motorcycle sports are on the rebound, with a sharp increase in promoted events. Supermoto races are being held on kart tracks and parking lots. Dirt track racing is popular on horse tracks at county fairgrounds. The modern motocross bike is an ideal platform for a custom supermoto or DTX bike. Although an MX bike is legal to race with changes to the tires and brakes, there is a standard profile of component changes to make a bike more competitive in supermoto and DTX.

Tryce Welch was an innovative developer of the DTX bike during its inception by the AMA. Welch worked closely with Jeremy Wilkey on suspension valving changes, such as spring force, damping, and travel bias as well as tires and wheels, gearing, and steering damping. Welch was the driving force in the development of the modern DTX bike and has built bikes ranging from 50 to 505cc, raced by generations of racers in the AMA Amateur Nationals.

The growing sport of supermoto is thick with dirt track racers. DTX bikes are ideal for conversion to supermoto. Here are some tips from Welch on customizing an MX bike into a DTX or supermoto racer.

CHASSIS MODS

Modifying the chassis for better handling starts by lowering the center of gravity. Options for accomplishing a lower CG include reducing the travel of the forks and shocks with spacers, an aftermarket triple clamp with adjustable offset and rake angle, and linkage bars.

HANDLEBARS AND CONTROLS

AFAM offers a special set of swept-back handlebars for DTX bikes. Many pro riders are switching to MX-style bars.

WHEELBASE

Wheelbases for the SM and DTX bikes vary with the brand but end up between 55 and 56.5 inches. There are some modifications possible, but the linkage systems restrict how short you can go.

SWINGARM ANGLE

Track conditions dictate the perfect swingarm angle, but 5 degrees is a good starting point. Adjustable links to fine-tune the angle are starting to become popular.

FORK RAKE AND TRAIL

The best steering head angle is between 24 and 25 degrees. There really isn't any need to modify the frame to achieve this angle as it is very close to a stock MX bike and can be dialed in by the front ride height. Offset triple clamps are useful in fine-tuning a DTX bike. Stock MX bikes run 50 to 52 millimeters off true offset, not triple clamp offset. The DTX

Sidestands make life easier on a motorcycle, particularly when you ride off-road. Pro Moto Billet units are well-made and unobtrusive. *Mark Frederick*

bike will push in the fast corners unless the front end is pushed out about 10 millimeters. Baer aftermarket DTX triple hand guards protect the rider in case of a crash and enable the bike to slide on the pavement. Magura inboard reservoirs protect fluid from spilling on the pavement during a crash.

Supermoto racing rules require that all engine oil filler and drain plugs are safety-wired. Also, a spill reservoir, or catch can, must be fitted to the bike to collect spills from the coolant, lubrication, and fuel systems. Traditional coolant must be replaced with distilled water.

Clamps are perfect for the DTX conversion, as they allow offset and fork angle with a simple adjustment knob.

STEERING DAMPERS

Due to space limitations caused by the radiators, steering damper selection is space restricted. WER, Ohlins, and Scott make rotary-style dampers that work well for DTX and supermoto. WER offers a special damping profile for DTX bikes that concentrates the damping effect just over center since these bikes have limited steering movement.

LINKAGE SYSTEMS

Aftermarket linkage systems are great for changing the rear ride height. They should not be used to actually lower the rear. Lowering the center of gravity by limiting the travel needs to be done by modifying the internals of the shock and fork.

SUSPENSION SYSTEMS
Valving

The changes in valving of the suspension components are as important as the spacing to limit travel. Supermoto and DTX bikes need both stiffer compression and rebound damping as compared to an MX bike.

Springs

It's possible to shorten the springs with the travel and make the spring rate stiffer, which is also better suited to supermoto and DTX. Traditionally, a suspension tuner will shorten the travel with aluminum spacers, stiffen the damping (LSC and LSR), and then install a shorter, stiffer spring to complement the valving changes.

Titanium springs are lightweight and starting to gain popularity. Otherwise, steel springs are readily available. Some tuners choose to shorten stock springs, which compensates for the lesser travel in two ways: It makes the spring shorter to fit the shock and stiffens the spring rate.

WHEELS AND TIRES

The only restrictions on MX bikes are the tires. Supermoto and DTX events won't allow knobby tires because of limited traction, braking, and the possibility of erosion to the track. Dual-sport tires are the only alternative for the stock MX wheels, but smaller diameter wheels and wider rims are the most competitive choice. Companies, such as Buchanan and FTM, sell rims and custom spoke kits for the do-it-yourselfer. White Bros. sells complete wheel kits based on Talon hubs and Akront and Excell rims. KTM sells complete supermoto wheels in its accessory catalog.

Supermoto wheels are 17 inches because that size has the best quality tires. DTX wheels are 19 inches, and there are several tires used for hard-packed and cushioned tracks. Typical rim sizes are: Minis, 2.75x17-inch (front and rear); 125cc bikes, 2.15x2.5-inch; and 250cc to 500cc bikes, 2.5x2.75-inch.

BRAKES

DTX bikes do not use front brakes, and the lever and caliper must be removed for competition. Supermoto bikes need oversized front brakes. Kits available from Braking and Gaffer use a larger disc with a longer caliper mounting bracket.

AUTOMATIC CLUTCHES

SM and DTX place similar demands on the clutch, requiring smooth power delivery and resistance to stalling during braking and cornering. Both slipper clutches and auto clutches are popular for different reasons. Slipper clutches are used in DTX for smooth traction on acceleration. Auto clutches are great for supermoto because they reduce rear wheel chatter on braking and the need to shift in the tight, twisty turns.

Z-Start and Rekluse are the two most popular brands of auto clutches for late-model dirt bikes. The Z-Start is a complete unit that replaces the clutch basket and pressure plate; it sells for about $800. The Rekluse auto clutch is just the pressure plate. It costs $300 and can be installed in 20 minutes.

DTX bikes are often lowered and fitted with 19-inch wheels and wider rims. Front brakes are not allowed in DTX. Engine mods typically include a slipper clutch, flywheel weight, and high-rev valvetrain.

The RadiX is a kit that mounts to your dirt bike which consists of a driven rear track unit in place of the rear wheel, with a ski up front. A Radix-equipped motorcycle can go through deep powder and up steep slopes.

The bolt-on unit is a solidly built piece of engineering that looks simpl, but incorporates more than 252 patent claims. The overbuilt unit consists of a 10.7-by-93.0-inch track with 2.1-inch lugs mounted on a custom-designed aluminum frame. The track uses super low-friction polyethylene slides similar to the hyfax sliders used on snowmobiles

The track is chain driven, and the over-engineered billet drivetrain is designed to handle more than 100 horsepower with ease. The track can pivot left and right on a rear linkage, a feature that helps the machine sidehill so well. A large disc brake on the jack hub slows the machine down.

An adjustable six-inch-wide dual-carbide Simmons FlexiSki and a 6061-T6 aluminium extension bolt to the stock front suspension. The rear suspension offers 15 inches of travel at the rear of the track, and uses two shocks. One is an Ohlins shock that mounts to the motorcycle and moves with the swingarm. The other is a custom unit on the track frame that damps the front of the track.

Developing this machine took about 12 years and more than 15,000 hours of engineering time. The engineering is subtly innovative and the key to unit's rideablity is years of refinement.

The kit adds about 40 to 50 pounds of weight to the motorcycle. The RadiX can be adapted to nearly any current off-road motorcycle—check http://www.2moto.com/ for specific applications and a dealership near you.

The 2Moto conversion allows you to navigate snow-covered backcountry terrain, and will navigate up to three feet of powder. This Red Bull bike is David Pingree's personal race bike. *Ken Faught*

The 2Moto track can be fitted to most modern dirt bikes. The conversion of David Pingree's bike took less than 40 minutes. Owners who are unfamiliar with the process will typically take 90 minutes to do it on carbureted bikes, and about 2.5 hours to convert EFI bikes. *Ken Faught*

The 93-inch-long track has 2.1-inch rubber lugs and can be equipped with an optional stud kit for riding on ice. *Ken Faught*

PROJECT 14
How to Install Hand Guards

Time: 30 minutes

Tools: Basic mechanics tools and stand, Allen wrenches

Experience: 2

Cost: $$

Parts: Hand guards, possibly new grips

Hand guards have been in existence since the 1980s, and they are a dirt bike rider's savior as they protect your hands from getting hammered by trees and rocks. Hand guards come in many varieties but fundamentally come in two versions. Version one is the classic; these have a two-point mounting and attach to the end of the handlebar, wrap out and in front of the hand and controls area and attach to a second point farther down the bars. This design is the strongest and will handle the most abuse. The second version is the open-ended version. These guards only attach to the inside of the handlebars or to the lever mounts. These are designed more for roost control than bouncing off of objects. The two basic designs are refined and modified to meet the needs of the specific user, and they are available in a rainbow of colors and spoiler designs.

Hand guards provide hand protection from trees, rocks, brush, saplings, and other riders. They also make the bars stronger and less prone to bending. Some argue they take some of the feel out of the bars, but that's a small few. The benefits far outweigh the slight downside. Hand guards will make your ride safer and more enjoyable.

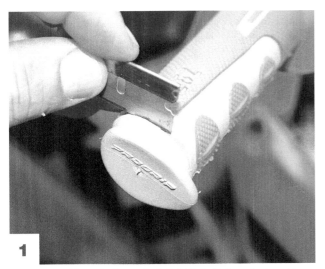

1 Using a razor, cut the ends of your grips just slightly inside the ends of your bars, leaving a small portion of the bar exposed. If your throttle body has a closed end, loosen it at the mount and slide it out about 1 inch. Then cut the end of the throttle body off with a hacksaw. Clean up any rough edges with emery cloth. Once the end is open, loosen the mount and slide the throttle body over back to position, exposing 1/8 inch of bar.

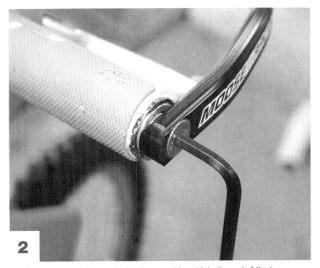

2 Assemble the bar end mounting hardware and insert into the end of the bar. Tighten until slightly snug. Note the space between the bar and the throttle body/grip.

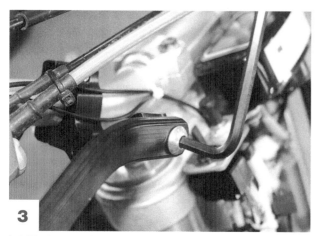

3

Install the inner mounting bolt to the inner mount end. Lightly snug this bolt. Next we will install the back of the inner mount.

4

With the hand guard level, install the back of the inner mount on the bar. Snug the bolts. Check for level one more time. Make sure the controls and cables don't interfere with the guards in any way. Failure to do so can result in serious injury. Once everything is well fit, tighten the inner mount tight.

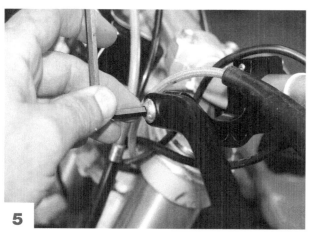

5

Now tighten the outer bolt on the inner mount.

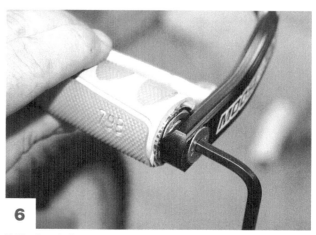

6

Tighten the outer bar end bolt, checking to insure the throttle moves freely. Recheck that the controls and cables move freely and work properly. Repeat the installation process on the clutch side.

7

Spoiler installation: Using the supplied hardware, position the spoiler on the hand guard in the correct position. Using a screwdriver, install all the screws into the mounting hardware. Do not tighten until all of the screws are installed.

8

Now that all the screws are installed, check to make sure none of the controls or cables interferes with the hand guards. If all is clear, tighten the screws to the manufacturer's specifications.

Index

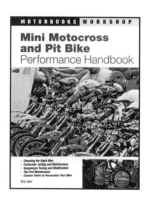

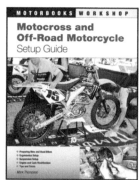

CPSIA information can be obtained at www.ICGtesting.com
Printed in the USA
LVOW01s1956291014

410901LV00002B/2/P